Consumer Behaviou

MW00984839

Consumer Behaviour and Analytics provides a consumer behaviour textbook for the new marketing reality. In a world of Big Data, machine learning and artificial intelligence, this key text reviews the issues, research and concepts essential for navigating this new terrain. It demonstrates how we can use data-driven insight and merge this with insight from extant research to inform knowledge-driven decision making.

Adopting a practical and managerial lens, while also exploring the rich lineage of academic consumer research, this textbook approaches its subject from a refreshing and original standpoint. It contains numerous accessible examples, scenarios and exhibits and condenses the disparate array of relevant work into a workable, coherent, synthesized and readable whole. Providing an effective tour of the concepts and ideas most relevant in the age of analytics-driven marketing (from data visualization to semiotics), the book concludes with an adaptive structure to inform managerial decision making.

Consumer Behaviour and Analytics provides a unique distillation from a vast array of social and behavioural research merged with the knowledge potential of digital insight. It offers an effective and efficient summary for undergraduate, postgraduate or executive courses in consumer behaviour and marketing analytics or a supplementary text for other marketing modules.

Andrew Smith, BSc MSc PhD, is currently the Director of the N/LAB at Nottingham University Business School, UK where he is Professor of Consumer Behaviour. He is also an associate of The Horizon Institute (for digital economy research). Professor Smith has published numerous papers on consumer behaviour and worked on a number of funded research projects for Research Councils UK, ESRC, EPSRC, DFID, ERC, Bill and Melinda Gates Foundation, European Union, The Office of Fair Trading and Innovate UK among others. These projects have involved various multinationals and NGOs (including Walgreens Boots Alliance, World Bank Group, Tesco, IPSOS and Experian, among others).

Consumer Behaviour and Analytics

Andrew Smith

Routledge
Taylor & Francis Group

LONDON AND NEW YORK

First published 2020
by Routledge
2 Park Square, Milton Park, Abingdon, Oxon OX14 4RN

and by Routledge
52 Vanderbilt Avenue, New York, NY 10017

Routledge is an imprint of the Taylor & Francis Group, an informa business

British Library Cataloguing-in-Publication Data
A catalogue record for this book is available from the British Library

Library of Congress Cataloging-in-Publication Data
A catalog record has been requested for this book

ISBN: 978-1-138-59264-3 (hbk)
ISBN: 978-1-138-59265-0 (pbk)
ISBN: 978-0-429-48992-1 (ebk)

Typeset in Bembo
by Newgen Publishing UK

Contents

Figures

Tables

Preface

It's useful to contextualize the ethos and function of *Consumer Behaviour and Analytics* (*CB&A*). This preface therefore outlines the aims and approach for the benefit of students and teachers alike.

Consumer marketing has been at the centre of a social and economic revolution in the last two decades and the forces driving this change continue to exert significant influence; specifically the abundance of data and pervasive digital technology. The digital tsunami has already happened; consumer marketing has fundamentally changed.[1] However, a sound understanding of extant consumer research is still essential for intelligent analytics-driven marketing.

CB&A is a practical book on an applied subject. From the outset it aims to align with practice. For example, consumer marketing often begins with analysis of transaction data; the starting point for *CB&A*. Business students need scholarly insights into customer behaviour, particularly those elements most relevant in the digital era. *CB&A* provides an accessible tour of these insights. It explores how they can inform actionable decision making with specific attention to the challenges and opportunities in the age of analytics and big data. However, *CB&A* is not a data science textbook, nor is it a manual for the underlying mathematics (absolutely not). The core objective is as a consumer behaviour textbook suitable for the new normal, a book that regards the principles of contemporary data science whilst focusing on the core domain; consumer behaviour and consumer insight. In other words, a managerially focused, practical guide to data and knowledge in consumer behaviour (one that is cognizant of the fundamental changes to marketing and the world outlined above). The data and knowledge in question are two-fold; (i) the generic knowledge generated by academic research, (ii) the insight that can be derived from the analysis of consumer transaction data and other commercial data. *CB&A* explores how we can blend these streams of knowledge more effectively to underpin sound managerial decision making.

The desire to understand consumer behaviour is a microcosm of the quest to understand human behaviour in general. It is a daunting task and in response

CB&A does not try to be an encyclopaedia – instead, the book distils the essential elements and most salient and relevant insights in the age of pervasive analytics and digital technology. The book is therefore a 'way in' to the topic and not the last word on the topic.

More words or pages doesn't necessarily mean a topic is more important, it simply means that a subject requires more explanation and exposition. So, some very important topics are dealt with in a parsimonious way if the topic is readily explained. Likewise, some topics require wordage out of proportion to their perceived importance if they are inherently more complex.

What prior knowledge is assumed? Not much. The book assumes that you have some familiarity with marketing terms and some knowledge of the contemporary business environment. It assumes that you can assimilate basic mathematical terms and ideas.

CB&A employs a blend of techniques and exhibits from direct questions posed within the text, worked examples and more complex explanations through to fictionalized scenarios to illustrate ambiguity and complexity; the book has numerous exhibits of data and summarizes knowledge in tables and schematics. *CB&A* deploys many abstracted examples. Abstraction ensures that a number of examples are not tied to specific cultural contexts or geography.

CB&A is designed as a core text for consumer behaviour, consumer analytics, marketing analytics or related courses of study. It might also serve as a useful secondary or supplementary text for numerous other modules on marketing or business analytics.

The book is designed to be read from start to finish. There is an underlying narrative structure and topics are not arbitrarily ordered within chapters or from chapter to chapter. However, chapters and sections are also designed to be read independently for reference and revision. Books are linear whilst the subject is not. The subject of consumer behaviour is like a lattice or network of interrelated concepts not a chain. There are therefore numerous signposts to help cross-referencing but these are not deployed *ad nauseum* given that many concepts are interrelated. The book is not formally split into parts but Chapters 1 to 3 deal primarily with the 'windows' on consumer behaviour provided by transactional and other data streams. Chapter 4 introduces the concept of 'exogenous cognition' as a link between the individual (consumer) and the distributed system of analytics. Chapters 5 to 7 review the plethora of extant research most pertinent to insight in the digital era. Chapter 8 proposes a format to apply knowledge, research and data-driven insight into coherent analytics and marketing. The eight chapter structure gives teachers room for manoeuvre in a ten (or 20) unit module structure where *CB&A* is the core text. For example, two chapters could be taught over two sessions if required (Chapters 2 and 7 cover a lot of ground but are best presented as discrete).

Specific points are referenced; generic, conflated and uncontentious elements typically are not.

Online interaction with the author is encouraged for teachers and students alike via https://consumerbehaviouranalytics.wordpress.com – see you there.

I hope that you find this book insightful and useful.

Note

1 Analytics-driven marketing will not go away. It is not a fad or fashion; generation of data will continue and increasingly sophisticated ways of gathering it and exploring it will occur. Unless someone lets off a nuclear device in the upper atmosphere, thus creating a sufficiently powerful electromagnetic pulse to wipe the digital slate clean and send us back to the stone age (let's hope that never happens), then data-driven lives will be the norm, and we'll be more data-driven as the digital revolution reaches terminal velocity.

Acknowledgements

Very special thanks go to James Goulding, Gavin Smith and John Harvey of the N/LAB for various insights and support, and to anyone associated with the N/LAB and Nottingham University Business School. Thanks also to Sally Hibbert for advice on elements in Chapter 7. The author would also like to acknowledge the impact of two funded research projects in particular; 'Neo-demographics: Open Developing World Markets by Using Personal Data and Collaboration' EPSRC EP/L021080/1, which supported a significant and timely programme of work in consumer analytics and sowed the foundations of the N/LAB, and 'From Human Data to Personal Experience' EPSRC EP/M02315X/1 that also facilitated the same.

Chapter 1

An introduction to consumer analytics

Introduction

This chapter introduces some key issues and concepts that lie at the heart of an analytics-driven approach to consumer marketing. The chapter reviews the various types of inquiry and inference, cause-effect, descriptive and predictive analytics. It also reviews the various forms of purposive data capture used to augment analytics insight (e.g. surveys, ethnography, neuroscience etc.). A key premise is that marketing education has a greater chance of relevance if aligned with (or cognizant of) practice; this underpins the rationale for starting with issues central to behavioural analytics insight (the 'engine room' for contemporary consumer marketing practice). Those who have not read the preface should do so now, since it sets out the overall approach to the topic and the ethos of *Consumer Behaviour and Analytics (CB&A)*.

The context of contemporary marketing

Consumers and marketing have changed radically in the last decade or so. Consumer marketing is increasingly analytics-driven and data-driven. This has become the new normal. Seemingly, practitioners are in a position to 'know' more about what customers actually do than ever before. This knowledge is increasingly reliant on insights generated by algorithms leading to 'automated marketing'. However, humans oversee the configuration of data processing, the interpretation of output and the subsequent tactical and strategic decisions that this data processing informs. Figure 1.1 exemplifies the mindset required to interact with this new reality.

The functional boundaries between 'technical' aspects of data science and the 'traditional' skills of the marketer are blurring (if not within individual actors' skill sets then within organizations or teams). The modern marketer needs to be able to see things through the lens of the data scientist (see, for example, Provost and Fawcett 2013). The functions cannot be divorced or discrete, as depicted on the left of the diagram. At the very least they are required to overlap, as

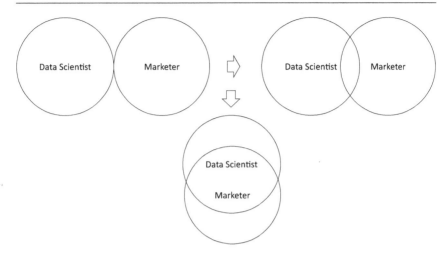

Figure 1.1 The contemporary mindset and skill set

the upper right Venn illustrates. Data scientists need to be able to think like marketers and marketers like data scientists. So, the lower Venn is the ideal; a blending of the mindset and even skill set. Commercial organizations (and not-for-profit ventures) need to ensure that these functions are blended with cross-disciplinary teams and individuals. If they are siloed and compartmentalized then the outcome is bound to be sub-optimal. For example marketers will pose research questions which are not viable and interpret data and output in a way that is questionable (or just plain wrong). Conversely, data scientists will tend to pursue actions and projects that might not lead to actionable marketing or posit research questions that already have answers (via the back catalogue of academic/generic consumer behaviour and marketing research). So, these human intermediaries require sources of extant knowledge (regarding marketing and consumer research), such as that summarized in *CB&A*, and insight into analytic thinking (as discussed in this and subsequent chapters).

Why data-driven?

There are distinct imperatives that explain how and why data-driven marketing has come about:

Operational imperatives

Why ignore all that data?

Data capture has never been easier. That is, transactional and other behavioural indicator data, or verbal and written (sentiment) data. It would seem perverse to ignore that data. It has obvious self-evident potential. Indeed, data streams can only get richer. Amazon Echo or Google Home point the way to the future, as does the internet of things (the network of smart devices that can autonomously communicate – e.g. smart refrigerators). There are more windows on our thoughts and our behaviour than ever before in the history of humankind. We used to leave a few pot fragments behind us for archaeologists to dig up; now we have a gargantuan data library on everyone.

Ostensibly the mobile phone or tablet is there for your convenience, to help you live your life; this is true. But it is also telling people what you're doing, where you are, what you're buying, who you know and many other things, too numerous to list. It is performing these functions ceaselessly and continually. Google is a data management company that makes its money from targeted marketing communications (MC); it sells the insight to other businesses. It epitomizes the new economy. It provides services free at the point of use in return for you 'paying' with data. It is truly global, truly cross-national.

Cost

Data capture is less costly than it was. Moreover, many businesses capture data as a matter of routine in order to operate their services. The data is there. However, the notion that data capture and use is cost-free is a fallacy. Additional costs include the storage of data, high performance computing (HPC), the expertise required to process the data (in-house or outsourced), the infrastructure and organizational changes to ensure that the data leads to strategic usage and data-driven decision making. Nonetheless, analytics-driven marketing appears to be cost-effective.

Analytical imperatives

Let's find out what people actually do before we attempt to explain it

The late Andrew Ehrenberg was critical of (academic) marketing's deductive approach. Models and ideas about consumer behaviour can be generated *ad nauseam*. 'Models without facts' as he put it (Ehrenberg 1988). This is possibly a questionable label but it exemplifies a period when academic and practitioner marketing research often tried to explore and explain behavioural drivers and antecedents, or rely on reports of behaviour (via surveys) before conducting so-called descriptive research on what people are actually doing. If we're not sure of what people are doing and how they are behaving, should we really be asking the question 'why are they doing it?'

His work and the work of fellow travellers and associates remains singular and influential. It led to some rare 'laws' of consumer behaviour and the methods and analytical model developed have been widely used in commercial market research. However, this body of work did not spawn a flurry of data-driven, more inductive work. This is explained by inertia and prevailing orthodoxy dating back to the genesis of scholarly and commercial consumer behaviour research. A brief account of these origins is essential; it is executed in Chapter 4 (the most suitable location in terms of this book's narrative).

Pre- and post-war marketers used to rely on anecdote and instinct about what the customer required and desired. However, a series of unexpected product[1] failures provoked a rethink of their approach to customer insight and new product development and targeting. This culminated in customer segmentation and categorization exemplified by the Values, Attitudes and Lifestyle approach (VALs) in the 1970s. Suffice to say that the approach attempted to predict consumer preferences by psychographic measurement. This means that consumers were categorized according to their psychology, aspirations, their intellectual and financial resources and crucially their motivations. The VALs method was influential and its impact still reverberates. Segmentation is still core to modern marketing (many things need to be aimed at groups or blends of groups not individuals) although the starting point is increasingly transactional/behavioural data. Questions remain over the ability of psychographics to predict behaviour. In the age of analytics-driven consumer research, psychographics have found a role in *explaining* observations on behaviour or providing evidence to support the conclusions drawn from behavioural data.

Data identifies individuals/households

This might seem normal now but it was a long time coming. Financial services have always required identity. However, prior to the loyalty card or online purchase many retailers and service providers struggled to link purchases with people. Knowing who bought what is taken for granted now. This allows marketing communications to target individually rather than through channels or media (i.e. like traditional advertising). Most products are still not individualized, communications increasingly is.

The upshot is that retailers and those last in the chain/closest to the consumer are the new 'druids'. If you are further upstream (i.e. if you make fast-moving consumer goods – FMCGs) then you need the entity who sells on to the consumer to help you understand behaviour. In past decades you would have relied on market research companies and surveys for insight. Now, it's the retailer or internet service provider. Online and offline retailers and service providers are simultaneously in the data business in a big way and can sell the insight back down the supply chain.

Data and insight

There are numerous ways of classifying data (from the statistically focused to those based on typologies for research methods). Table 1.1 and Figure 1.2 present two ways of categorizing data that help us understand the scope and potential of consumer analytics. Neither provides an exhaustive list, since the sources of data are myriad, however, these are the principal sources and certainly those most relevant to *CB&A*. Table 1.1 delineates via three dimensions; access, dynamism and whether the data is harvested as an integral part of the service or transaction or whether it is collected for a particular research objective (purposive). Data is behavioural if it gives objective insights into behaviour (location, routine, actual purchase) as opposed to sentiment (thoughts, ideas and opinions). Behavioural insight data is often spatially and temporally dynamic (with time and location indicators – see Chapter 2 for details); purposive data is static (associated with a specific time and location). Transactional data refers to any data that is primarily related to the service in hand. Social media data is quasi-transactional in the sense that it is collected as a result of the social interaction via the platform in question. A lot of data is proprietary and not freely available.

Figure 1.2 locates various types of data on a continuum of transaction and interaction. In reality many of these forms of data are both transactional and

Table 1.1 A data typology

Example data source	Access	Static/dynamic	Transactional or purposive
Loyalty card data	Closed – proprietary	Dynamic temporally & spatially (locates store)	Transactional/ behavioural
Online transaction data	Closed – proprietary	Dynamic temporally & spatially (locates user)	Transactional/ behavioural
Call detail record data	Closed – proprietary	Dynamic temporally & spatially (locates user to high order)	Transactional/ behavioural
Smart device data	Closed – proprietary	Dynamic temporally & possibly spatially (if the device is portable)	Transactional/ behavioural
Social media data	Closed – proprietary Open – public	Dynamic temporally & spatially (potentially)	Quasi-transactional
Census data	Open – public	Static	Purposive
Market research survey	Closed – proprietary	Static	Purposive
Neuroscience Study	Closed – proprietary	Static	Purposive

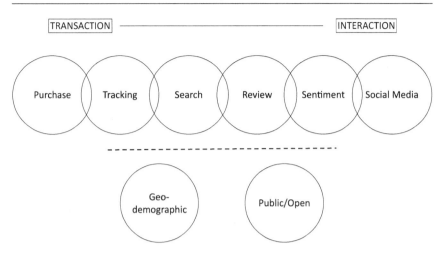

Figure 1.2 Data sources and streams

interactive and the continuum is therefore a simplification, but it emphasizes the fact that some data sources are based on a specific commercial exchange or service deployment or relate to a purchase (e.g. a product search or review) as opposed to a more ephemeral expression of sentiment or discussion on social media with oblique commercial relevance and significance (for example a discussion about diet that gives underlying insight relevant to the food market as opposed to a review about a specific product). Purchase records are primarily transactional. GPS data or other forms of tracking data (e.g. call detail record – CDR – cell phone data) are essential to the provision of a service but track the consumer. Search data can relate directly to a purchase process (i.e. looking at alternative products) or be more contextual. Review data relates to purchase but is essentially communicative, whilst sentiment and social media data might not relate to a specific transaction.

   The figure positions geo-demographic and open data (e.g. census data) sets as distinct. Geo-demographic data sets, collated by companies like Experian, are conflations from various data sources (census and other open data; purposive market research) that classify households by postcode/zip code according to numerous dimensions/measures and propensities (e.g. income, ethnicity, media habits, eating habits, lifestyle, values and attitudes). Whilst they are static they are extremely useful for cross-reference. For example, if you have access to an online transaction data set you will have customers' postcodes/zip codes. You can therefore interrogate the data to explore the possible relationships; to relate the inferences from the purchase analytics to the geo-demographic data as a 'check' of the veracity of your findings or to facilitate potential explanations for your insight.

There is more data than ever before and this creates challenges and opportunities. Contemporary data streams are rich, and if conflated they are even richer; however, the picture of the consumer is partial, the data artefacts are fragmented (e.g. you might know what a customer buys when they shop with you but not when they patronize your rival). The notion of 'truth' is elusive and fraught with epistemological (theory of knowledge) pitfalls; these have been debated *ad nauseum* elsewhere (e.g. Kincaid 1996), although the following section does address pertinent issues briefly and parsimoniously. Inference is a more useful and workable objective; data is evidence (analysts are like the archaeologists of the near past). The consumer is 'knowable' to some extent both individually and collectively via intelligent inference (via machine learning or data interpretation by analysts or both). A simple protocol for inference and interpretation is proposed below (based on a few questions).

Data are artefacts that have the potential to be information; the potential to be insight and knowledge. In analytics this often means traces and indicators of behaviour or sentiment (in the case of social media). The term 'digital footprint data' or 'digital data' is largely meaningless nowadays; the word digital is now superfluous since almost all data are captured and/or held via digital channels, receptacles and systems. Analytics often raises questions as well as answering them and these questions often need augmented methods; other methods to address the question raised or to test or verify the inferences made from the transactional data. These other forms of data capture are briefly reviewed below, however this book assumes that the starting point of inquiry are insights derived from analytics; data processing driven by machine learning. Why? Because this is the order of inquiry that is dominant in the real world of consumer marketing and *CB&A* is an applied book that aims to align itself with practice as stated in the introduction.

Consumers are complex. Consumer behaviour is, self-evidently, about understanding and explaining human behaviour and human behaviour has myriad causes, drivers and antecedents. Analytics-driven marketing has been accused of dehumanizing the consumer and there is evidence that data scientists and analysts can fall into the trap of seeing consumers as cases or rows in the data matrix; certainly this is a concern in the practitioner sphere (Strong 2015). This book endeavours to take a humanistic view of the consumer. What does that mean? Well, it tries to remember that there's a person behind that data; that the data is a representation of the person, it *is not* the person (Cluley and Brown 2015). This separation between person and data, between representation and human is crucial to the ethos of *CB&A*. This also relates to an essential point of ethics. Individual people generate data. They are the data producers. Google, Apple, Amazon, Microsoft, Experian, HSBC, Verizon, China Telecom etc. are the *custodians* of the data. They profit from it. As alluded to above, Google's whole business model is based on mining, leveraging and trading the insights from the analytics function. The browsing and location services (Google Maps) are free services that capture data. Data assigned and associated with an individual. This data is valuable, giving up the data is the price you pay; it is the other side of the transaction for the advantages of accessing and using the service. The hope is that the data is used in ways that ultimately benefit you as a customer (through targeted and tailored services and marketing communications or through efficiency gains – e.g. electronic assistants). However, this creates a fundamental change in how we make decisions as consumers (this is unpacked in Chapter 4) and is a major imperative of this book. We are outsourcing decisions to machines that base their proxy decisions and recommendations on analysis of our past behaviour (and those others we appear to resemble).

Analytic inquiry

Analytics is often characterized as being data-driven, underpinned by mathematics and statistics (enacted through machine learning). The resulting insight typically leads to privileging breadth over depth (i.e. insights from high volume data/lots of people as opposed to depth/study of individuals). A lot of analytics is about finding patterns, identifying causes, or making predictions. *CB&A* seeks to explore the advantages of analytics-driven approaches but also questions the efficacy of analytics and explores prior knowledge of consumer behaviour and the employment of other forms of data capture (in order to augment insights from analytics). Frankly, analytics often fails; it is imperfect science, when it fails then it is adapted and re-deployed in short order (it 'learns').

Table 1.2 provides a simple delineation of the three core types of reasoning relevant to *CB&A*. Abductive reasoning is the most commonly deployed to explain any observed patterns or feature in data derived from transactions (in descriptive analytics). For example, after some exploratory analysis (data mining such as clustering) we might observe that consumers are associated by their patronage times, the times that they browse or logon or come into a store and buy. We might infer that home work-life patterns drive and enforce consumer behaviour in this instance. This is logical and probably the most obvious explanation, but we have no 'proof' as such. This is the essence of abductive reasoning (owing its origins to Ockham's Razor and the law of parsimony; the hypothesis with the fewest assumptions is more likely to be correct). This observation might lead us to form a theory or model of behaviour, that in market X work-life patterns are the key descriptor of behaviour. We can then employ other forms of enquiry to test this idea, perhaps with a cross-sectional survey or with an experiment (e.g. online A-B test – explained below) or a mixture of depth and breadth methods. Now we are entering the realm of deduction, once we attempt to look for 'truth' or attempt verification or falsification we are testing our ideas and inferences in a particular way. Another way of 'testing' the veracity of our ideas is by seeing if the initial observation holds in other samples of data, i.e. other data sets that are comparable. This is not deductive, it is a form of inductive research because the observation is being specified. In the analytics sphere the most common occurrence of induction is:

A. Via targeted or depth research.
B. Through the transition from abduction to induction – when we attempt to find the observed pattern in multiple data sets as described above.
C. Arguably through the application of an 'inductive machine' (Popper 1963) via predictive analytics (described below).

Here's an illustrative example for case A. We might interview consumers about their work-life pattern in the context of grocery purchase. They might refer to the impact of work-life repeatedly, this also manifests itself in an online survey of a large panel of consumers. They are providing evidence for a specific observation that might lead us to the hypothesis that we can then seek to test by other methods. We will return to these ideas later in the book, and it is important that you are clear on the basic differences between the three protocols of reasoning and research in Table 1.2. Why? Well, it is crucial that we understand the limits and the benefits of analytics-driven marketing from the outset.

In terms of extant research (therefore potential explanations and causes of observed behaviour) *CB&A* draws on various 'base disciplines' because our knowledge of consumers has been built on varied inquiry from a disparate band of scholars. In fact, this poses a problem because the volume of research into consumers and consumption is vast and diffuse. A good deal of this insight is psychological in nature, but economics and sociology and compound disciplines and sub-disciplines such as economic psychology or consumer culture theory also offer insight (this issue is dealt with in detail in Chapter 4).

Cause, effect and inference

Issues of cause and effect are crucial to marketing analytics. One key attribute of the analyst is the ability to determine explanations of observed behaviour. These explanations might appear or manifest as correlations or other forms of non-linear or 'submerged' statistical relationships when data is mined/explored (Chapter 2 reviews the potential nature of these relationships). Figure 1.3 shows how a consumer switches between brands of soft drinks (synthesized from a real data set). The figure plots the purchase of one person's soft drink purchase in sequence; all purchases are 330ml cans. The data is in-store and derived from a loyalty card. These purchases are plotted in sequence from first bought to last bought. The numbers represent brands or product variations as per the

Table 1.2 Types of inquiry

	Observation	*Outcome*	*Truth or false?*	*Example*
ABDUCTIVE Inquiry	Incomplete	Best explanation	Maybe – requires further inquiry	In some transaction data soft drink consumers appear to buy more in the summer; this is probably due to being dehydrated in hotter weather.
DEDUCTIVE Inquiry	Model/rule	Specific explanation	Yes or no. Verifiable (but verification may be partial or contingent)	A hypothesis is posited that people buy more soft drinks on hot days. This is tested on data and we establish that on average, consumers drink 30% more on hot days. The explanation or overriding explanatory variable is the air temperature – any other explanation is speculative until proven.
INDUCTIVE Inquiry	Specific	Generalized explanation	Maybe – requires further inquiry	A series of interviews with a segment of consumers about the effect of the weather on consumption reveals that they do more exercise in the summer and this drives an increase in soft drink consumption.
BLENDED Inquiry	Conflated	Blended	Consilience	Taken together, the inferences and findings above provide a variety of insights that co-relate.

legend. The numbering/coding is weighted according to purchase frequency and sequence. So, the most favoured is coded as 1, next favourite is coded as 2, etc (the legend also clarifies this). If a product is bought as many times as another then the first bought is given the lowest/first number. The purchase sequence plot is an example of a *data transformation* (i.e. converting raw data into something interpretable and illuminating). Take a minute to look at the plot. If you don't understand what it is showing then read the explanation above once again. Write down your observations and ideas about Person A's soft drink purchase even if they seem obvious or simplistic. Subsequent paragraphs explore the potential inferences from this fragment of data in a systematic way.

Figure 1.4 gives the frequencies for each of the brands in Figure 1.3 and the associated legend. The juxtaposition of the two exhibits demonstrates the value of cross-referencing exhibits and representations of data. Figure 1.3 indicates that three products are preferred and that there is a sub-repertoire of favoured products, but this is a little obscure in Figure 1.3. Figure 1.4 gives a very clear indication of the dominance of these three products.

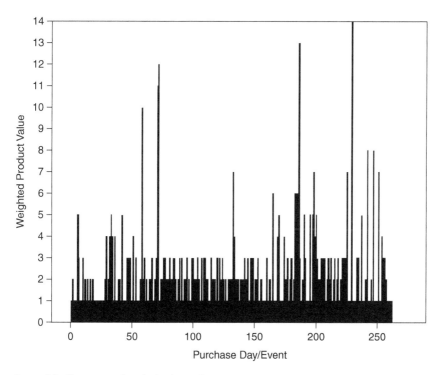

Figure 1.3 One person's soft drink purchase in sequence
Legend: 1=Diet Coke; 2=Cherry Coke; 3=Orange Fanta; 4=Diet Sprite; 5=Mountain Dew; 6=Fever Tree Tonic; 7=Dr Pepper; 8=Lipton Ice Tea; 9=Pepsi Max; 10=Lemon Fanta; 11=Appletiser; 12=Belvoir Elderflower Presse; 13=Irn Bru; 14=Lipton Ice Tea Peach.

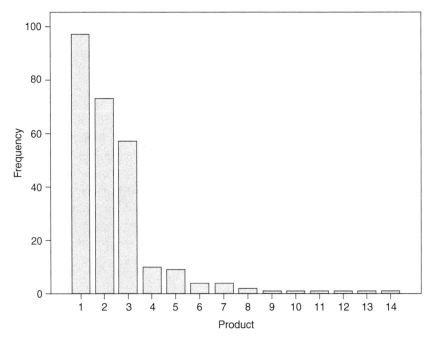

Figure 1.4 Frequencies for Figure 1.3 purchase sequence plot

Even these simple reduced exhibits tell us quite a lot. They also raise a number of questions and the fact that they do is equally as valuable. Five categories of questions or elements of inference help us to add some structure to any observations we derive from the analysis of the two figures. The following example of how we might follow this question-based protocol is illustrative and not exhaustive (another analyst – perhaps yourself – might approach it quite differently). This is normal; data requires interpretation and interpretation is biased and personal even if we strive to make it objective and neutral.

1. What are they; what do they denote?

It is useful to begin with a very basic account of what the data exhibit essentially is. This allows us to delineate the boundaries of the data; to remind ourselves what we are looking at and to audit what we are looking at:

Figure 1.3 depicts the weighted values for products in sequence of purchase for soft drink from one retailer only (since it is based on an outlet brand specific loyalty card) and for one person only. It shows a purchase sequence of 14 distinct products and over 250 purchase events. The horizontal axis is not a true time axis but simply a sequence axis. Figure 1.4 is a histogram of the frequencies of products in Figure 1.3.

2. What do they seem to indicate?

Here we move from denotation to connotation and possibly to abduction (indeed stages 2, 3 and 4 are liable to co-relate):

The favourite brand/product is Coke, the level of first brand loyalty (the proportion of purchase of the most favoured brand) is high. We can also determine the proportion for each of the other products. There is a sub-routine or repertoire of the three favoured products. Many of the products are only bought a small number of times. There appear to be phases of purchase; for example from event/purchase 0 to roughly purchase 70 the phase can be characterized as dominated by the three favourites but interspersed with significant but occasional acquisition of the less favoured/lower weighted products (less stable – higher entropy). The second phase (from around 70 to 170) characterizes a more stable period in which the buyer rarely buys any product outside of the three favoured ones. The third phase more closely resembles the first.

3. What might it indicate?

We now move further in the realms of abductive inference and even conjecture in which we posit potential explanations and/or make logical suggestions for the observations at stage 2:

For this category Person A seems to display a high level of behavioural loyalty/repeat purchase rate for the three favoured products given the overwhelming frequency of these three. It is reasonable to assume that this is based on a preference of these although it might be influenced by other factors (such as availability and price/sales promotion). The other 11 products are only bought occasionally. The most likely explanations for this are variety seeking, availability, sales promotion and value responses, the impact of marketing communications or buying on behalf of others. The favoured brand is a sugar-free formulation, whilst the other two most purchased products are full sugar formulations. Perhaps this indicates someone who is conscious about their sugar consumption but still drawn to sweeter tasting products.

4. What questions do these exhibits raise?

The key questions stemming from the exhibits relate to the motivation and context of the purchases (the stage can overlap with stage 5 to some extent but is best kept discrete). For example, why do they buy high and no-sugar formulations? What provokes the purchase of the outlier products? Are there any available covariates or variables that can potentially explain these tendencies and phases? Do they exhibit similar repertoire biases and phases for other product categories in the wider data set? What products do they buy alongside these products (i.e.

basket analysis)? The information is insufficient to reach unequivocal conclusions about the apparent motivations and propensities observed above.

5. What don't they show?

A huge amount of potentially useful data and information is missing. If someone presented you with this exhibit then the following preliminary audit of the most obvious blind spots would allow you to contextualize, assess and critique the veracity of their findings (or your own conclusions). What about purchase from other outlets? This is not the totality of Person A's purchase, their overall pattern of soft drinks purchase is unknown. So, the observations must be qualified. There is no indication of time scale or time and place of purchase. Is the data for one year, three months or one week (actually it is for a two-year period)?

Most transactional data sets will record many other useful variables; these would allow some of the issues raised in points 3, 4 and 5 to be addressed or diminished. One key lesson here is the complexity and ambiguity even in the representation of a very reduced and simplified data set. Just one product for one person for two years from one outlet. Imagine the volume of data generated for all of Person A's purchases at this convenience retailer and then imagine the volume generated by the whole customer base; this is why data gets 'big' and hugely complex.

The explanation of behaviour is a more tricky and complex task and might ultimately prove elusive. Imagine that we find a mathematical relationship between sales promotion and choice. In other words, there appears to be a relationship between the price variations and the product bought – not just for Person A, but across an entire data set. Such a relationship will never explain the variation 100%. Correlations simply suggest a relationship, they do not establish a 'true' relationship. This is why an archaeological model of discovery is proposed. The archaeologist cannot travel back in time to check their conclusions; the consumer analyst can never be completely sure about their explanation. They might even check their conclusions by commissioning a study to ask consumers about why they switch products – this might appear to corroborate their initial conclusion. All of this evidence and data should be treated with caution. Consumer behaviour is complex and even if there is overwhelming evidence for a dominant explanation it will never be the only factor driving behaviour for an individual or for a market.

Key elements of analytics

Here we review some of the core concepts of contemporary data science. A non-mathematical and accessible review of these is required in order to help define the analytics mindset and to understand the context of data-driven marketing. Moreover, subsequent chapters refer to these core terms repeatedly.

Descriptive analytics

Description is powerful. At a very basic level, descriptive analytics looks for patterns and trends. Segmentation is a salient example of descriptive analytics application in marketing. Increasingly segmentation is now based on processing transactional and behavioural data (as opposed to subjective survey output). Another example of descriptive analysis are time series of purchase or sales for a particular product. The output, the segmentation map or the purchase time series gives insight but does not test anything. Descriptive analysis can lead to soft (abductive) prediction; for example we observe that a consumer segment has previously been amenable to direct marketing, and we assume that this will continue. So, it allies with abductive or inductive inquiry. On an individual level, consumers can appear to behave 'randomly' (Goodhardt, Ehrenberg and Chatfield 1984); data is often noisy (i.e. patterns or consistencies are often obscure at the individual level). Often, individuals are best understood as components of a whole; patterns emerge when a number of cases are explored *en masse*; perversely the individual behaviour is best explained by the analysis of the group or market. Despite the individualization of marketing communications many products are still aimed at groups or types; it's not possible to individualize offerings for many product categories. Therefore segmentation (via clustering) remains a ubiquitous analytical tool. However, there have been significant innovations in terms of the ability to undertake segmentation on very large, complex (high dimensional) data sets and the underlying mathematics. A key innovation is the emerging ability to cluster (associate) people simultaneously not just by *what* they buy but *when* they buy.

Figure 1.5 illustrates a possible outcome for grocery retail. Proximity is mathematically determined and relates to association between groups; the closer the greater the relationship according to the two variables on the axes. The potential features (variables) that could be used to derive these axes are explored in Chapter 2 (Chapter 2 also covers association, clustering and segmentation in more detail). It is also significant which quadrant the cluster/segment is in. So, 'City Slickers' go high on convenience and premium spend; 'Grey Foodies' cook from scratch but like premium/quality; 'Busy Bees' score neutral on value but have a bias to convenience; 'Thrifty Nifties' go for value lines and convenience whilst 'Austere Trads' go for cheap and high effort/prep food. These groups are going to require differentiated offerings and communications. Once the market has been successfully and meaningfully delineated by behaviour then a next step is to explore the other characteristics of the segments (e.g. socio-demographic, attitudes, lifestyle etc.) via other available data or purposive research.

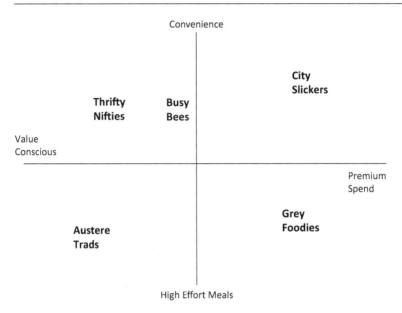

Figure 1.5 Behavioural segmentation example

Data mining

Data mining is a very broad term that encompasses a range of largely descriptive techniques used to indulge knowledge-driven discovery (KDD). This is essentially about knowledge building of a pre-existing data set. An analytics team or lone researcher will employ a range of techniques to generate an array of outputs and visualizations of the data in order to understand its structure, limitations, potential and scope. This is typically and broadly in line with the five stage inference protocol outlined above. One powerful method of initiating this process is via 'vertical sampling' in which various researchers take a data file of just one individual and construct a narrative around that data. This approach was pioneered by Smith and Sparks (2004) in order to show the potential power and limitations of digital purchase records. Converting outputs and exhibits into a vignette of a person also helps to humanize the data as well as illustrate its potential and limitations.

Predictive analytics

Predictive analytics seeks to estimate something in the future by trying to identify the determinants of past behaviour. For example an online retailer might want to predict when a consumer is most likely to move house, since some descriptive inquiry has indicated that when consumers change address they spend more on certain categories of product six months after moving (e.g. sofas and furniture). This information is useful and can be used for targeting marketing communications and offers in a more timely and efficacious way. A predictive model is required to do this. Without diverting too much into the myriad of mathematical concepts surrounding predictive analysis, certain steps are required. The dependent variable is the one we are trying to predict – the house move. The analyst will try to identify relationships between the independent variable or features in the data (known as feature extraction – see Chapter 2 for example features); this process is typically iterative. These features might be well defined in the transactional data (e.g. spend per month) or a feature embedded in the data that needs to be calculated or extracted (e.g. a behavioural tendency like brand loyalty). Suppose that various variables/features and parameters are tested in various combinations (via machine learning or more traditional techniques) in order to test their ability to predict a house move on a portion of the data where a house move is clearly indicated (e.g. by a change of address). This is done on a portion of the data (not all consumers who change address); if machine learning is employed then this is the sample on which the data or model is 'trained'. The efficacy of the model and its ability to predict will then be tested on a holdout sample (the portion of the data set not used in the 'training' or testing stage); in order to see if it can discriminate between households that are likely to move and those that won't. The outcome will not be 100% robust but even if it is 50% effective at predicting a house move six months prior to the event then that is powerful in mathematical and practical terms. For the sake of this example, let's imagine that the key features that predict a move are a marked reduction in overall spend in the two years prior to the move (abductive reasoning would suggest that this is due to saving up for the move) coupled with an increase in spend on home improvement products (abductive logic or even evidence might suggest that this is due to the current property being enhanced and improved in order to maximize its saleability and value). These features in the data can then be monitored automatically in order to identify consumers who might move house.

A simple example of the logic of prediction is given in Figure 1.6. 'X' depicts the event that an analyst is trying to predict. In this case the event is the emergence of a secondary delivery address, seemingly a second home or holiday home as the primary address is retained. Spending on furnishings and homeware peaks around this time (line A). Spending on 'B' (summer and holiday, sports and leisure associated products) peaks in the preceding months beforehand. This might indicate that the amount of time abroad or at leisure is increasing. If the data indicates that this tends to happen towards retirement age for more affluent consumers then a likely scenario is that consumers are spending more time at leisure, in a different locality either actively engaged

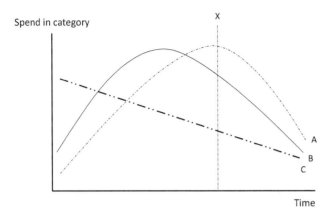

Figure 1.6 Prediction of second home

in a property search or perhaps the purchase of a secondary home is inspired by this time at leisure. There may be other clues in the data. The analysis also indicates that spending on attire and apparel associated with employment (e.g. formal wear, certain types of technology product etc.) declines in advance of the event that the analyst wishes to predict (Line C). An algorithm is then constructed to identify these changes in spending in order to predict the purchase of the secondary property. This prediction has obvious advantages to the marketer. Offers on homeware can be made well in advance of the critical event in order to ensure that spend is captured and not lost to competitors. Online marketing communications and purchase prediction is dependent on this kind of approach.

One issue with predictive analytics relates to a concept dealt with in more detail in Chapter 4 of this book, specifically analytics' reinforcement of existing behaviour; a consumer buys a lot of product x, therefore the consumer is targeted with offers for product x or its variants. This makes it more likely that they will continue to buy product x. So, the predictive attempt is actually moulding behaviour.

Predictive model design is not like traditional model design. The process of feature (variable) extraction is arguably an inductive method of building a model; it does not begin with a theory or idea. Once the most efficacious model has been determined then it might not be clear *why* it works; just that it *does* predict to an agreeable level. The context-mechanism-outcome configuration pioneered by Pawson and Tilley (1997) provides a method of deriving explanations that might help here; in the sense that the predictive model takes account of context and outcome but not mechanism (see also de Souza 2013). So, it follows that theorization is required to describe the intervening mechanism (this can then be tested by other means).

Machine learning

Contemporary data science relies on what we might call traditional statistics and established methods (linear regression) and 'automated' algorithm-based methods; machine learning (ML). ML is an offshoot of artificial intelligence and is important because it allows marketing analytics systems to react in real time to consumer behaviour that leaves any kind of data trail; facilitating automated real-time marketing in the digital sphere (via online algorithms). Machines are stupidly intelligent. We can train a machine to recognize a giraffe in photos, but the machine does not know what a giraffe is. Likewise, it will learn that you tend to buy a certain product on Amazon but it might not establish that you are buying these items for someone else or someone else has used your device and will therefore target you with inappropriate offers and ads. At least this might be the case initially. In time it might learn that it's not you (there may be clues in the data). Chapter 4 considers the cognitive interface between machines and people.

Machine learning has taken over in the commercial sector. It is the present and future. In the academic sphere there is a sluggish attempt to account for this sea change. Data-driven investigation and automated data processing are often described as a 'black box' approach; opaque and void of theory. This is not a productive or accurate view. Theory and generalization can be attained via data-driven methods; certainly with the help of them as outlined in Table 1.2 and elsewhere above.

Algorithms

An algorithm is simply a set of rules that solves a problem or determines an outcome or action. Algorithms can be expressed in flow schematics (flow diagrams). This flow diagram is then converted into machine code to facilitate automation. Figure 1.7 illustrates a simple example that is self-evident. Offers will continue to be sent if they are redeemed; the schematic has a loop. This algorithm might connect with myriad others. The potential complexity of algorithms is virtually limitless.

Purposive research

'Traditional' market research is still hugely important. Purposive research refers to the acquisition of data in order to address a specific question; as opposed to the interrogation of pre-existing transactional data. *CB&A* advocates research designs and managerial structures that are led by behavioural data analysis (however, the sequence and design can be reversed); in order to align with practice in real-world marketing. This section explores the scenarios and research questions

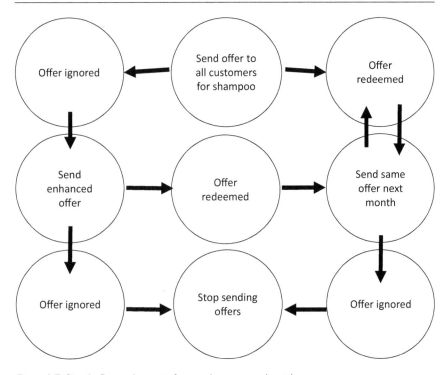

Figure 1.7 Simple flow schematic for an elementary algorithm

that these kinds of approaches can address and the aspects of consumer psychology and behaviour they are best placed to uncover. It does not provide an exhaustive exposition of these techniques (other books are better placed to do this); it simply outlines their potential role in an analytics-driven environment.

Survey

A survey is an attempt to glean insights by means of questions. A representative and statistically robust sample of consumers is used (i.e. representative of the population in question). The population might be defined by geography (e.g. a country or region), behaviour (e.g. purchase of cars), psychology (e.g. impulsive individuals), lifestyle or demographics or a conflation of these (e.g. geo-demographics and behaviour). In other words, the various base variables for customer targeting and segmentation. If a whole population is surveyed then it becomes a census.

The questionnaire is the data capture instrument and can be complex (e.g. an omnibus survey about various attitudes and behaviour or a psychographic survey running to 100 or more questions) or simple (e.g. a single question poll of voting intention prior to an election). This is a very complex area indeed in its own right (see Rossiter 2002). A survey can be administered (face-to-face or by phone) or not. These days, a survey is typically delivered via online mechanisms. The instrument of data capture might be app-based or via a web page. This is less costly than the human administered approach, although the greater expense might be deemed worth it if the topic in hand requires it. For example, a survey of vulnerable groups (e.g. children) might require the presence of parents and would also provide more reliable data if administered face-to-face. For many commercial applications cost concerns are likely to prevail over any marginal advantages achieved through direct human oversight.

In order to understand how this fits with an analytics-driven approach, then, we need to consider the types of data that surveys can capture in more detail and the strengths, and weaknesses, of surveys. Surveys formed the basis of market research and market intelligence from the 1960s through to the start of the 21st century. Table 1.3 reviews their contemporary deployment and pertinence.

One pervasive problem with survey-based research is the inherent subjectivity and variability in questions and answers. Asking someone's age is a relatively objective task, whilst asking someone how often they buy shampoo relies on memory and judgement, asking them their opinion about a brand requires a very subjective judgement. Answers can be open (an expression in the respondents' own words) or closed; requiring scoring (on a Likert scale for example), ranking, selecting various pre-ordained answers. The data types/answer formats elicited are consistent with those reviewed in Chapter 2 (i.e. cardinal, ordinal, interval and nominal).

Responses to questions can be misleading. People lie, forget and will present themselves in a positive light in relation to prevailing social norms (social desirability bias – SDB). Reports of behaviour are notoriously unreliable when compared with behavioural/transactional data. However, as Table 1.3 outlines, they are a useful tool for augmented inquiry in analytics-driven projects.

Depth and interpretive studies

There are various forms of depth inquiry in which the objective is not breadth *per se* but nuance and intensity. Interviews of small cohorts are often deployed to understand the anatomy of an issue or topic. Complex issues are the most appropriate for depth interviews, not for example a depth investigation of why people buy cat food (presumably because they, or someone they associate with, have a cat). They are therefore more suited to issues such as the ethical

Table 1.3 Survey applications and issues

Applications	Salient example	Rationale	Fit with analytics-driven approach	Challenges
Customer satisfaction	Hotel stay rating and appraisal	Satisfaction is subjective and based on fulfilment or not of expectations (expectancy disconfirmation). This is a subjective factor.	Whilst we can infer that a repeat patron is satisfied, behavioural loyalty can be specious (see Chapter 2). Satisfaction surveys can be cross-referenced with behaviour as monitored in a hotel loyalty scheme.	Satisfaction is subjective and multi-dimensional. Consumers who have had a bad experience might be more motivated to fill in the form. This can be overcome by offering incentives (e.g. loyalty points etc.).
Recall or knowledge	Advertising effectiveness	Advertising offline is difficult to assess. A spike in sales after a campaign might be due to other variables (e.g. hot weather for soft drinks). Recall (remembering) is a basic requirement for impact on behaviour.	Recall and response to marketing communications (MC) can be cross-referenced with transactional data.	Consumers struggle to recall accurately, given the 'white noise' and clutter of marketing communications and the fact that they have many more things on their mind that have greater salience.
Service or privilege sign-up	Online retail sign-up or loyalty programme sign-up/registration	This basic information is required for delivery and ID verification but the addition of other questions is possible, e.g. 'Do you have children?'	This makes data that is unlabelled (raw transaction data) labelled. It is a crucial opportunity to glean extra information at a point where consumers are receptive to a (limited) number of questions.	Too many additional questions might provoke a questioning of trust or motive, respondents may make errors or even provide fallacious data.
Attitude or perception	Antecedents of repeat patronage	Repeat buying can indicate loyalty that is 'true' (see Chapter 2) but it might be 'spurious' and driven by lack of choice or income constraints. Knowing why people repeat patronize is important.	This motivational insight can be cross-referenced with the transactional data.	The reasons uncovered are dynamic and any survey is out of date as soon as it is complete.
Psychographics	Personality associations with purchase	There might be indications in the transactional data that suggest certain products. Historically, such studies have often failed to provide consistent/generic 'rules' of association between psychological attributes and behaviour. Nonetheless, the idea that consumer behaviour can be predicted by psychographics remains seductive.	Once again, the prize is the opportunity to cross-reference or 'explain' behavioural data patterns or trends.	Psychographic rating scale surveys can be long and fatiguing or complex for respondents.

Part of an experiment	Test of responses to product or communication variants	Lab-based experiments often have a survey or questionnaire element in order to assess respondent reactions or to influence behaviour.	Experiments are useful for hypothesis testing; in consumer analytics the hypothesis is derived from the behavioural data.	Lab-based experiments (as opposed to A-B tests or field-based techniques) can be costly and complex.
Concept testing	New product development	Questionnaires can be deployed in order to gauge survey reactions to a concept that is unfamiliar to the consumer.	Transactional data can only give insight into the adoption of similar products; it cannot test a concept.	Surveys need to be balanced and allow the negative reactions as much space and potential as the positive reactions. Initial reactions to new things can be unreliable and the true test is in the marketplace.
Non-buyers	Increasing market penetration	You will not have data on non-buyers unless you acquire out-of-house behavioural data or commission a survey to find out how you can reach them via product variants or new communications.	Non-buyers occupy the most obvious data 'blind spot' in analytics-driven applications.	As stated before, survey responses can be biased and misleading. Excellent sampling and design are always essential.
Ground truth	Geospatial 'check'	Analysis of CDR data can be a good way of generating socio-economic maps in areas of fast population change in developing economies. Surveys provide a useful check of ground truth and the veracity of initial inference.	The issue is once again triangulation and cross-referencing. The survey may identify anomalies in the data and suggest ways to improve feature engineering.	There may be logistical problems in reaching some groups and communities.
Hypothesis test	High value customer attributes	The purchase data might suggest that high value customers share some other attributes – this might lead to the generation of a hypothesis that requires testing.	See those for experiments and psychographics.	See those for experiments and psychographics.
Segmentation	Underlying attributes of behavioural groupings	Segmentation can incorporate many of the applications above.	See those for experiments and psychographics.	See those for experiments and psychographics. Establishing the basic objective of demographic attributes is more reliable.

dimensions of decision making or the exploration of contexts (such as family decision making and dynamics; i.e. where a narrative account is required).

Ethnography (and the online step-sister netnography) rely on passive (covert) observation or participant (overt) observation (sometimes augmented with interviews and other interrogative techniques where appropriate). For example the researcher might observe how people behave during clothes shopping in-store. They might record this data via video or make field notes or both. This approach can be used to address questions raised by the analytics; often leading to a reduced form of observation that isn't true ethnography. For example, how sequences of purchases occur; whether people select core items then accessories or vice versa. The transactional data will have these bundles of products in the same basket but will not indicate the 'path' through the store (virtual 'click paths' are readily determined for online contexts).

Experiments

Experiments are good for testing the effects of 'treatments'; a treatment being the variable or stimulus that you are changing in order to test a differential response. For example, which web page configuration users prefer. This can be done covertly online by simply randomly exposing two groups to the two different configurations. If the dependent variable/objective is time on site then you can readily determine which website configuration leads to greater engagement (this concept is revisited in Chapter 3). This is an example of what we call an <u>A-B test</u>. The overt/active lab-based experiment is most suited to studies seeking to determine psychological factors (though the lab can be virtual/online) and generally these are the preserve of academic inquiry. A company could employ a lab-based experiment to test differential reactions to two forms of packaging, for example. The problem with the lab experiment is that it tends to isolate a stimulus or effect. People make decisions and buy things in the real, noisy world where various other things influence and distract you. Conversely, the A-B test occurs in the real world.

Neuroscience

There has been some hype about the potential impact of neuroscience on marketing. Essentially, neuroscience maps brain activity during an occurrence or episode. It requires specialist equipment and can only be carried out in a suitable facility, not in the real world. This means that it is haunted by the same issues as the lab-based behavioural experiment. It is well suited to very specific questions: for example, emotional responses to certain marketing communications images.

Conclusion

Many of the themes, topics and issues introduced here are revisited and developed throughout *CB&A*. It is important that you are comfortable with the core concepts and issues introduced here; if you aren't then a re-read of certain sections might be advisable. Analytics really comes down to two simple approaches. It either seeks to find patterns and describe and classify behaviour and sentiment or it attempts to predict and influence it. It is a strange form of science. It is better equipped at investigating *what* people do rather than *why* they do it. However, *what* isn't a bad starting point… is it?

Note

1 The book refers to offerings as products whatever their blend of tangible and intangible elements; a product is taken as anything sold whether a physical artefact or a digital virtual good (DVG).

References

Cluley, R. and Brown, S.D. 2015. The dividualised consumer: Sketching the new mask of the consumer. *Journal of Marketing Management*, 31(1–2), pp. 107–122.

de Souza, D.E. 2013. Elaborating the Context-Mechanism-Outcome configuration (CMOc) in realist evaluation: A critical realist perspective. *Evaluation*, 19(2), pp. 141–154.

Ehrenberg, A. 1988. *Repeat-buying: Facts, theory and applications*. Oxford: Oxford University Press.

Goodhardt, G.J., Ehrenberg, A.S. and Chatfield, C. 1984. The Dirichlet: A comprehensive model of buying behaviour. *Journal of the Royal Statistical Society. Series A (General)*, 147(5), pp. 621–655.

Kincaid, H. 1996. *Philosophical foundations of the social sciences: Analyzing controversies in social research*. Cambridge: Cambridge University Press.

Pawson, R. and Tilley, N. 1997. An introduction to scientific realist evaluation. In E. Chelimsky and W.R. Shadish (Eds.), *Evaluation for the 21st century: A handbook* (pp. 405–418). Thousand Oaks, CA: Sage Publications, Inc.

Popper, K.R. 1963. *Conjectures and refutations*. London: Routledge and Kegan Paul.

Provost, F. and Fawcett, T. 2013. *Data science for business: What you need to know about data mining and data-analytic thinking*. Sebastopol, CA: O'Reilly Media, Inc.

Rossiter, J.R. 2002. The C-OAR-SE procedure for scale development in marketing. *International Journal of Research in Marketing*, 19(4), pp. 305–335.

Smith, A. and Sparks, L. 2004. All about Eve? *Journal of Marketing Management*, 20(3–4), pp. 363–385.

Strong, C. 2015. *Humanizing big data: Marketing at the meeting of data, social science and consumer insight*. London: Kogan Page Publishers.

Chapter 2

Purchase insight and the anatomy of transactions

Introduction

This chapter aims to summarize behavioural aspects and biases; including loyalty, customer value and variety seeking. It also determines how we can assess and characterize purchase dynamics. In doing so, it explores a variety of core concepts and techniques; from data classification to data dimensions and visualization through to correlation and association. Latterly it considers the various ways in which we can make sense of consumers at the individual level and aggregate level through various forms of analysis of transaction data.

Behavioural biases and customer value

Loyalty and repeat purchase

Customer loyalty is a much abused term. The academic literature on business practice uses the term to refer to a multitude of related concepts, from emotional bonds to a brand to how often you buy it. As far back as 1978 Jacoby and Chestnut cited 53 definitions. Figure 2.1 builds on the work of Dick and Basu (1994) to delineate between these in a summarized and accessible form.

Previous research has tended to focus either just on the dynamics of repeat purchase and/or on the attitude and cognitive processes underpinning that behavioural manifestation of loyalty. Here the term *Relative Attachment* is used to incorporate cognitive and emotional elements (the latter being important but often neglected in extant research). Attachment is high if you have a positive attitude and affective or emotional disposition to the product, low if not. If you like it then attachment will be high, if you don't it will be low. *Repeat Purchase/ Behavioural Intensity* (sometimes referred to as Repeat Patronage) refers to the percentage of time that you (individual or household) purchase the product in a given time period (100% − 0%). What is a high rate of repeat/velocity of purchase? That is an excellent question. The short answer is it depends on the market and the average repeat purchase rate for that market. Let's say for the snack market the average is 50% and Consumer Z purchases their favourite

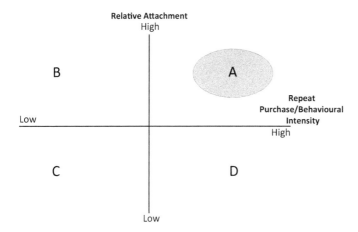

Figure 2.1 Dimensions of loyalty

70% of the time in a year – this constitutes a higher than average rate. But it is also a function of frequency, if Consumer Z only makes two purchases of snacks a year then this reduces the overall significance of their repeat purchase rate – so we should always factor in frequency (see also recency, frequency and monetary value – RFM below). So, a repeat purchase or repeat patronage score can be a function of frequency and the repeat rate. There are various ways of reflecting this mathematically, however that is beyond the scope of this section. So, we can think of the behavioural component in terms of behavioural intensity; as a function of the repeat purchase rate relative to the average, velocity or frequency of purchase. The zones or quadrants in Figure 2.1 are explained below.

A. *Composite Loyal.* Consumers in this category buy the product at relatively high rates of repeat purchase or intensity and are also positively attached to the product in hand. In this sense they are true loyals.
B. *Constrained Loyal.* This customer has a positive attachment to the product but this does not manifest in behaviour and purchase. This could be because the consumer likes a brand that is out of their price range, not available in their locality, or perhaps seeks a cheaper brand out of choice.
C. *Disloyal.* This is self-evident; the consumer does not like or buy the product a great deal. They may still purchase at low rates due to availability or price issues on occasions (perhaps it is on offer and a low involvement good or necessity).
D. *Specious Loyal.* The Specious Loyal doesn't like the product or brand but buys it nonetheless. No, they aren't mad. This can happen due to lack of income and/or availability or other constraints (e.g. convenience). For

example you might only have one grocery store in your town. You may use it a good deal without thinking it is much good because you can't be bothered to drive anywhere else.

The problem with behaviour only (transaction) data is that it will not discriminate between Specious and Composite Loyals. Discrimination between these groups would require us to survey and cross-reference with the behavioural data. Likewise, transaction data alone cannot delineate between the Disloyal and the Constrained Loyal unless some sentiment or review element is present.

The cycle of purchase is a factor; repeat purchase will tend to be lower where variety seeking may be a factor (see below), and it does tend to be lower for goods with numerous substitutes and for FMCGs as opposed to high involvement goods like automobiles, where attachment might be strong enough to create more Composite Loyals. Ehrenberg (1988) and his fellow travellers have also demonstrated that there is a relationship between product preference and market penetration. They all help to provide an actionable taxonomy of manifestations of loyalty and related concepts:

- *Sole brand loyalty.* Sole brand loyalty is quite simply being entirely loyal (in terms of repeat purchase) to a product. It is quite rare in FMCG markets (numerous studies have demonstrated this), but many people still use the term loyalty to indicate 100% adherence or purchase when in reality it is a special case. Dirichlet modelling research has also shown that in fast-moving markets sole brand loyals are often light buyers. However, digital virtual goods (DVGs) and subscription services have inbuilt inertia. For example, a consumer might have one mobile phone network provider, subscribe to one streaming service or have only one bank. If Spotify 'has' all your music then there is a cost to leaving them. Inertia effects and the impact of marketing analytics on them are revisited in Chapter 4.
- *Repertoire.* In many FMCG categories (e.g. coffee, beer, shampoo etc.) with fast purchase replacement cycles we buy in repertoires of products (we're multi-brand buyers). The repertoire is simply the number and composition of products you buy in a given class of product (e.g. soft drinks) over a given time frame. The slower the cycle of purchase or replacement the longer period of time we would need to get a meaningful assessment of repertoire (as with repeat purchase rates). This should not be confused with the concept of the Evoked Set – this is the set of brands that you would *consider* buying, not necessarily that you actually buy.

- *First brand loyalty*. This is the percentage of time you buy the favourite (most bought) brand in your product repertoire as defined above.
- *Footfall*. Simply refers to the act of setting foot in a store (not necessarily to purchase). The online equivalent would be visits to a purchase site in a given time period.

Routine and habit

Routine and habit are circumstantial (commuting) or enforced by a psycho-logical bias (risk aversion) or loyalty. For example, a transactional data set might indicate that an individual consumer buys a given basket of products on a repetitive and frequent basis on weekdays. They might buy their lunch from the same retailer most mornings around the same time, this 'habit' might be due to time poverty (the general business of their life and need for lunch on the go) and a function of convenience. It might also be underpinned by some psychological tendencies to habitual behaviour or laziness. The behav-ioural data cannot distinguish readily in terms of the drivers or motivating factors. Although, an individual may display a number of indicators of habit, e.g. similar shopping times outside of the apparent work days or adherence to certain products. Confirmation of these factors requires some kind of interactive data capture like a survey (see Chapter 1). So, we can distinguish between *true habit* or habitual tendencies and a *derived habit* not strongly underpinned by psychological tendencies – this being a form of circum-stantial habit often underpinned by work-life routine (or other routine). Spatial data traces are helpful. If the regular lunch purchase is associated with a store some distance from home then abductive inference suggests this is a work time purchase. Spatial and temporal dimensions are explored in more detail below.

Customer value

'Man walks into a pub...'

Miguel and Pablo go to the same pub on a regular basis (*El Perro Leal*). Miguel goes once a year – on a Saturday – for his birthday celebration and puts €2,000 behind the bar and everyone there gets free drinks until the money runs out. He never goes there at any other time. Pablo goes there every Saturday for a few drinks and some food and spends €37.00. Pablo spends €1,924 per annum (nominally the same as Miguel). Who is the most loyal? (Pablo does look forward to Miguel's birthday...)

The 'Man walks into a pub' cut-out illustrates and raises various issues about the assessment and measurement of customer loyalty and customer value:

- Both customers are worth approximately the same in terms of their crude overall value within a given period (a year).
- Both Pablo and Miguel exhibit very predictable and regular behaviour – once a week and once a year respectively.
- Their relative frequencies are utterly different: 52 times per annum and once per annum.
- Prior to his birthday Miguel won't have visited *El Perro Leal* for 364 days, whilst Pablo is there every seven days.
- Their behaviours are entirely distinct and they present very different challenges to the publican (these are reviewed below).

If we use certain measures then Pablo and Miguel will 'cluster' together or be associated as customers with similar attributes. Both spend a similar amount over the year and both are very regular in terms of their behaviour, so if those two variables are privileged in any analysis then they will appear similar (though we know that they are not in terms of some crucial attributes). If we only calculate for a six-month period, one that doesn't capture Miguel's birthday blowout, then we will get a very different picture. This emphasizes the importance of time frame selection; data will look different depending on the temporal span chosen (day, week, month etc). Average spend per week over the year will be roughly the same; again this is potentially misleading and spurious in managerial terms even though the mathematics are robust. Their differences are as important as their similarities from an analytical and operational point of view. It would seem sensible and justifiable to account for these differences without losing sight of the near equal contribution to income. Analytics should inform operational issues. Miguel's behaviour has implications for cash flow and operational issues like stock and staffing levels (the publican should mark Miguel's birthday on the calendar and be ready for it).

RFM

An attempt to reconcile some of the questions and issues that arise from the example above is exemplified in the Recency, Frequency and Monetary value model and its variants (adapted for different sectors). This model is a simple calculation of customer value and not synonymous with the more complex notion of customer lifetime value (CLV – see section below). There are numerous mathematical formulations for RFM, but they all account for three essential elements:

- Recency – When was the last purchase or interaction?
- Frequency – How often do they purchase/interact?
- Monetary Value – How much do they spend/interact?

The methods of assessing the three elements should be adapted to context, but most methods assign a score for each and these three scores can then be weighted according to sectoral concerns (for example, recency might be given more weight for pay-as-you-go cell phone users than would be the case for an online clothes retailer). The key issue is how each element is measured; once again this should be adapted according to the sector/market and situation.

1. *Recency.* The principal factor here is the choice of time frame – what is recent will vary from market to market as the example above illustrates. For example, whether they have visited in the last month would be relevant to an online retailer like Amazon but less relevant to a car part retailer or perhaps an airline. If the publican in the example above regards someone who hasn't been in for a drink in the last month as a 'lost' customer, then he will categorize Miguel as such – but will do so fallaciously (see *churn* below).
2. *Frequency.* Once again, what time interval is appropriate if the intention is to derive an average rate of purchase or visits? This is sector dependent – the faster the cycle of purchase, the faster moving the market then the smaller the appropriate time interval. So, months for grocery and longer for automobile purchases. If the publican in the example above chooses average visits per month then Miguel will score 0.083 (1/12th), while Pablo 4.3.
3. *Monetary value.* Again, monetary value over what time frame? The answer depends on judgement and the purpose of the analytics undertaken.

People can be given a score according to the actual value or assigned to quartiles of groups based on that score (this essentially converts the data into interval data). RFM scores can then be cross-referenced with other variables; perhaps demographic variables or other dimensions of behaviour (purchase basket profiles). There are variations of RFM with duration (D) or engagement (E) sometimes augmenting or replacing M. This variant is often used for assessing traffic to a website that does not rely on a transaction with the user to make money but harvests income from advertising relating to traffic (e.g. TripAdvisor). Some versions specifically incorporate non-purchase interactions (response or receptiveness to direct marketing – for interactions) whilst others account for churn rate:

- *Churn rate.* How many customers are lost in a given period? If a bank loses 3% of its accounts in a year then the rate is 3% churn per annum.
- *Retention rate.* 100 minus the churn rate, e.g. 100% − 3% = 97%.

One difficulty with churn rates is the fact that there are many reasons that a customer might disappear off the analytics radar screen only to return later. If the indication threshold is too strict then customers who travel regularly or who fall ill or experience a period of financial hardship might be spuriously identified as lost to churn when in reality they will return. This issue can be addressed by purposive data collection or identifying features and markers in the data that indicate travel, variant income etc.

Churn prediction is a huge area of predictive analytics in its own right. The analyst and the resultant algorithm will endeavour to identify changes in the behaviour of customers who subsequently leave in order to identify customers who are at risk of leaving (exhibiting the features of 'exiters'). For example, a gradual reduction in spend may be a prelude to zero spend in the final event. Other factors might be more subtle and more tricky to identify. For example, changes in preference in behaviour related to life stages or significant life events.

Customer lifetime value (CLV)

CLV essentially extends the logic of RFM and attempts to incorporate other elements; quite often it will use churn rate. The actual formula applied will vary from company to company and market to market. The basic principles of CLV are best illustrated through a simple worked example that distils the essential elements (see Gupta et al. 2006 for a comprehensive review of more complex approaches).

A simple distillation (for an online grocery retailer):

(Average monthly spend * Margin per customer) / Monthly Churn Rate
Case A: (£100 x 25%) / 3% (expressed as 0.03) = £833.33 = CLV
Case B: (£200 x 25%) / 3% (expressed as 0.03) = £1,666.66 = CLV

Clearly, in this example, the function has two constants (margin and churn). So, double the average spend will produce double the CLV. Envisage a situation in which the retailer establishes that a particular segment has a higher churn rate that relates to certain patterns of purchase and blends of goods purchased together (baskets); perhaps value-conscious families with limited discretionary income represent the principal occupants of this segment. Linking CLV with other data can prove invaluable.

Case C: (£100 x 25%) / 5% (expressed as 0.05) = £500 = CLV
Case D: (£200 x 25%) / 5% (expressed as 0.05) = £1,000 = CLV

The higher churn rate results in a lower CLV, since the churn rate is essentially a probability that the patron will exit from the retailer. So, although the average monthly spends and margins are the same as Case A and B, the resulting CLV is markedly different. Equally, the retailer may establish that certain segments have differential margins (profitability). This will have self-evident effects on the CLV (i.e. the higher the margin the higher the CLV).

Let's assume that a machine learning/autonomous algorithm-driven approach is able to extract consistent features that individualize the calculation of CLV in order to move beyond a segment-based approach. In this case churn rate (or margin – since this will vary according to the product lines purchased and will even vary from purchase event to event) can be adjusted per person not just by segment. For example the retailer may establish that customers prone to discounted high value purchases who have purchased for over five years consistently have a much lower churn rate of 1% (therefore a retention rate of 99% or 0.99).

Case E: (£200 x 25%) / 1% (expressed as 0.01) = £5,000 = CLV

This case describes a customer with an average monthly spend identical to Case D but with five times the CLV (they may only purchase once a month, so would score low on a crude Repeat Purchase Rate assessment). Whilst the retailer shouldn't become fixated with the highest CLV buyers, they will account for more revenue and possibly profit (depending on the margin for those individuals/that segment) than a similar number of lower CLV customers. Conversely, the retailer may decide to drive up the CLV of lower value groups through sales promotion (perhaps driven by an acknowledgement of their high margins).

CLV validity can be further enhanced by the application of a Discount Rate (DR); the interest rate used to calculate the value of the cash flow for the customer over time. Net Present Value (NPV) can also be employed; this being a formula to calculate the present value of the investment (the customer in this case, since servicing them costs money, margin representing the per customer profit) according to spending in the future. These elements are commonly employed in accounting and investment and they highlight an advantage and a drawback of CLV analysis (dealt with below).

CLV should be used very cautiously beyond the short to medium term and in this sense the word 'lifetime' is potentially misleading. Lifetime more accurately reflects the customer's 'life' or their worth during their sustained patronage. However, actual life expectancy can be taken into consideration. How? Well, spending patterns might help to indicate social groups and this can be cross-referenced with any demographic data. Although this might sound morbid, it is worth doing in markets with very low churn rates; for example banking and insurance (where inbuilt inertia might be linked with perceived high switching costs to militate against churn). Likewise, some loyalty programmes (those that have run for some decades) are a testament to the fact that a significant proportion of the customer base can display very high rates of *Composite Loyalty*. For these customers, projection of true 'lifetime' value is a possibility. Although, generally speaking, the further ahead in the future the projections of income and spend then the greater the dangers of spurious prediction. However, the function of forecasting is not prediction as such, it is estimation. Analysis of older *Composite Loyals* might provide a basis for predicting the future spend and worth of comparable younger patrons (who display spending consistent with their older associates). This is not as far-fetched as it sounds.

Greater sophistication and hopefully accuracy can also be derived through allowing a variation in the churn rate and margin over time as well as the more static approach described above (metrics become reflexive). For example it may become evident after analysis that churn rate increases as spend on high value items increases (perhaps purposive investigation establishes that this is driven by higher discretionary incomes over time).

The adoption of CLV marked a subtle but important shift in emphasis in consumer marketing. As already stated, loyalty is used to mean various distinct things. CLV is a more precise measurement, although there are issues with the fundamental and even more sophisticated methodologies, it broke ground by seeing the customer as a financial asset. This might sound dehumanizing but in crudely commercial terms this has some advantages. It overcomes some issues raised in the 'Man walks into a pub…' narrative. Fixating on CLV can mean that a humanized approach to marketing is at risk, however. This can lead to a mechanistic form of marketing that has various pitfalls:

- Focusing on financial dimensions can lead to a reductionist approach.
- The neglect of 'low value' groups or segments who are still strategically important (perhaps with high future value or potential).
- That CLV is perceived as definitive or 'real' as opposed to a useful tool for forecasting or estimation.

How churn and switching manifests in reality

Figure 2.2 exhibits forms of commonly observed behaviour. It depicts a time series/sequence of brand choice for an FMCG over a 40-day period using the weighted time-series technique introduced in Chapter 1 (here we assume the series accounts for all purchases; in fact one per day). The following forms of behaviour are market specific and it does not hold that a consumer with a tendency to the caricatures of behaviour below in one market will exhibit the same

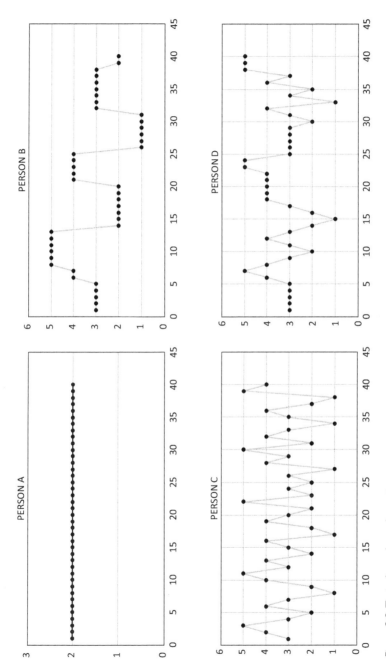

Figure 2.2 Typical purchase dynamics

tendency in another. It is quite possible to be a Composite Loyal (or Specious Loyal) to a brand of skin cream based on perceived effectiveness and utility whilst being a variety seeker when it comes to soft drinks. There is mixed evidence that people have general biases across the board in all markets, however some people are more habitual and risk averse whilst others are more adventurous. Marketing interventions can also drive switching. In short, the picture is a complex one with competing explanations for churn, switching and loyalty. Subsequent chapters deal with many of the determinants for choice dynamics.

The following cases are illustrative and in reality the series will be more 'noisy'.

Person A: Sole loyal

This is self-evident and Figure 2.2 is merely a graphical depiction of the concept of sole brand loyalty as discussed above. One brand/product/offering is consumed in the monitored time period with no or limited deviation. The explanations for this behaviour are indicated in Figure 2.1 and the subsequent commentary (i.e. composite loyalty, specious loyalty, habit etc.).

Person B: Sessioner or step-change

This is a form of behaviour brought about by 'serial monogamy'. The consumer repeatedly buys the same brand (perhaps with some limited deviation). This could be induced by 'chasing' sales promotions. For example, a consumer tends to buy the shampoo on offer. This would suggest that they are driven more by value than brand or utility. In turn this could be due to economic circumstances or a more subtle value seeking tendency (frugality or bargain seeking). The behavioural pattern could also be the result of other factors, changes in location over short time frames (affecting availability and preference), seasonal effects, a true form of serial loyalty with changes provoked by new product variants, or a susceptibility to marketing communications campaigns. It could also be the result of a slow-moving form of variety seeking – perhaps a consumer buys the same beer for a period and simply gets bored of it and switches every so often (therefore the pattern is the result of a stimulation function and elements of a short-term composite loyalty). Once again, a conflation/complex of causes and influences can be responsible for this in reality.

Person C: Oscillator

It is quite common to find that consumers move or switch within a repertoire of products, this gives the 'oscillating' effect illustrated in Figure 2.2. If the frequency of purchase is fast (daily) then this is unlikely to be caused by sales promotion, which tends to run over weeks rather than days (although other forms of marketing communication may have determining effects, as indeed may many other variables). However, it could be induced by price sensitivity relating to different outlets or locations or availability (e.g. a brand that is only available at the store near work). Another likely explanation is a form of 'routinized' or limited variety seeking; the consumer wishes to avoid consuming the same variety all the time but has clear preferences and limits. The definitions and possible causes of variety seeking are explored below.

Person D: Stager

Person D demonstrates a situation in which the consumer exhibits hybrid forms of purchase. They might stick with a product for a period then indulge in switching or derived or true variety seeking. This form of dynamic is quite common and a result of the complexity of drivers of choice and the potential explanations described for the other categories above (temporal variations in price, availability, or preference; preference biases are dynamic and not static). Marketing analytics spends a good deal of effort exploring the manifestation of 'entropy' or variety, switching, stability and instability.

Variety seeking

A key distinction is between *derived* variety seeking and *true* variety seeking; i.e. product switching not necessarily due to seeking variety as such but due to other explanatory variables such as price promotion or availability and variety seeking driven by the desire for change. Without other data besides transaction data, we cannot be sure that variety seeking is true, this would require us to survey and cross-reference with the behavioural data (or eliminate the other explanations if relevant variables and covariates are available in the transaction data). The Optimal Stimulation Level (OSL) explains the degree to which individuals indulge in variety seeking behaviour and is derived from work in psychology on exploratory behaviour (e.g. Van Trijp 1995). Essentially it explains variety seeking in terms of the requirement to be stimulated; the requirement to avoid boredom. A lower OSL will mean a reduced tendency to consciously seek variety and vice versa.

Data forms and dimensions

Data types

It is useful here to review the forms that data comes in prior to a discussion of dimensionality and a review of the various sources of data relevant to consumer analytics and their essential characteristics.

Cardinal

Cardinal data is quite simply numeric count or measurement data. For example the price of a given shopping basket or visit or individual product. There are two distinct categories of cardinal data: *continuous* and *discrete*. Continuous values are not constrained; they are expressed as any number or value between two values (e.g. 0 and infinity ∞ – although the upper limit might be constrained by a practical maximum). For example, the duration of a cell phone call could be a fraction of a second or many hours. This value can be expressed to many decimal places, however for transactional or charging purposes this degree of accuracy is not required and, as is typical in such data, the figure will be rounded. For example, the cell phone network provider will likely record the duration of the call to the nearest second. GPS location can be expressed continually or within given time intervals. Discrete values are expressed as whole numbers or values. For example footfall (the term used to describe store visit events). There cannot be half a visit to a store, it has to be a whole or discrete value, but it might be between 0 and a very large upper limit (e.g. number of visits to a given shopping mall in Hong Kong). Both of these forms of cardinal data are very common in transactional and other data. A key issue is how they manifest in time, the temporal realm; a section below deals with this crucial point.

Ordinal

Ordinal data is numeric data with a direction or rank. Table 2.1 gives two examples. Scale data is often used to capture expressions of opinion or attitude (often from purposive data capture), for example in a hotel satisfaction questionnaire administered on departure. In that case the number is a mathematical abstraction of something that does not actually exist. The second example of ranked data can be derived via survey or by converting (transforming) cardinal data described above (you convert the continuous value and categorize by rank).

Table 2.1 Ordinal data examples

Level type	1	2	3	4	5
Scale	1 = Like very much	2 = Like	3 = Neither like nor dislike	4 = Dislike	5 = Dislike very much
Rank	Most visited store	Second most visited store	Third most visited store	Fourth most visited store	Fifth most visited store

Interval

Interval data is collected in that format (for example in a survey) or by converting (transforming) cardinal data described above (you convert the continuous value and categorize by interval). It is less common in transactional data unless the data transformation is built into the data capture. Table 2.2 gives two examples.

Interval data are commonly used in survey types of data capture via online questionnaires or service sign-up. It is useful for capturing data on self-revealing cardinal data such as income, as we know that respondents are more likely to answer truthfully and accurately if an interval scale is used (as opposed to asking for their exact income). During the analytical process it might be expedient to convert cardinal data into categories; this might be necessitated by preference for a given technique.

Nominal and categorical

Nominal or categorical data has no mathematical 'direction' and is not numeric. This type of data is common in analytics; product names and brands and product stock-keeping categories are clear examples. Nominal and categorical data can be converted or transformed into numeric values with some 'meaning' as in Figure 2.2 (product brand name into a weighted value to reflect purchase frequency). Often any numeric coding is arbitrary and mathematically meaningless but useful. For example converting gender orientation into a number after recoding it as a category; this transformation is arbitrary and the analyst should not then treat this data as truly numeric data. It can also be derived from the analysis of text and pictures (via machine and 'deep' learning techniques) to derive themes or topics from complex data (e.g. social media, purchase bundles). For example we can take Facebook page text and mine it for indications of well-being and happiness and categorize people accordingly (there are various practical and ethical challenges with this kind of analysis).

Table 2.2 Examples of interval data

Category example	1	2	3	4	5
Income per annum	¥0–49,999	¥50,000– 99,999	¥100,000– 149,999	¥150,000– 199,999	¥200,000+
Age (years)	0–19	20–39	40–59	60–79	80+

Transaction data in reality

The variety of these various data types within a data set will determine and constrain the 'traditional' statistical techniques employed. More complex methods and the application of machine learning can often address these, however the mix of data types within the initial data matrix is a key point. Table 2.3 provides an illustrative example. In reality, there may be even more columns and the exact configuration will vary from data set to data set.

The configuration of data is not necessarily optimized for analysis. Transactional data serves other masters. For example, stock-keeping and inventory management, taxation obligations, with its primary purpose being a record of the transaction for income inflow. The customer insight team will need to use the Transaction ID and the No of Items (number of identical items) columns to create a 'basket', i.e. all the products bought at the same time/transaction. Event 1 and 2 have the same transaction ID and therefore the same time and store stamp, but these are recorded discretely. The Store Code will identify the store location and is the only spatial indicator. The item description will also have a numeric code (this has been omitted here for the sake of economy and readability of this table). The account number is the same and therefore this fragment of data is for one person/cardholder (though they may have bought on behalf of others).

The matrix above is superficially very simple. However, a careful examination of this very small slice of big data illustrates the inherent complexity of such artefacts. The matrix contains nominal and cardinal data, and these can be cross-referenced with time and a crude spatial indicator. The following observations are elementary but important starting points:

- Purchases are made on consecutive days.
- Two stores visited.
- Three visits/baskets.
- Baskets are small.

Various questions arise. The questions below are not exhaustive, they are examples of the analytic potential of the data in practical managerial terms. Analysis of a larger slice of data will address these if appropriate techniques are applied:

- How often does this person visit stores?
- What times do they visit stores?
- Which stores do they visit in a given time frame and can we extrapolate a work/life or home/leisure pattern in the data?
- How varied are their baskets?
- Which products occur most frequently?
- What do they spend/redeem loyalty points on?
- What are the seasonal patterns in the data?

Table 2.3 Example of convenience store loyalty card data

Case/event	Account no.	Price	No. of items	Transaction ID	Store code	Product description full	Product category/ merchandise group	Date and time	Points accrued	Points or offers redeemed
Item 1	28998989	01.40	2	55858858	68787	Fresa Strawberry Snack Bar 50g	Long-life snack	13.09 27.7.22	0.28	0.00
Item 2	28998989	10.99	1	55858858	68787	Lobster Sun Cream 250ml	Skin care – summer	13.09 27.7.22	1.10	0.00
Item 3	28998989	01.49	1	34544544	68787	Pokey Cola Diet 330ml can	Soft drink	10.26 28.7.22	0.15	0.00
Item 4	28998989	01.49	3	44464666	89899	Pokey Cola Diet 330ml can	Soft drink	15.56 29.7.22	0.43	0.00
Item 5	28998989	04.29	1	44464666	89899	Gourmet Gluten-free Veggie Feast Wrap	Pre-packed sandwich	15.56 29.7.22	0.43	0.00

The retailer will want to determine any individual patterns in the data and also determine whether segments/clusters within the data reflect these tendencies and patterns or biases – in other words, are there consistent usage patterns of the store? These might associate with the location of stores (see Figure 2.4). For example, a store in a transport hub might have a distinct usage pattern in terms of the items bought, basket mixes, peak times and frequency of use. So, the Store Code becomes more than a number, we can derive a nominal variable for the store; for example Airport, Small Neighbourhood Centre, City Centre etc. or something more sophisticated grounded in the data. The key point here is that we are adding a variable or feature to the matrix above. We can also label the transaction ID with basket categorizations derived from analysis of the whole data set. For example, 'Snack only', 'Drink only', 'Non-food led' etc. If this categorization is automated then the algorithm can learn to improve and enhance the categorization. We can then associate the matrix with external variables, the weather (sun = more drinks and sun cream), significant events, the demographics of the account holder, the list is potentially very long indeed. Now, imagine that same matrix/data set for 8 million regular purchasers and for ten years' worth of transactions. This allows us to interrogate issues around seasonality and even explore changes in locality and employment (indicated through using different stores).

Data complexity and dimensionality

At its most basic level, dimensionality relates to the number of variables (columns) in the data matrix (see Table 2.3). The rows in the matrix are the cases (e.g. events, people, purchases etc.). The mix of data types within that matrix complicates and creates dimensionality/complexity. Dimensionality is also a factor of any spatial and temporal realm; the presence of both of these simultaneously combined with a mix of variable types (cardinal, ordinal, interval, and nominal – COIN) leads to data sets with high dimensionality. Data sets that are high dimensionally and rapidly expanding with a high velocity of capture (e.g. smartphone record data) present practical and analytical challenges. They are vast and complex and expanding – so-called Big Data.

In order to navigate this issue the following three aspects of dimensionality and data richness or complexity are reviewed and then applied to commonly captured forms of commercial data streams: activity, time and space.

Activity

The essential nature of the activity recorded will vary in terms of the mix of COIN variables. Data will often record purchase or other activity (browsing, usage etc.). It will typically record the activity based on the following generators (or units) of activity:

1. *Individuals*. Phones, cards and accounts are often linked to individuals. Purchase data linked to an individual (via a loyalty card or online) will allow individual targeting and personalization. However, a note of caution: individuals often buy or act on behalf of others. Some data capture is clearly linked to an individual or lead purchaser (e.g. cell phone usage via SIM ID), others are more ambiguous in terms of whether they represent individual or collective (e.g. household activity); for example a grocery store loyalty card. The data itself will provide clues to this question (e.g. child-related products).

2. *Households*. Smart electricity meters are an example of household or address-based forms of rich data capture. However, households are sometimes single person households, i.e. individuals. Store cards can also fall into this category (the issue of household composition and decision making is comprehensively dealt with in Chapter 7).

3. *Centres of activity*. For example an offline store. Individual consumers' usage and patronage may occur and provide rich data streams even without individual identifiers. Store cards identify the individual whilst an offline store without a store card scheme may have no way of tracking the individual patron (unless they tag the payment card). They will have electronic point-of-sale data (EPOS data). This will record activity and enable the analysis of baskets and allow them to characterize at the basket/purchase event level or store level (an example is given in a subsequent section) rather than for the individual purchaser. Footfall is also based on visits to a centre of activity (store or site). Footfall is sometimes recorded via facial recognition. The store or mall will tag a face and know how many faces have visited within a given time frame and how many faces have visited more than once.

The units of activity generation all provide data of variant richness and complexity. This will vary according to data capture protocols and formats. Footfall via facial recognition will provide simple counts with a temporal dimension, for example. It represents a relatively simple data set with a binary (visit; no visit recorded with a time stamp). This makes the data set relatively low in richness. Many commercial data sets are far more complex.

Data dimensions

1. *Time*. Some data streams will provide temporal data that is continuous. A smart meter in a household will provide continuous data. Even if no electricity is being consumed this is valid data. The time series of usage will

simply revert to zero. This will give meaningful indicators of the household usage pattern: all devices get turned off in this house at night, this house is empty, they go on holiday for two weeks in June each year. Data that is not continuous is called *point data*; indicative of a *point progression*. A classic example is store/site visits/patronage. For each given day (or hour or week) there may be many non-visits. Visits may be sparse.

2. *Space*. Spatial data can be continuous or *point/static*. Smart meters are located in houses, so are smart devices like Amazon Alexa. Alexa will give indications of spatial 'tendencies', for example asking about good restaurants in a given locality miles from home. Smartphones provide GPS and cell tower locality. When turned on the device may effectively provide a continuous spatial trace. Online purchase or in-store purchase provide static indications of locality; store codes or ISP addresses. They do not track you on a continual basis.

When temporal and spatial data are effectively continuous then the dimensionality of the richness of activity or usage recorded is complex (Table 2.4 summarizes some examples in terms of time and space). Intertwine continuous spatial traces and continuous temporal data and you have a data set that becomes very large very quickly. For example, the data captured by the Android operating system on a mobile phone. If the data recorded is also multi-dimensional in terms of the activity richness then the potential of the data is considerable in theory; however, the noise in the data is likely to increase and the potential analytical challenges may also correlate. The larger and more complex the data set the greater the challenge of summary and data reduction. High dimensionality and complexity will mean that visualizations reliant on two dimensions will need to be capable of 'collapsing' those dimensions (for example via dynamic topic modelling – DTM). A very crude rule of thumb is: 'the more complex the data the more complex the mathematics'. Complex forms of analysis can sometimes provide output that is harder to interpret or to apply to data-driven decisions; however, it may also hold gems of knowledge that would otherwise remain submerged in the data. Moving from complex raw data to actionable and interpretable output is a key challenge in consumer analytics; the process is related to concepts such as *sense-making* and *data-driven decision making* (D^3); these issues form the spine of Chapter 8. Visualization of data is a key issue: exhibits (tables, graphs, schematics, maps, heat maps, animations etc.) provide accessible summarization of complex data and output. They are a key component of the process. Output is meaningless and useless if it cannot inform sound managerial decisions. We will review the forms of visualization below and explore how the various dimensions in the data can be represented in order to inform D^3.

Table 2.4 Example data categories and dimensions

Data type	Dimensions		
	Activity and data categories	Time	Space
Loyalty card	Transactional	Yes – but point process so only has a time stamp when activity occurs	Yes – not continuous – stores are static
Online retail	Transactional	Yes – point	Location potentially available through ISP address
Call detail record – basic	Transactional	Yes – continuous (unless device is off – even when not in use – the null data is useful)	Location through cell tower usage. Continuous if device on.
EPOS data (no individual identifier)	Transactional	Yes	Yes – but stores are static
Smart device (portable)	Multi-dimensional activity Transactional	Yes – continuous	Location through cell tower usage or GPS. Continuous if device on
Smart device – static not interactive e.g. Smart Meter – Smart Fridge	Transactional	Yes – usage/function determines whether continuous or point	Static
Smart device – static – interactive e.g. Amazon Alexa	Multi-dimensional activity	Yes – point	Static
Financial services	Transactional	Yes – point	Static
Browsing and ISP Data	Multi-dimensional activity	Yes – point	Dependent on device
Social media	Multi-dimensional activity	Yes – point	Quasi-static – depends how data is accessed
APP usage	Activity	Yes – point	Quasi-static – depends how data is accessed and app usage/ function
Footfall by facial recognition	Behavioural – static	Yes – point	Static

Data dimensions and visualization

This section gives a brief overview of the topic. Subsequent sections and chapters will provide various examples relating to specific applications (conceptual and empirical). Some examples have already been given in Chapter 1 and the first part of this chapter. Marketing likes to collapse data to two dimensions. Why? Well, because pages, slides etc. are two-dimensional. A third dimension requires some form of pseudo three-dimensional graphic. Although, the 'DNA' examples in the next section represent various features or dimensions in a two-dimensional form, they are essentially transformations of simple charts. It is crucial not to confuse the dimensionality in the data with the dimensions of data visualization. Multi-dimensional data can be represented in two dimensions in terms of visualization.

The simple map of two 'meaningful' dimensions (where each axis represents actual variables) is useful for any bivariate comparison (see Figure 1.5, Chapter 1). It is still very common in consumer analytics because it requires very little explanation (three-dimensional representations are possible with the appropriate software; indeed virtual reality allows data to be explored as a 'space' but these applications are not yet ubiquitous). Any simple two-dimensional graphic can have the quadrant lines imposed upon it (these should intersect at the mid-point or average/median of both variables). Data visualizations are representations of data indicating things from real life; they are not 'real' in themselves. They are essentially crude models. Like all models they are useful but their limitations should never be forgotten.

The two dimensions used are often mathematically meaningful but do not represent variables found in the raw data (or reduced data). The representation is then multivariate not bivariate. The example in Figure 2.3 could be

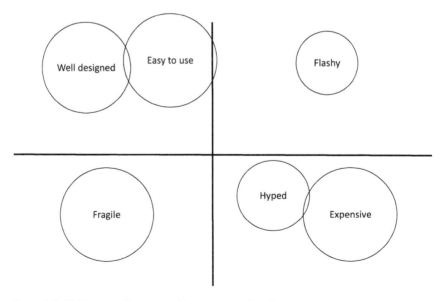

Figure 2.3 Multivariate distance and importance of topics

derived from topic modelling (e.g. Jacobi, van Atteveldt and Welbers 2016). The topics can then be 'mapped' (via a technique such as principal components analysis); the axes do not represent variables as such but are mathematically meaningful. The example here associates words from some web-scraped data relating to a discussion of a brand, however, such a technique could be applied to any text-based nominal data (any forum or social media data). Figure 2.3 depicts the distance of the derived topics and also their importance (depicted by the size of the circles). The larger the circle the more important or prevalent the topic, closer proximity or distance of topics demonstrates association in reality. The closer the topic the more likely to be in the same piece of text/post/review.

The heat map depicts the importance of something or the intensity of an activity by the size and/or colour intensity of an actual geographical zone (e.g. a region or ward or cell tower Voronoi regions). This is a useful device for summarizing data with a spatial dimension and is very common. It is useful for convenience showing store usage intensity as depicted in Figure 2.4. The darker the store the greater its weekly revenue. The stores are then spatially mapped according to the boundary of the urban area in question in relation to the principal transport routes.

The map is self-evidently useful if the spatial distribution is the overriding subject of interest. If animated then the time dimension can be incorporated (in order to show seasonal changes of activity or perhaps consumer spend patterns in a city in the day vs. the night). This requires numerous versions of Figure 2.4 for each week or month, for example.

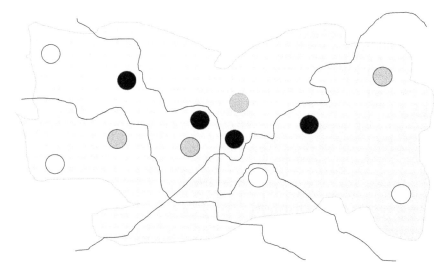

Figure 2.4 The heat map

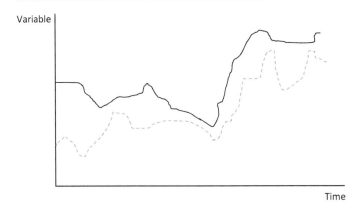

Figure 2.5 Simple time series

Time series are simple two-dimensional graphs of one or more variable over time. When depicting multiple variables each line is signified by a colour or other form of discrimination as in Figure 2.5. The time axis is, by convention, the horizontal axis. The key factor is the level of aggregation or unit size of the time axis. A time series depicting weekly sales will look very different from one depicting daily sales over the same time frame. The level of aggregation should be determined by the research question (e.g. identification of daily busy hours or busiest days for staffing purposes).

The exposition above is not exhaustive, it is illustrative. As already stated above, *CB&A* provides numerous examples of exhibits to explore applications and demonstrate various aspects of method and consumer behaviour. A crucial point to emphasize here is the power of visualizations when they are presented in an array and cross-referenced. For example, a map of store types as shown in Figure 2.4 can be accompanied by the typical weekly spend per hour of those stores (like Figure 2.5). An important example dealt with in Chapter 3 is the network. The network shows 'traffic' or flow between nodes (people, places or websites etc.). It can incorporate elements of the heat map, where the size and shade of the node signifies importance or intensity of activity (for example a highly active Twitter account).

Features, correlation, association and relationships

Features at the individual level

Feature extraction (or variable if the analysis is more conventional) is a key part of machine learning based analytics. It concerns the identification of meaningful and significant tendencies and characteristics in the data. The data matrix (like the one in Table 2.3) provides the initial variable but not the features. The crude data has potential to provide features. For example a tendency/

propensity to derived variety seeking across various product groups must be derived or extracted from the raw data; there is no column for it in the matrix. Feature extraction allows personification and personalization of scores and the collective categorization of an individual according to these features. So, it can lead to descriptive or predictive analytics. Personification of individuals or other centres of activity (e.g. stores) is a possibility. Data mining and exploratory analysis are often used to generate and derive features. Once they are exposed then consumers can be assigned scores according to those features in the data; grocery customer 'DNA' as illustrated in Figures 2.6 and 2.7.

Take some time to cross-reference the feature descriptions for Person X and Person Y in Figures 2.6 and 2.7. Positive scores show high tendency/spend; negative show low evidence of feature (or inverse of feature). Some of the features are essentially opposites (e.g. Traditional vs. Adventurous) but it is possible to score moderately in both. In sum, Person X appears to be health-,

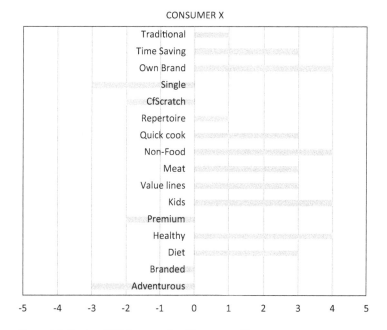

Figure 2.6 Feature/DNA scores for Consumer X

Feature descriptions: **Adventurous** – A measure of entropy/variety and the tendency to buy new and innovative lines. **Branded** – Tendency to buy branded lines as opposed to own label lines. **Diet** – Propensity to buy diet and low-fat lines. **Healthy** – Tendency to buy products associated with a healthy lifestyle. **Premium** – Purchase of more expensive lines with cheaper alternatives. **Kids** – Child-related products. **Value lines** – Purchase of lines badged as value. **Meat** – Meat purchase. **Non-Food** – Proportion of spend on non-food. **Quick cook** – Degree of purchase of microwave food. **Repertoire** – Size of repertoire for various product groups. **CfScratch** – Purchase of lines suggesting food is prepared from scratch. **Single** – Degree of single portions bought. **Own Brand** – Proportion of purchase of retailer's own brand. **Time Saving** – Purchase of lines designed to cut down cooking and preparation. **Traditional** – Purchase of lines deemed to represent the conventional foods for the group in question.

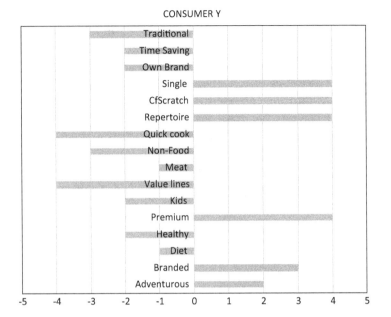

CONSUMER Y

Figure 2.7 Feature/DNA scores for Consumer Y
Refer to the notes to Figure 2.6 for full feature descriptions.

value- and time-conscious and also a family buyer. Person Y is the mirror image (to a large extent); they are disassociated. On an individual level these DNA scores can be used to target them with variant marketing communications and offers. If segmentation analysis incorporates this data then they will be in different clusters/segments. Features can be extracted from any transactional/ behavioural data set. The more complex the data the more likely that the feature list is elongated. For example a leading smart device ecosystem operator bases analytics on more than 200 features (from derived personality, various tendencies, politics, mobility, morality, kids, pets etc.).

Correlation

'Are we related?'

Antoinette has been working late, mining data for a men's apparel online SME retailer with no dedicated analytics department. She is not a maths specialist and relies on spreadsheet-based software and 'plays' with the data until she finds something useful. This has worked on several previous occasions – she has a keen instinct for the market and is no fool. One night, after ordering pizza she makes a breakthrough half-way through a slice of Nicey-Spicey. She discovers that there is a relationship between hat size and repeat purchase rates for briefcases. The correlation is high, strikingly high. This leads her to spend significant funds on a direct marketing communications campaign targeting men with large heads for a new luxury brand line of briefcases. It fails…

Antoinette is a particular kind of data scientist. She *is* a data scientist, perhaps feral, untrained and reliant on her intellect and her market nous; but if you play with data you are doing data science whether you like it or not, in the same way that someone who cycles regularly is a cyclist. They have no chance of winning the Tour de France but they are a cyclist (and they can only improve). *CB&A* is based on the premise that the Antoinettes of the commercial world require some readily consumed 'atlas' of consumer behaviour and analytics (not a course in applied mathematics and statistics – nonetheless we can't avoid the underlying issues in the maths). She is not a rare breed. Many SMEs rely on people like Antoinette, even if they outsource some of their analytics functions and rely on 'off the peg' solutions (e.g. Google Analytics). Even the most mathematically gifted data scientists can make 'mistakes' (in fact they are slaves to trial and 'error'), they do not make an enemy of error. Mistakes really aren't mistakes when you realize why something doesn't work. As soon as that happens they become learning. That is not as trite as it sounds. It is true. More precisely, Antoinette has discovered the hard way that correlation (the search for a robust linear relationship between two variables) can be beguiling and lead to sub-optimal managerial decision making. A mathematical relationship can happen by accident/be fallacious or it can be real. Perhaps she has uncovered something real, but perhaps there is an intervening variable or feature that links the two that she has concluded is insignificant. Perhaps she has found out something entirely spurious. More skill, training and mathematical insight will help her; but some fundamental appreciation of the complexity in transaction data is a start. The following sections explore issues around complexity, association, correlation and relationships between variables and things.

Patterns and structure in consumer data

The maths to find the structure in the examples in Figure 2.8 needs to be more sophisticated than simple correlation tests (like Pearson). The figure depicts various scenarios for the relationship between two variables (A and B – e.g. spend vs. age). The cases powerfully emphasize the effectiveness and importance

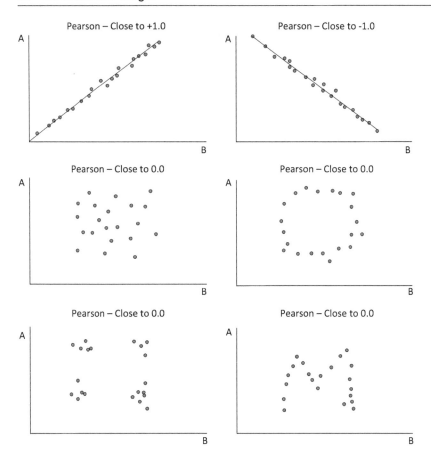

Figure 2.8 Correlation and the lack of it

of visualization, though. The structure in the data (or lack of it) is self-evident in each case. Correlation looks for a line. Where there is no line then it will not find it. Dispersion, or non-linear structures will give low correlation scores as Figure 2.8 illustrates. The examples below are for a bivariate relationship (the relationship between just two things in isolation). As identified above, many transactional data sets are multivariate, complex and multi-dimensional. No one ever said data science and consumer analytics was easy.

Association at the individual and aggregate level

Analytics is often about the search for patterns, hidden or obvious structures in data, association and relationships. Data is a soup, analytics is the search (sometimes forlorn) for the recipe. It is a form of reverse engineering; exploring the anatomy of things that have already happened. There are numerous ways and methods of searching for these associations (these can feed into the DNA style features above). This section reviews and discusses commonly employed examples, their limitations, advantages and some underlying issues:

Individual level

Basket analysis is ubiquitous. It seeks to associate products bought at the same time by the same purchaser (again, bear in mind that they may be/will be purchasing on behalf of others). Table 2.5 illustrates a typical purchase event or bundle of products bought at the same time.

Mr C Bellamy is seemingly a creature of habit. His basket varies but it is consistent enough for him to be categorized as someone with limited 'entropy' or variance in his spend. A newspaper, a chocolate bar, some bread, nappies and a bottle of wine. As illustrated before, various conclusions can be made about his life from this data (these conclusions have potential pitfalls as well as potential gains for the marketer). He *might* consume the bottle of wine on the way back from the shop… It is more likely that he is simply buying it for evening consumption. Whatever, the basket level analysis is a useful unit of analysis. It records a visit to the store or site. It goes beyond a simple count of products bought within a given time frame and locates purchases as part of an 'event'.

Association rule mining is often used to undertake basket analysis (Ma and Liu 1998). This simply seeks to determine which products are bought together. Basket analysis is ubiquitous in retail analytics. If robust associations are made between specific products or product groups or classes then this can be used to inform product placement in-store (or online), marketing communications (bundling offers or 'unrelated' products together). An extension of this is the construction of product constellations. Product constellations essentially extract classes or categories of product or product function/utility or usage from the analysis of baskets or overall purchase over a given time frame (e.g. products associated with a healthy lifestyle). The picture generated can indicate various lifestyle and behavioural factors. Topic generation (based on topic

Table 2.5 Mr C Bellamy's typical basket (8.00 am local convenience store)

Product	Price	Quantity
The Daily Gleaner	1.00	1
Choco Moco Choc Bar	0.80	1
French Baton (Family Size)	2.00	1
Nappies/Diapers	5.00	1
La Sloerve Merlot – 75cl	10.00	1

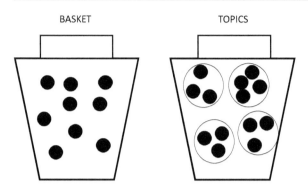

Figure 2.9 Basket vs. topics

modelling) is also very important and potentially powerful. It attempts to associate products bought together consistently within a given data set. Analysis
applies to the data set as a whole but the unit of analysis is the individual.
Topics are bundles of products bought together consistently within a data
set. They may not be in the same product/stock-keeping class (e.g. hair care);
in fact they often are not. However, they are bought together. For example,
a 'male grooming topic' might associate hair gel, shaving gel, face balm and
shampoo. A 'travel/holiday' topic might associate sun cream, sunglasses and
motion sickness pills. Figure 2.9 illustrates the logic of the topic vs. the basket.
Dynamic topic modelling (Smith, Goulding and Smith 2016) allows us to
cluster topics by adding a temporal dimension (it can discriminate between
'male grooming' Saturday spend and weekday lunchtime). This could also be
applied to digital virtual goods (DVGs); for example genres of streamed music
accessed at any given time of the week.

Aggregate level

At the aggregate level, segmentation is the most obvious and widespread
manifestation of the search for association between individuals. Figure 2.10
takes four of the examples from Figure 2.8 and simply imposes axes at the
intersection of the median points for the two variables in order to demonstrate the essence of clustering. For the sake of continuity let's assume that the
two variables are A=Spend, B=Age. This is the essence of segmentation, the
imposition of structure on dispersed or uncorrelated data. If the variables are
correlated (like the first two cases in Figure 2.8), then a continuum is exposed
(e.g. older = higher spend). A continuum does not require two dimensions,
and whenever bivariate segmentation diagrams show a linear relationship then
abandon them; since they will add little to an analysis of association and disassociation. One can simply represent the market as a continuum or linear

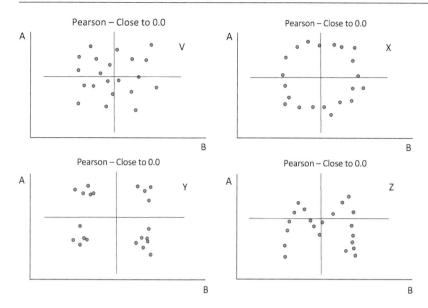

Figure 2.10 Dividing uncorrelated data

equation or function; this is justifiable but it isn't really segmentation and it certainly isn't clustering.

Once again, the power of visualization is self-evident. The median axes provide quadrants and illustrate the strengths and the potential dangers and ambiguities of this approach. Case Z is unambiguous. There are four distinct groups, one in each quadrant (low age – low spend; high spend – high age; low spend – high age; low age – high spend). However, clustering is not usually this neat and clear (more sophisticated techniques are covered below; they often produce more ambivalent results). In case V each quadrant is populated but there are a number of cases that are close or even on the margins of another quadrant. Simple or more advanced clustering analysis often gives rise to this. These cases (consumers) might therefore be regarded as conflations or transitory zones in the map; they are marginal and we could choose to see them as out with the more evident cluster (some more advanced analysis allows multiple membership and allows 'overlap'). In cases X and Z the quadrants don't 'explain' the underlying structure (these can be expressed mathematically); however, the division into quadrants does allow the imposition of some alternative structure. This is more actionable in case X than Z. In case X a good number of cases lie within the 'depths' of the quadrant although the 'margins' are also populated. In Z the strength of the quadrant imposition is even less clear.

Practitioners do employ this form of manual bivariate segmentation (often by selecting two overriding features or conflating features from customer DNA

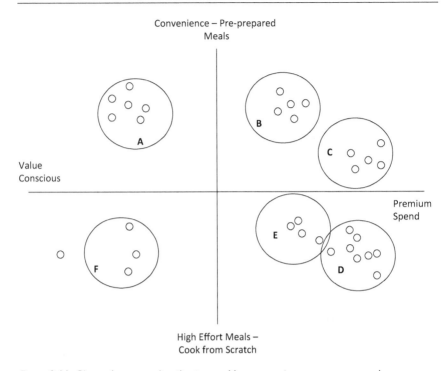

Figure 2.11 Cluster/segment distribution and homogeneity – grocery example

Note: Each dot represents 100,000 customers.

Cluster A: Is quite tightly defined by the two axes. This should make it easier to target with store/site specifications and marketing communications informed by the segmentation variables.

Cluster B & C: Are in the same quadrant but distinct. Sometimes it might be appropriate to target them as one cluster or segment, to an extent it depends on the homogeneity of the other features within the cluster as discussed below (each might be composed of groups with very distinct demographic features, for example). C and E could be considered as a 'meta-segment' since they are both close to the median for the vertical axis. If their membership is associated by demographics or other meaningful features then this would strengthen the case for treating it as a dispersed or diffuse segment.

Cluster D & E: Again a decision needs to be made about the benefits of regarding the two as operationally distinct. We could regard the two dots on the margins of the cluster as a sub-segment in their own right. Once again, more information on the further characteristics of the membership of the cluster is required.

Cluster F & the Outlier: F is distinct and diffuse. There is a clear outlier grouping of 100,000 very value-conscious consumers. Nonetheless, they are all in the same quadrant of value-conscious consumers who tend to cook from scratch.

scores). Figure 2.11 depicts variables used by a major multinational grocery retailer. If this managed or 'manual' method of axis choice is adopted then the choice must have some underlying logic; it must be justifiable and it should be actionable (provide clusters/segments that inform/are useful for marketing decisions). The following issues must be considered:

- In order to achieve a bivariate solution a number of variables and features can be conflated. In Figure 2.11 the axes (Cook from scratch/Pre-made meals vs. Premium spend/Value-conscious) are derived from similar features in Figure 2.6 and 2.7. Various features (e.g. spend, premium product purchase) might indicate affluence, for example, and they can be combined into an overall affluence score (usually via weighting the values for each feature). Likewise value consciousness can be indicated by the propensity to take up offers and sales promotions, the magnitude of purchase of value lines, overall spend per annum, average basket spend etc.
- The variables or axes must have a good chance of discriminating and delineating, there is no point in experimenting with axes that don't split customers up. If overall spend is not distributed and quite consistent in your customer base then it is futile to use it as a discriminating variable/ axes in a bivariate segmentation approach. Therefore, checking the distribution of variables is a good idea.

Key issues are therefore the distance from other members and other clusters, the size and compactness/diffuseness of the cluster, proximity to the median/ medoid/centroid (or extreme) on any axis and the homogeneity of the cluster beyond the two discriminating axes. The other characteristics, features or variables of the cluster must be known so that the anatomy of the cluster can be better understood. The segments can either be homogeneous or heterogeneous beyond the two variables used to cluster. Some of these other variables and features might reside in the transactional data set. An additional option is to interrogate the cluster with purposive research, for example a survey to explore the lifestyles of the cluster members.

Many clustering techniques (e.g. k-means) generate axes with mathematical significance (and more complex conceptual meaning) and employ more than two input variables; they are multivariate. The mathematics of these techniques are complex and varied. Some basic terms and concepts are dealt with below. The primary function of the discussion here is to contextualize the use function and limitations of clustering and classification in consumer analytics not to explore the mathematics. Figure 2.12 provides an abstract example.

The cluster solution in Figure 2.11 is derived through four input variables:

- An RFM-based score for CLV.
- The average spend on food items per month over the last year.
- The average spend on non-food items per month over the last year.
- An income assessment based on the postcode/zipcode moderated by other evidence in the purchase data (premium item spend etc.).

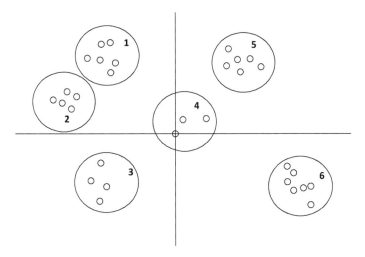

Figure 2.12 Multivariate cluster solution

How are these variables/features selected? Preliminary knowledge building analysis can establish the variables that have the greater potential for explanatory power. There is an element of trial and error with any protocol to establish the features for cluster analysis.

Cluster summary descriptions (low, medium, high – the exact location is determined by actual values):

1. Low RFM score, high spend on food; low spend on non-food, medium income.
2. Low RFM score, medium spend on food, low spend on non-food, lower income.
3. Medium RFM, high spend on food, medium spend on non-food, medium income.
4. Medium RFM, medium spend on food, medium spend on non-food, medium income.
5. High RFM, high spend on food, high spend on non-food, medium income.
6. High RFM, medium spend on food, high spend on non-food, high income.

If values are assigned accordingly (1 = low; 2 = medium; 3 = high) then the transformation depicted in Figure 2.13 is possible.

Segmentation and other forms of descriptive analysis serve a valuable summarization function. However, their use should always be subject to questioning. They present models of the market but segmentation is never 'true'. It is healthier to see any segmentation 'solution' as a window on the data. Indeed,

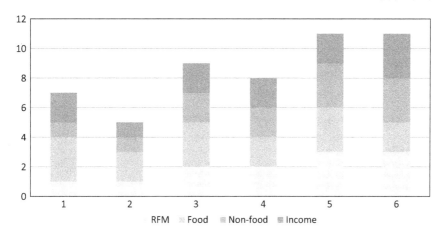

Figure 2.13 High, medium and low scores for each cluster for each variable
Note: The vertical axis depicts the score vs. the segment number (horizontal axis).

multiple solutions with different numbers of clusters, different input variables can be generated; each of these may provide valuable insights that can trigger further informed investigation.

Conclusion

This chapter has explored various metrics, concepts and methods that we can employ in order to understand and think about the consumer behaviourally and transactionally. The essential quest in consumer analytics is for association and disassociation between products, features and people. These can also have temporal and spatial manifestations. Transactional data sets are highly complex and dynamic; this chapter represents an elementary introduction to the topic. It is sufficient for the purposes of *CB&A* (i.e. a tour of core concepts sufficient to inform the content of subsequent chapters and the terms of reference of the book). However, this should not obscure the inherent complexity of the under-lying issues and data dimensions.

References

Dick, A.S. and Basu, K. 1994. Customer loyalty: Toward an integrated conceptual frame-work. *Journal of the Academy of Marketing Science*, 22(2), pp. 99–113.
Ehrenberg, A. 1988. *Repeat-buying: Facts, theory and applications.* Oxford: Oxford University Press.
Gupta, S., Hanssens, D., Hardie, B., Kahn, W., Kumar, V., Lin, N., Ravishanker, N. and Sriram, S. 2006. Modeling customer lifetime value. *Journal of Service Research*, 9(2), pp. 139–155.

Jacobi, C., van Atteveldt, W. and Welbers, K. 2016. Quantitative analysis of large amounts of journalistic texts using topic modelling. *Digital Journalism*, 4(1), pp. 89–106.

Jacoby, J. and Chestnut, R.W. 1978. *Brand loyalty: Measurement and management.* New York: John Wiley & Sons.

Ma, B.L.W.H.Y. and Liu, B. 1998, August. Integrating classification and association rule mining. In *Proceedings of the Fourth International Conference on Knowledge Discovery and Data Mining.*

Smith, G., Goulding, J. and Smith, A. 2016. Beyond customer segmentation – Temporal topic modelling for big retail data. In *American Marketing Association Winter Conference Proceedings*. Las Vegas, NV.

van Trijp, J.C.M. 1995. *Variety-seeking in product choice behavior: Theory with applications in the food domain.* Wageningen: Netherlands Agricultural University.

Web and social media activity

Introduction

Much of the material in the previous two chapters is applicable to the realm of browsing, social media and DVGs (e.g. inference, data types and dimensions and visualization). This chapter seeks to address the remaining key topics relevant to this arena of consumer activity. One notable aspect of the new paradigm of consumption is the vast record of non-purchase activity; search, sentiment, review, tracking and comment etc. Insight into pre and post purchase is now abundant for many brands; in the analogue era purposive research was required to access such insight. Chapter 3 reviews various metrics and measures and KPIs that have been relevant in the analogue era and those that are more relevant to web and social media applications. As with previous chapters the coverage biases towards the underlying principles as opposed to the mathematics of analytics and to understanding the opportunities to gain insight into the consumer and customer via these interactions (and some of the difficulties and pitfalls). Subsequent chapters explore the social and behavioural science behind consumer motivations and communication. This chapter focuses on the consumer as revealed by analytics.

Monitoring in the digital space

The digital evolution of marketing has blurred some lines. Direct marketing is merging with advertising. Messages appearing on web pages are being individualized in terms of the targeting and even the content but the artefact appears or resembles a 'traditional' advert nonetheless. Pure/traditional advertising is targeted through the channel of delivery (website or publication or media channel etc.) whilst direct marketing is sent to a personal identifier (email address or postal address etc.). If the message is adapted to data on an individual (perhaps based on browsing behaviour) or personalized in any way then it ceases to be pure advertising. Perhaps direct advertising is a more useful term to encompass the emerging and growing space in between pure or traditional direct marketing (e.g. spam) and adaptive or individually tailored 'ads'; such as those that might appear on your web page offering you a bespoke discount on a set of products you recently browsed.

Non-transactional consumer activity in the digital sphere relies on the following types of surveillance. Subsequent sections refer to each of these themes or types in more detail:

1. *Counts.* Simple tallies of activity are useful. For example hits on a web page or the number of likes. However, they are limited in isolation. Although we can track them over time and spatially, which adds to their explanatory and predictive powers.

2. *Tracking.* The ubiquitous cookie is the classic example. The cookie is a much talked about thing. Cookies are still the source of misconception and controversy. A cookie is a text file that the web user can 'pick-up' when visiting a site. It identifies a device not a person *per se*. Your browser stores the text file – called cookie.txt. When you request another page from the server, your browser sends the cookie back to the server. Cookies are also nested in other people's sites. Cookies can 'talk' to other cookies and therefore can track your activity on the web in order to tell the cookie originator (e.g. an online retailer) the following about your browsing behaviour and features:

   • Your search engine (e.g. Google, Bing, Ecosia).
   • Device ID.
   • Browser (e.g. Chrome, Explorer).
   • Location.
   • Time stamps.
   • Pages viewed.
   • Links clicked.
   • Exit pages (last page on site before departure).
   • Paths through a site or browsing session (i.e. 'click paths').
   • Return visits.
   • Bounces.
   • Conversion.

   That is quite a list. It is self-evident why the humble cookie.txt is reviled and revered in equal measure by the privacy lobby and online marketers respectively. The cookie facilitates many of the measures outlined in this chapter.

   Click paths (the pages and specific items and links on the web) are also a good example (see Figure 3.2). The key concern is to trace the individual's journey so that marketing communications target effectively and usability is optimized.

3. *Sentiment.* Any measure of opinion or thoughts. This is usually accessed via the analysis of text; e.g. automated analysis of social media or reviews (via online algorithms). Sometimes it might be purposive but online (e.g. a survey after purchase).

4. *Connections.* Various 'maps' of association will give insight into connected concepts (e.g. brands, words, attitudes). This provides for networks of association to be constructed (e.g. social network analysis – SNA).

Once again, it is helpful to provide a complementary but alternative structure in order to give a more comprehensive picture. Figure 3.1 classifies the range of functions and activity that delineate and define the diverse range of monitoring associated with 'web analytics'. Web analytics refers to a constellation of activities that are diverse but complementary. This creates a problem managerially since the term is widely used and is polysemic; the term refers to a plethora of monitoring and metric actions. In isolation the term is therefore vague.

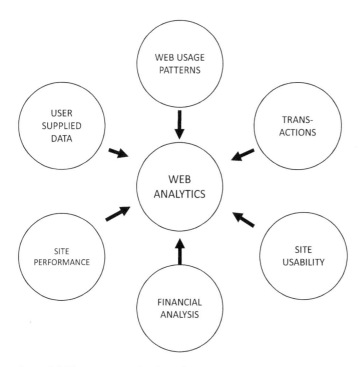

Figure 3.1 The anatomy of web analytic activities

Table 3.1 Traffic origins

Traffic origin	Definition and issues
Direct	User-driven – simply typing in the URL or the company name into the search engine or by using a bookmark.
Referral	Link-driven – through a link that is sponsored, promoted and often paid for. This is the direct result of marketing communication and therefore a very active space for analytics and performance monitoring.
Organic	Search-driven – the result of a search that reveals non-sponsored links. However, search results are biased and informed by 'preferences' and past browsing behaviour. Person A searching for something on Google will likely have the search results revealed in a quite different order than Person B. The ordering of results is informed by algorithm-based analytics and their online 'persona'.
Social	Social media driven – the result of a recommendation on a social media platform. Social network analysis is therefore relevant here.

The best way to arrive at a comprehensive understanding and appreciation of the anatomy and application of web analytics is by exploring its component parts and the variety of applications whilst acknowledging that these areas overlap and augment each other. Web analytics at its best and most effective is comprised of a series of layers.

The following list describes some key terms that are common in the lexicon of web analytics; in principle they relate to the monitoring of key objectives:

1. *Community growth.* The community in question could be the customer base or the site users or a social media grouping or following. One issue here is the ability to discriminate between 'real' and 'fake or fallacious' users, followers or customers. Many people may follow someone on a social media platform but their engagement with the platform may be shallow or inactive. Customers on a website might be buying on behalf of someone else or might be frequent visitors who buy very little. Intensity of use is therefore a key issue. Table 3.1 outlines the origins of traffic.

2. *Impression and reach.* These are dealt with in terms of metrics in Table 3.1. Reach refers to the number of prospects/people exposed to a site or message, whilst impression relates to a measure of frequency or intensity of reach (how many times is the person exposed to the site/message?).

3. *Engagements.* Quite simply, this refers to user-driven actions that indicate interaction. For example 'likes', reviews or 'shares'. These are commonly counted or tallied and provide very basic metrics of activity:

a.   *Visits*. Self-explanatory. A landing on a page or site.
b.   *Conversion*. There are various forms of conversion and associated metrics and they are dealt with in Table 3.3, for example conversion ratio from visits to purchase.

Web analytics is very metrics-driven, as described in Table 3.2. Artefacts refer to marketing communications actions (email, advert etc.). Whilst many of these measures are not mathematically or conceptually complex there are some problems with their inputs, outputs and application (the table identifies some of these).

These simple measures should always be regarded with caution; they are best used in conjunction with each other and augmented with the techniques and insights elsewhere in this chapter. One key issue is eliminating the effects of other variables for ROMI, Reach and DRM in order to determine the effectiveness of your communications effort. If you replicate and sustain your marketing communications efforts over a long period of time then you will have a better chance of controlling for the other impacts on sales. If, however, your campaign is short and coincides with a competitor's price fall and myriad other changes then your chance of identifying or isolating the effect of your MC effort is tricky. If you sell novelty t-shirts in Scandinavia and promote them heavily via a sponsored link campaign for one month in the summer, a month that happens to coincide with unseasonably hot weather, then you may struggle to work out which factor led to which sale. In reality the effects will conflate. Consumers will not consciously think 'It's hot and I like your ad; these two issues are affecting me equally' and this factor is reflected in the aggregate data. If you have historical data on the effects of the weather and other factors then you have a chance of working out the *approximate* impact; if not then you are effectively guessing. Assessing advertising and MC effectiveness has long been addressed by the application of increasingly complex econometric models and more recently machine learning. It remains an inexact science. Metrics specific to online analytics outline how this problem can be overcome (to some extent). Table 3.2 reviews some of the common measures of online communication effectiveness and measures of activity.

These are all elementary. This is their strength and weakness. As with the more traditional or 'analogue' measures in Table 3.2 they are best considered together and require the insight from various other sources of evidence as discussed below.

Online tracking does present an opportunity. Cookies and other tools and techniques do allow the marketer to determine and link a person (or more accurately a device) with a chain of actions that lead to purchase or not. If you

Table 3.2 Basic marketing communications metrics

Measure	Dimensions		
	Definition	Formula/mechanics	Constraints and problems
Return on Marketing Investment (ROMI)	Return on cost of marketing action	ROMI = [(Increase in Revenue x Margin) − Cost of Marketing] / Cost of Marketing e.g. ROMI = [(£50,000 x 50%) − £10,000] / £10,000 = ROMI of 1.5	Isolating exact marketing costs and isolating uplift due to actions (and not other factors e.g. weather) is easier said than done.
Reach:	*Exposure to artefact:*		All need to be cross-referenced with up-turn transactions and profit.
Basic reach	No. of persons exposed to artefact	Simple count	
Frequency	No. of times person exposed to artefact	Simple count	
Pass along rate (PAR)	No. of times artefact is shared	Simple count	
Cost per mile (CPM)	Cost per thousand of artefact delivery against exposure	CPM = (Cost / Gross Impressions) = Cost per person; multiply by 1000 e.g. Cost = $100,000; Gross Impressions = 200,000, cost per person is $0.5 − CPM = $500	Easier with direct marketing − emails etc.
eCPM	Gross impressions (audience size) − online equivalent		
Direct response measures (DRM):			
Sales uplift	Increase in sales due to action	Simple or complex calculation of sales uplift during campaign	Isolating exact marketing costs and isolating uplift due to actions (and not other factors e.g. weather) is easier said than done.
Take rate	Outcomes against messages sent/artefact intensity − expressed as %	e.g. 500,000 website hits from 1,000,000 emails x 100 = 50%	
Acquisition costs per outcome	Ratio of costs of action vs. outcomes	Campaign costs / achieved outcomes cost. Euro 100,000 / 500,000 hits = 0.2 Euros per hit.	
Recognition and recall	A survey of how many people remember what an ad was for or remember anything about the ad	Often represented as a simple percentage of audience who can recall the ad or what it was for − requires a survey.	Not a reliable measure of effectiveness as the artefact might be recalled but not effective − i.e. might be memorable but otherwise a bad ad.
Purchase intention	How many people exposed to the artefact or campaign intend to purchase as a result of it	Often represented as a simple percentage of audience that intend to purchase based on the marketing comms campaign or artefact − requires a survey.	Intention is not the same as purchase. Various factors can interrupt intention.

Table 3.3 Common web specific measures and revenue formulas

Measure	Dimensions	
	Definition	*Formula/mechanics*
Transaction conversion rate (TCR)	Record of conversion to transaction/sale from action (e.g. click)	e.g. 50 conversions from 1,000 clicks gives a TCR of 5%
Other conversion:		
Visit to purchase	How many visits convert to sale	e.g. 2,000 visits for every 400 sales gives a rate of 20%
New vs. returning	A simple record – self-explanatory	Achieved by monitoring ISP address or cookies or user ID
Bounce rate	Website visitors who leave without purchase	e.g. 10,000 visits with 7,000 not buying = bounce rate of 30%
Pay per click (PPC)	Payment by client according to number of contacts for online marketer (e.g. Google)	e.g. £0.01 for every click
Cost per acquisition (CPA)	Charge for every new customer/ purchase stemming from click/ contact	e.g. 1% on every purchase attributable to the online marketing

click on a link in an online ad or direct marketing (marketing aimed at an individual – a letter, email or bespoke link) it has been easier to assess, even in the analogue era (if you respond to a call then you can be tagged and the marketer will be able to mark you as driven by the communication). Direct Response Advertising (DRA) used to rely on you calling a number in the ad; now DRA has become the norm online. Click on the ad and in all likelihood you will be identified and tracked. The marketer will know if you were influenced by the ad. This ability to track has changed marketing communications and has allowed the likes of Google to proliferate and prosper; the individualization of the assessment of effectiveness forms the basis of a good deal of online consumer analytics (web analytics). When longitudinal response data is processed it can provide opportunities for profile and persona construction (dealt with below).

User and usage insight

Imagine that you have established that a million people (ISP address or IDs) visited your site this month. You know how many have been before, how many times they have come back, how many of them have bought and what they have bought, you know how effective the sponsored link strategy is, bounce rates etc. What should you do next? In short you add detail to the above, often by exploring the following:

1. *Audience composition.* A logical next step is to mine the transactional and website usage data (behavioural data) and any data that you have or can acquire on user demographics and attributes (previous chapters have comprehensively discussed transactional data). Insights into user demographics can be gleaned by using standard/off-the-shelf databases based on postcode/zip code and the characteristics of residents in those codes.

2. *Website usage.* There are various ways to track users' navigation of the site. Cookies provide a useful source of information and inputs for analytics. Time on site is one example. However, some more sophisticated methods are also available for deployment. The most salient are briefly reviewed in turn:

    a. *Heat maps and eye tracking.* The movement of the mouse on the web page can be tracked; this requires the use of appropriate script and software by the domain owner. Numerous commercial enterprises offer services to site owners that will generate heat maps based on the movement of the mouse. This allows the web designer to determine the elements and sections of the web page that draw more attention from the user. The web page can be reconfigured on the basis of this information; the maps could also be used to classify or segment different user types or styles (this can be cross-referenced with other data on users).

        Eye tracking requires the use of wearable technology or augmented computing and is therefore in the realm of purposive data capture. The technique records the object of the users' gaze and provides a record in the form of a heat map. The usefulness of the data acquired is consistent with those derived from mouse movement, but the data is not so readily captured. Mouse monitoring does not require additional equipment and is more cost-effective (the data is captured by users in the real world). Eye tracking might be more appropriate to web design prior to launch.

    b. *Click paths.* Figure 3.2 depicts the reduction of some hypothetical analysis of how consumers tend to click through a website. In fact, A, B, C, D and E could be websites, pages on one site or even sections on a page. Click paths are applicable to various units of analysis. The

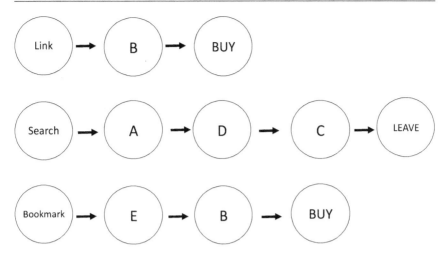

Figure 3.2 Click paths

example here assumes that the letters refer to pages on a given site; it is clearly simplified and illustrative. The analysis reveals three common paths (clearly in reality the derivation of such data is through processing highly complex and noisy data – the case above is parsimonious). The three dominant paths illustrate various features and questions of managerial relevance, for example:

- Why do people bookmark Page E and not the homepage (Page A)?
- Non-buyers have the longest click path but still leave.
- Page B precedes purchase and non-buyers avoid that page (perhaps they can be directed to it).
- Direct and referral are working, organic is not.

c. *Subjective factors.* Site enjoyment, ease of use and satisfaction are very important but subjective factors will require purposive research (e.g. survey or wearable technology). A consumer/user panel can also be employed in order to test and inform innovations and changes. Alternatively changes can be tried out using an A-B test.

d. *A-B testing.* A-B tests are field experiments (a brief definition is given in Chapter 1). One group of consumers (subjects), group A, are exposed to distinct stimulus A, the other group (B) are exposed to stimulus B. Any difference in reaction or response can then be assessed (notwithstanding the noise caused by conducting experiments in the field, i.e. in real settings). They have various useful applications and can provide significant insights into cause and effect and behaviour in general. A-B tests are relatively easy to execute on the web since they are cost-effective and technically relatively straightforward to implement, design and execute. For example a homepage can be reconfigured for one set of users vs. another set to test if the new configuration results in more purchase or more time on site. The examples in Figure 3.2 could lead a site owner to ensure that new users who access the site organically are presented with two different homepage configurations. The owner can then determine which page performs best in terms of purchase outcome.

Words and talk

Much of the data on the web relates to posted opinion and sentiment in the form of reviews, posts, blogs and social media. If a company controls a forum it will have access to the text generated. Otherwise this data needs to be acquired from ISPs or web-scraped. Web-scraping is manual or automated. Web-scraping is not theft, it is the extraction of data in the public domain. It doesn't necessarily provide data linked to individuals, although this is possible where such data is volunteered. For example it might involve an analysis of all the words used on Twitter and provide aggregate counts. Even relatively basic analysis of such data can provide valuable insight. Figure 3.3 provides an elementary example.

Simple topic or content analysis will count and monitor phrases used in social media and forums. The use of 'Expensive' is stable, 'High quality' references decline after some stability as do references to 'Cool'. References to 'Bling' (which could be positively or negatively valenced/framed) and to 'Rip-off' increase. This should concern the brand owner as the overall picture is of negative sentiment. There is a peak of activity in May and the reasons for this need to be determined if they are not obvious. This analysis can be used to inform countering marketing communications or even inform price changes and product development. Likewise, this information could be web-scraped and used for their own advantage. They can highlight the negative perceptions vs. their own brand via marketing communications and messaging.

Sentiment analysis attempts to assess and categorize the voice or attitude of the subject via the automated analysis of text. The analysis will attempt to classify and summarize the opinion, sentiment or attitude towards a particular object or concept (e.g. a brand, a location, a celebrity). It can be based on web-scraped or proprietary data (this is often incorporated into persona construction, discussed below).

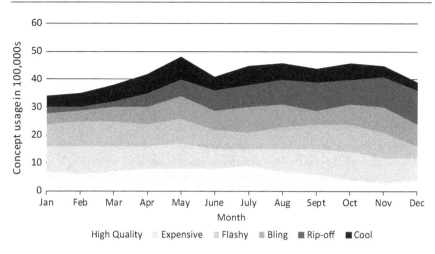

Figure 3.3 Concept or topic usage relating to Brand Z over time

'The curious case of Colin's holiday'

Colin returns from a well-earned holiday and posts this on TripAdvisor and on his Facebook page.

Had a *really* good holiday in Turkey. I'd like to thank the manager for his enviable talent for invisibility. I never thought that hotel managers worked undercover. He was excellent in this regard. I was very impressed by the ability of the hotel staff to consistently convert my meal order into something entirely unexpected. I particularly enjoyed the game of "trace the sock" initiated by the laundry team. The impromptu night-time enter-tainment around the pool (visible and audible from my balcony) had me in hysterics. A big thank you to the other guests. Highly recommended.

A simple or unsophisticated analysis of this text is hazardous. The adjectives, verbs and phrases employed are superficially positive ('really good; enviable talent; excellent; very impressed by the ability of the hotel staff; enjoyed the game; in hysterics' etc.). If these are extracted without some method of assessing the overall context and frame then an entirely inaccurate impression of Colin's holiday will be the result. Some automated approaches may not detect Colin's sarcasm even though all but the most dim-witted person will detect it. These and related issues are well-known to exponents of sentiment analysis but they still challenge application. Language is extraordinarily complex. We take it for granted, but codifying it is fraught with difficulties. Sentiment analysis is as good as the algorithm employed and as good as the human interpreters and overseers.

This example leads to a wider issue with the analysis of text; the basis of reviews and social media (along with the photo which can also be subject to auto-analysis, recognition and classification via deep learning). This distils to the 'say' vs. 'do'. Sometimes sentiment and actions are harmonious, sometimes they are dissonant. The so-called 'attitude-behaviour gap' has provoked much thought and some angst in consumer research. There are two ways in which this can manifest itself via social media and sentiment data:

 i. The person is subconsciously misrepresenting themselves. The methods employed to record people's attitudes and views are at fault or more likely the instruments used allow for biases. This could be due to social desirability bias (SDB).
 ii. The person is knowingly misrepresenting themselves.

In reality the two explanations are related. Even with scientifically calibrated scales and questions it is still a challenge to glean 'the truth' from the consumer. People have a tendency to represent themselves in a positive light in respect of prevailing social norms (e.g. recycling behaviour) and whether they do this consciously or unconsciously on social media is difficult to ascertain. Virtue signalling is real. It's gratifying to get a lot of supportive messages about your virtuous views or reports of your virtuous actions. People also exaggerate and lie. We do this all the time in 'real' life; why assume we don't in the digital realm (in fact it's even easier; we can even Photoshop our selfies)? The social media space is 'public' – either in the broadest terms possible or within a clique or defined group. It is certainly conspicuous, that is the whole point. A version or representation of the self is provided, often idealized. People will show themselves in the best light on social media (unless the forum focus is life's problems). Social media and other sentiment data should always be interpreted and analysed in relation to actual behaviour if at all possible (i.e. cross-referenced with transactional data).

Social network analysis

Social Network Analysis (SNA) describes an array of concepts and techniques used to explore the connections and associations in a community or other entity. Online traces and identifiers make the construction of such networks relatively easy (in comparison to analogue/offline communities). Figure 3.4 depicts a simple network.

Each dot is a *node*. A node can represent any discrete entity in a network (e.g. a person, a website). We'll assume that in this example each node is a

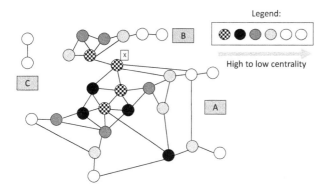

Figure 3.4 A simple network map

person and the form of connection is via social media. A is the primary network with the bulk of nodes. B is a *clique* that is connected to the rest of the network by virtue of person x. Person x is a *bridge*. Without them A and B are not connected. C is a discrete clique, these do occur but are a rare case. Person x is important because of their status as a bridge. If your aim was to market to community B and A then x is a crucial link. If you target them with marketing communications or offers they are likely to share then they have a disproportionate ability to reach both sub-networks. Identifying such nodes is a major preoccupation for network analytics. An additional preoccupation is the measurement of node *centrality*. In Figure 3.4 this is based on a simplified measure and notion of centrality; other methods are discussed below.

In elementary terms, centrality is the measurement of the importance or influence of a node in the network. The legend indicates that the red and yellow people in the network are the highest scoring in terms of a basic measure of centrality. The following three measures and definitions of centrality are commonly employed (there are other variants and methods).

Conceptually simplest is degree centrality; defined as the number of links to a node. Closeness centrality (or closeness) of a node is the average length of the shortest path between the node and all other nodes in the graph (i.e. how many nodes between them and another node – the lengths of the lines/ connections in the figure is abstract and does not indicate closeness). Thus the more central a node is, the 'closer' it is to all other nodes. Eigenvector centrality (also called eigencentrality) is a measure of the influence of a node in a network. It scores all nodes in the network based on the notion that connections to high-scoring nodes contribute more to the score of the node in question than equal connections to low-scoring nodes (used by Google PageRank). Person/page **x** and their immediate southern red neighbour will

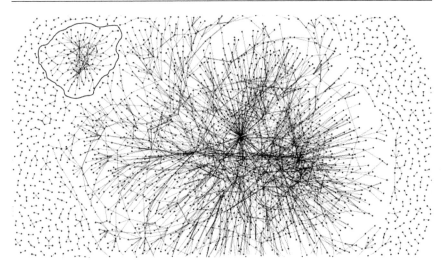

Figure 3.5 Excerpt of a real social media network

have the highest score on this basis. Multiple measures can be employed and conflated to provide a composite score of centrality overall (possibly with a weighted value for each measure). Centrality scores identify influential consumers (gatekeepers) or websites.

Figure 3.5 depicts a relatively small social network based on real-world data. The density of the dominant high centrality sub-network contains some high centrality people/nodes (the dark ones). One smaller relatively discrete sub-network is delineated on the left. The periphery of the diagram shows numerous small discrete networks like those in C in Figure 3.4 (many dyadic – two people, or triadic – three people).

Reciprocation and direction are key concepts in network analysis. The flow of contact between people or websites, whether two-way or one-way, is important (e.g. does the website act as a referrer or gatekeeper for another site or as the receiver? What is the nature of the relationship between the two connected nodes?). The network in Figure 3.4 gives no indication of the direction of connection, it simply depicts the existence of a connection. Figure 3.6 provides illustrations of six different types of relationship by showing the flow between node triads (this flow could be messaging on a social media platform, for example).

A: This triad shows the situation of a taker. They receive but do not give out. A Twitter follower who never posts.

B: This shows a giver. A Twitter poster who never follows.

C: There is some reciprocation (two-way flow) between two nodes. Contact is shared but one node is still a giver (more than a taker).

D: Reciprocation is occurring between one node and the other two although they have no direct contact. So, in this simple triad network the left-hand top node is central and crucial.

E: All nodes take and give but reciprocation is not total.

F: Total reciprocation.

Obviously there are more potential variants of these triads and the flows in reality will occur in highly complex networks. Another key factor is the volume of any flow (e.g. how many messages are posted?). If a person has a high centrality score and generates a high volume of traffic on a social media platform then this should signal their importance in the network. Social media is about influence and identifying the most influential nodes is critical.

Homophily describes the tendency for 'birds of a feather to flock together'. We know that there is a tendency for like minds to associate via social media, the so-called echo chamber effect, where a forum simply reinforces its own belief and attitudes. The homogeneity of a network or clique can be interrogated via sentiment analysis per node. This is one other example of the power of combining various sources of data and different forms of analytics to provide layers of insight and evidence.

These groupings/networks will respond to events. Figure 3.7 provides a summary of the analogue/physical and digital dynamics of various example events.

Temporal dynamics mean that the categorization in the matrix according to the two dimensions of physical manifestation and digital manifestation are not fixed. Things, specifically groups of people, have a life in the world and online and this varies over time. Their physical intensity and coherency and their

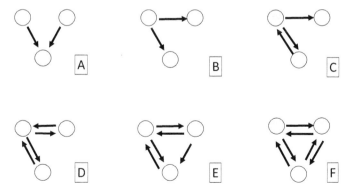

Figure 3.6 Relationship triads

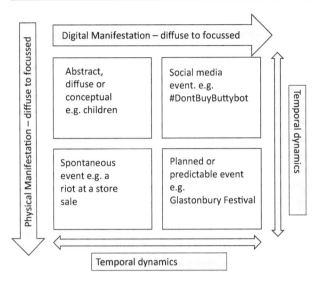

Figure 3.7 Dynamics of groups in the physical and digital realm

digital presence are related but will have differing temporal profiles and temporal dynamics. The logic of the diagram is best understood through the consideration of the examples within it and by cross-reference with Figures 3.8, 3.9, 3.10 and 3.11 (dotted lines depict digital activity, solid lines physical activity).

Case 1: Children

In Figure 3.7 children have a diffuse physical and digital manifestation and essentially constant time profile (Figure 3.8). They exist in the world but at the basic conceptual level they do not congregate *en masse*, they are not organized and are only an entity at the categorical and conceptual level. Digital communication relating to children in general is diffuse. If the example is an event for children in a given locality then it will move in the matrix (towards Case 4 in Figure 3.11). If your objective is to market a product that is relevant to children in general (e.g. a universally appealing game, toy or apparel) then you must address the fact that your market is physically and digitally diffuse. You will have to disaggregate in order to communicate by using a multitude of channels to reach this physically and digitally diffuse 'group'. The temporal dynamic is flat for children as a whole since they never form a coherent physical or digital whole.

Case 2: Riot at a Black Friday in-store sale

A spontaneous riot is a physical manifestation of high intensity, being geographically specific with a discrete and identifiable group presence. The digital

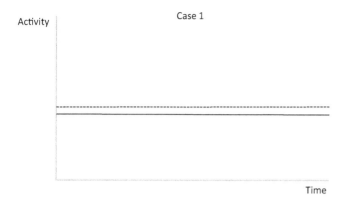

Figure 3.8 Temporal profiles for Case I

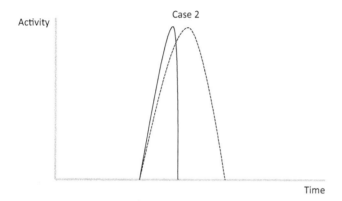

Figure 3.9 Temporal profiles for Case 2

manifestation (web traffic and social media) will lag and peak during/after the physical event (depending on its spontaneity and duration) as Figure 3.9 shows.

Case 3: #DontBuyButtybot

Buttybot is a fictional app that allows you to match your interest, behaviour and activities with other people so that you can hook up with them as new friends. Buttybot has experimented with their algorithm and conducted an A-B test. The A-B test meant that a sample of users were intentionally sent the profiles of people that the algorithm predicted they would hate (in order to calibrate the efficacy of the algorithm). The result is not pretty (the algorithm is good). There is a leak from an employee about this tactic. This in turn results in a huge social media backlash which then provokes a series of demonstrations at the offices

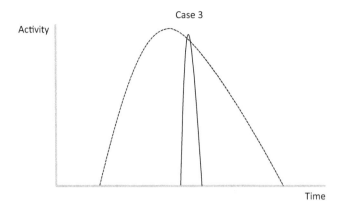

Figure 3.10 Temporal profiles for Case 3

of Buttybot in major cities. Here we have a grouping or event of high intensity digitally that gives rise to physically intensive events, but it is essentially derived from a virtual grouping or network (see Figure 3.10). If you were to try and cash in and make #DontBuyButtybot t-shirts then you need to pay heed to the physical and digital temporal dynamics. Start online and make sure you're selling at the demonstrations.

Case 4: Glastonbury Festival

Unlike Case 2 and 3, something such as Glastonbury Festival has a predictable temporal profile. In the physical realm this is an intense manifestation over a few days. In the digital realm this might well result in a slow build up of traffic up to the event followed by a spike during and immediately after the event with a decline of sharing and traffic afterwards (see Figure 3.11). This will follow a predictable annual cycle in the physical and digital realm (with the exception of 'fallow' years). A predictable cycle in the physical sphere combined with an equally predictable cycle of intensity in the digital realm provides a nicely pre-dictable proposition for marketers seeking to exploit this event. It is clear when they should marshal physical and digital activities to coincide with the event's online and 'real' life.

The lessons from these cases are self-evident to a large extent. One important point is the temporal dynamics as described above. No coherent event or group activity is entirely constant (i.e. Cases 2, 3 and 4). Fluctuations, or more precisely the ability to predict or respond to fluctuations, is an essential but troublesome issue for contemporary marketers.

There is a great deal of discussion around the subject of agility in marketing and this is entirely understandable. The primacy of the digital space has made

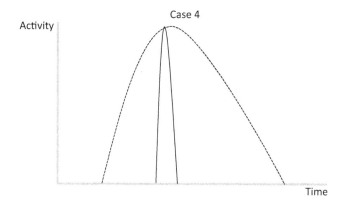

Figure 3.11 Temporal profiles for Case 4

marketing real-time, certainly in terms of marketing communications. Many established, but valuable, protocols for segmentation do not adequately account for the temporal realm. *When* people do and say things are as important as *what* they do and say. Techniques like dynamic topic modelling point the way forward.

Conclusion

ISPs and other web and smart technology mediators and product providers (like Apple) are in a position to attempt to construct and nourish complex virtual 'personas' (Turow 2012; Cluley and Brown 2015) based on the insight reviewed in Chapters 1, 2 and 3. These virtual selves might be accurate or inaccurate and can attempt to categorize us in terms of gender, location and mobility, preference, personality and almost everything else. This is also a concerted attempt to ascertain many of the features and drivers of consumer choice dealt with in Chapters 5, 6, 7 and 8 (i.e. extant consumer research as opposed to analytics insight) as well as behavioural indicators.

There is a potentially dark side to this or, at the very least, a sea change in the potential power of marketing. Data has biases and algorithms make 'assumptions'. If most buyers of product A are men then an algorithm charged with contacting potential buyers will target men even if this is questionable. It will tend to reinforce the bias. A prominent psychographic app, designed to locate people in terms of their personality, once assigned the wrong gender to a BBC presenter live on air. Web and social media data is noisy, messy and will contain false signals; its value is much hyped but it remains potentially potent in marketing terms. However, this does lead to some crucial ethical questions; these are unpacked in the following chapter.

References

Cluley, R. and Brown, S.D. 2015. The dividualised consumer: Sketching the new mask of the consumer. *Journal of Marketing Management*, 31(1–2), pp. 107–122.

Turow, J. 2012. *The daily you: How the new advertising industry is defining your identity and your worth*. New Haven, CT: Yale University Press.

Chapter 4

Extant research and exogenous cognition

Introduction

The internet, or any physical library, confronts us with a vast array of articles and monographs on any subject. Consumer behaviour is no exception. A cursory search on Google Scholar or the Social Science Citation Index will yield a bewildering array of articles. Superficially, the search for information and knowledge has never been easier. However, the sheer volume of work on the topic (a volume that increases by the day) is stifling for any newcomer to the topic. This is the inherent strength of the textbook. It provides a distillation, a handbook to navigate the space. This chapter seeks to review the history of academic consumer research (briefly) prior to a discussion of the seismic effects of the smart device and analytics on consumer 'thinking'. This is exemplified by the concept of exogenous cognition (introduced here); a concept which links analytics with consumers' 'internal' decision making.

The importance of considering extant research

There is a dualism of practice and academic research. They both regard each other and the relationship is reflexive and symbiotic but they exist in different realms and spaces. Academic research can have very clear managerial implications and lessons but sometimes (perhaps often) the implications for management or analytics in practice is obtuse or poorly communicated. Likewise research in the commercial realm often struggles to incorporate the essence of leading academic work; partly because of the vast and growing volume (it is problematic to navigate).

It is always good practice to understand what we already know before embarking on a study of consumers in practice. For example, if the focus is product choice in the FMCG arena then eschewing seminal extant academic research and generic insights in that topic would seem to be difficult to justify. Why avoid or ignore what we already know or the existing structures of understanding and interpretation? To do this is to undertake something essentially unscientific, i.e. to launch analytics without regard for what we already know. The danger is that the analyst finds patterns in data that are well-established and readily predicted by previous research or makes inferences about motivation that previous research has already discredited or are, at the very least, ambiguous.

A brief history of consumer behaviour research

At this point a very brief tour of the lineage of academic consumer research is valuable since it contextualizes the thematic structure adopted in the following chapters. Moreover, it is important to understand the lineage of the topic or avenue of intellectual investigation; without such an overview understanding of where we are and where we are going is bound to be stunted: if you want to know where to go then you should know where you have been. The following gives a brief overview of where these ideas have come from. Subsequent chapters reflect each tradition in more detail.

Micro-economic theory

The first concerted attempts to understand consumer decision making can be attributed to economics crystallized via Lancaster's consumer theory (Lancaster 1966) and concepts such as the indifference curve (exceptions might be socio-logical work such as Veblen 1899). The contribution is almost entirely theor-etical (notwithstanding later contributions by behavioural economists). Whilst the insights are of value, psychological variables and influences are treated in a somewhat arbitrary way; much is assumed or left mysterious. For example, indifference curves and utility theory cannot account for someone who buys cat food, doesn't have a cat and doesn't eat the cat food themselves. It is enough that they simply derive utility from it; the anatomy of the utility derived is seemingly not of interest. Clearly this is not enough to inform consumer-oriented business decisions. Nonetheless, the systematic approach employed demonstrates intellectual rigour and can claim to have started the conversation. The take home: utility and value are important.

Cognitive school

During the 1960s and 1970s business schools began to become more common at universities and marketing was studied systematically as a function of com-mercial practice. This coincided with the heyday of cognitive psychology (the conscious mechanics of the mind). The neglect of psychology in economic approaches was self-evident to the emerging marketing academy. The case is not difficult to make. Psychology is concerned with decision making, behaviour and influence in the main and it must have seemed obvious to mine the emerging insights, re-purposing them in the arena of marketing. This mirrored the acknowledgement in the commercial arena that psychology might prove decisive in business. The values, attitudes and lifestyle (VALS) attempt to provide a universal taxonomy of consumers for segmentation and targeting is a salient example of how these influences left universities and impacted practice. A number of ambitious attempts were made to describe consumer decision making in terms of generic 'global' models (e.g. Howard and Sheth 1969). These models describe consumers as conscious, essentially rational and mechanistic decision makers; exemplified with flow diagram (often complex) based schematics that imply a less than humanistic or holistic view of the reality of consumption and purchase and its various influences (what about fun, irrationality, emotion, manipulation and culture?).

The VALS kind of approach works to an extent but it is based on the partly fallacious assumption that overpowering or intransigent influences on the consumer can be isolated; that there is a Holy Grail or magic bullet. This idea persists to this day with the overblown claims of some analytics practitioners.

Behaviourist critique

By the 1990s the cognitive-driven approach had well and truly entrenched itself as the dominant paradigm. The only compelling attempt to challenge its core precepts was the behaviourist critique. Behavioural psychology had to a large extent lost out to the cognitive approach. However, in marketing it regained some traction. This counter was led by Gordon Foxall (e.g. Foxall 1995). Behaviourist approaches emphasize the stimulus–response paradigm and explore how people are influenced by external stimuli in order to elicit responses (usually through experiments or observation). The approach draws conclusions about the internal processes but these are not addressed directly; it draws logical inferences about why or how but the behaviourist approach looks at what happens after a stimulus (not why). This has some attraction in marketing since the internal processes, the anatomy of decision making is remote from the marketer. The lab-based cognitive psychologist will have their human subjects to hand and can furnish them with questions to determine why they have done something. The marketer can do this (via purposive research) but the natural relationship with the customer or consumer is one of stimulus and response; the marketer does something and the consumer responds or not; business and marketing has often been described as one huge field experiment (no amount of pre-market testing will guarantee that a product works). This is exemplified in the online A-B test (in which stimuli are adjusted for different groups of subjects/consumers). The reasons for any variance in response between two groups cannot be determined unless some purposive research is undertaken; if this is not done then the only finding is that the two stimuli give two variant responses (what not why). In the age of analytics the behaviourist approach has some renewed value and is a useful paradigm and touchstone.

Interpretivism, social and cultural theory

In the late 1980s and 1990s interpretivist approaches to understanding consumers gained traction. These approaches typically drew on social theory, cultural theory, sociology and deployed methods consistent with anthropology (e.g. ethnography) or more generic depth methods based on humanistic interviews. The analysis undertaken is typically text-based and not quantitative. The aim was often to generate theory not to provide generalizable rules of behaviour (this being based on a principle that consumption is socially constructed). This tradition is not empirical in the true sense of the word. Like all approaches it has its limitations. However, its legacy emphasizes the importance of meaning, nuance and the complexity of imagery and language used in marketing. In terms of analytics their greatest value is probably in enriching insight and informing depth purposive data capture.

An age of conflation and variety

In the 21st century work has been less polarized and an essentially pragmatic approach has emerged that acknowledges that various methods are required to understand the dynamics of consumer behaviour, from surveys to neuroscience. The conceptualization of knowledge is more complex and values the requirement to be 'scientific' whilst acknowledging a strong critical sense and caution regarding the nature of truth or certainty. There are still a number of researchers with entrenched positions but these allegiances are increasingly anachronistic.

Experimentation

The rise of behavioural economics (BE) has had a significant influence on the methods employed in consumer research in the academic and the commercial sphere. It has revitalized the cognitive-led investigations of consumer processes. BE is essentially a brand of economic psychology that seeks to find rules of behaviour via lab-based experimentation. It owes a lot to the work of Tversky and Kahneman (e.g. 1986) and the concept of framing (dealt with in later chapters). However, experiments have their restrictions. The question is whether the 'rules' established will hold in the noise and complexity of the real world.

Data-driven discovery – analytics-driven application

There is not as much as you might suppose in the academic sphere. It has not been 'fashionable' until now. Electronic transactional data has been around for decades but access to the data remains an issue for some (companies don't exactly want to give away their data to all and sundry). Ehrenberg and the Dirichlet model applications of brand choice were expeditionary, but these models are descriptive. The previous 'side-lining' can be explained by the dominance of the cognitive and interpretivist schools above (they have dominated the space and orthodoxy is created). Analytics and machine learning driven academic work is emerging. They represent the best prospects for examinations of large data sets in order to construct theory and find rules and patterns that hold for more than one data set. Generalizability is the key. Another contribution is in the area of method improvement. *CB&A* is one attempt to set the agenda for this emerging area and to explore how analytics applications can 'speak' to previous research and insights.

The challenge of context

The search for a universal model or framework for describing consumer decision making and behaviour has proved troublesome and elusive. Why? One major reason is the challenge of context. The factors affecting the consumer will vary in terms of their influence from market to market, situation to situation and from year to year. The key dimensions for variability are:

- *Product.* Originating a model of consumer choice that can account for the myriad of influences on everything from milk to automobile purchase is clearly going to prove problematic. All products are qualitatively different and will provoke quite different forms of decision making, even for a given individual.
- *Geography and socio-cultural.* The location, social and cultural context of purchase can vary hugely. You make very different decisions according to who you are with and where you are.
- *Psychological factors.* People have different minds and they have biases and individual tendencies. For example some are impulsive, others are inherently cautious.
- *Temporal dynamics.* Choice and behaviour evolve and change over long time frames and sometimes over very short time frames. For example, your behaviour might be quite different at the weekend, you might be more relaxed and more susceptible to certain forms of direct marketing (since you have the time to indulge them). You might have more money at the start of the month or at certain times of the year, in which case your perception of value and utility might shift significantly.

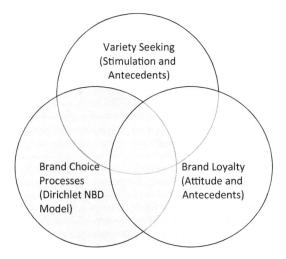

Figure 4.1 Topic overlap in consumer research

The challenge of complexity

A key problem in navigating the literature/extant research is the issue of overlap and complexity. Chapter 2 dealt with the issue of loyalty and other behavioural biases. Variety seeking and loyalty research are essentially looking at the same thing: choice outcome dynamics. The Dirichlet modelling research is looking at the same topic from a different angle (see Figure 4.1). These three topics link with other streams of research as well. However, if they are considered in conjunction then the outcome is likely to be more fruitful and more holistic. However, this also poses a challenge.

The challenge is the sheer amount of potentially relevant topics. This leads to a vast range of variables that determine choice and behaviour (essentially an extrapolation of the fundamental themes/traditions of consumer research reviewed above). For example, the following list of features/variables is indicative of the huge variety of potential determinants of behaviour:

- Price effects.
- Disposable income.
- Family structure.
- Emotional state.
- Behavioural biases.
- Susceptibility to marketing.

This list can go on and on.

The premise that all of the traditions and perspectives in extant consumer research have a contribution to make lies at the heart of *CB&A*; they often address the same topic even if they do so from very different angles. Any approach to holistic understanding that privileges one base discipline, say psychology, over other factors or vice versa is going to struggle to provide a coherent overview of consumer choice and behaviour. However, numerous variables and determinants are essentially psychological in nature although many of these are influenced and nourished by social commercial interactions (e.g. attitude). Many other variables are exogenously determined (e.g. marketing communications campaigns and targeting via analytics):

> *Understanding the consumer is as much about understanding interactions as internal processes – including interaction with distributed systems of consumer analytics.*

Conceptualizing the consumer solely as 'a decision making unit' (this phrase has been used by researchers in the cognitive tradition) is likely to lead to a stunted view. The consumer is an agent abroad in the world, not all decisions are deliberative or conscious or even controlled.

In order to address the challenge of context and complexity *CB&A* advocates and deploys an adaptive conceptual structure. This requires a review of the key features that determine and drive consumer choice. Prior to the initial explanation of this structure a novel concept is introduced and outlined; a concept that provides a direct link between analytics and consumer decision making and therefore between contemporary data-driven marketing and the consumer.

Exogenous cognition: the link between analytics and the emerging consumer

The Google refrigerator

It is March 2023 and Feng Mian is the proud owner of a new Google fridge. Her friends are impressed and jealous. Every time she runs out of something the fridge accesses her online grocery account and orders a replacement which is delivered the next day (if it's not in stock it will order the closest replacement subject to her approval). It is time-saving and convenient. So much so that she is considering buying smart cupboards too. Much of the time she waives her approval and lets the fridge order stuff without her intervention.

Her cousin Sheldon visits her from Australia. He stays for one month. Sheldon likes different food and fills the fridge with his preferred chilled items. After Sheldon leaves Feng Mian has to manually access her account and delete Sheldon-related items although she does keep one or two on the list that she has acquired a taste for. The fridge recognizes this change and continues to order Sheldon-related items. It also orders items that Feng Mian has never had before that it thinks she might like (having derived a variety seeking score for Feng Mian).

Feng Mian experiences something quite simultaneously mundane and sublime. Something that has changed and is changing the basis of consumer choice – although her fridge is an artefact of the near future; 'the internet of things' (smart devices that communicate with one another). The 'contracting out' of decision making for consumers is well under way and will soon be driven by semi-autonomous devices. IFTTT.com is an example of the desire for some of us to 'automate' many decisions in our life. Our choices are being informed and often contracted out to quasi-intelligent systems and artefacts (smart devices and automated processing of data). Much academic consumer research eschews the fundamental effects of this new marketing, or at best it simply takes them for granted (tending to focus on the micro issues and effects in academic marketing research). We cannot afford to sidestep the elemental impacts.

We defer to our smart devices continually. They are observing us and learning about us, feeding an ever growing data repository with our name on it. We can call this digital representation of our self and life as our *data self*. This data self is then reflected back at us (Estrin and Thompson 2015). Feng Mian's fridge is thinking, or more accurately acting on her behalf. Her fridge is one of the more simple examples of how our behaviour frames and dictates our future behaviour. More sophisticated algorithms will attempt to recommend things to us. This is replacing/augmenting the '*information search*' stage that the original cognitive models of consumer behaviour incorporated. We rely on review sites, likes and other online indicators of a product's efficacy and potential to fulfil the role required.

Traditional conceptualization of the consumer decision process

In the pre-digital era, if someone wanted to purchase a high involvement good such as a car then they would be likely to embark on a concerted search for information (if the purchase represented a significant slice of their disposal income). They would converse with friends and family, read car magazines and ultimately glean information from the salesperson. The whole process might have taken some time. One of the UK's leading car retailers estimates that in the 1990s customers would visit the showroom eight times prior to a final purchase. They now assert that the average is two visits. Smart technology has fundamentally changed behaviour.

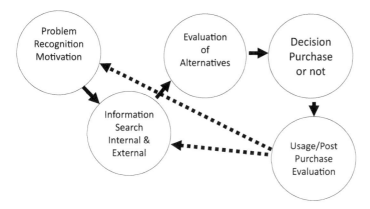

Figure 4.2 Reduction of the basic consumer decision model
Note: Dotted lines are feedback effects.

Figure 4.2 depicts a reduction/adaptation of the basic information pro-cessing search model. It still has some validity (at least for higher involvement purchases) and is a useful touchstone for a deeper appreciation of how perva-sive computing technology has impacted decision making. First we'll consider this process without explicitly addressing the impact of smart technology. The figure also depicts an algorithm (albeit basic).

- *Problem recognition.* A given consumer perceives a product/thing (let's say a TV) as under-performing, out of date, obsolete or entirely broken. The model couches this as a problem which needs to be resolved (therefore as an essentially cognitive and conscious process).
- *Information search.* The consumer accesses internal (memory, attitudes) and external information sources (e.g. friends, media, salespeople) to 'educate themselves' about the available alternative solutions (brands and product variations).
- *Evaluation of alternatives.* These alternative options are assessed according to salient criteria (e.g. functionality/style etc.). The notion of an Evoked Set of viable alternatives is a simple but useful concept to further augment our understanding of deliberative decision making (and even less delibera-tive scenarios). We will have brands that we are aware of and that we don't know about. If we know it and have a positive attitude towards it (and we can afford it) then it will likely belong to the Evoked Set – the brands that we stand a chance of buying subject to the effect of other determinants. If we are indifferent to a brand or don't know about it, it falls into the Inert Set basket. Brands that are not acceptable to us will be assigned or placed into the Inept Set. Of course, our ideas about brands will change

over time; some can move from the Inert to Evoked set via a marketing communications action (by raising our appraisal and/or awareness).

- *Decision*. The outcome is selected. This could be non-purchase; perhaps the consumer decides to watch TV on their computer from now on.
- *Post-purchase evaluation*. If a purchase occurs then the product performance is assessed and this feeds back (depicted by the dashed lines) into future information searches (internal) and also directly to problem recognition (perhaps the TV does not perform to expectations or malfunctions).

The impact of smart technology

Nowadays, when faced with a purchase choice, we will quickly consult the web. We'll look at review sites and ratings and rankings. Our search will provoke recommendations and marketing communications (informed by the direction of the search). We still use 'traditional' sources of information (e.g. family and friends, newspapers and TV etc.). However, the time frame is shorter; the ease with which we can retrieve information from multiple sources is notable. This has impacted all of the 'traditional' stages of the purchase process:

- *Problem recognition*. Smart devices can even recognize the problem. They might inform you that performance of a device is sub-optimal, or in the case of the smart fridge order an item that you always require but have run out of. In the case of a new TV the principal problem recognizer is still the person. However, 'problems' come in many forms. If the 'problem' arises as the result of marketing communications informed by your previous purchase behaviour then analytics and smart technology has had a hand in it. For example, imagine that MC informs you about a new TV at a great price that is self-evidently superior to your existing TV. The MC has provoked the problem. MC has always had this ability, in a sense the whole point of advertising is to provoke some dissatisfaction (to convince you to switch or to buy) or to reinforce existing choices. The MC capable of provoking the problem is individually targeted now and is informed by your browsing and your purchases.
- *Information search*. Smart technology and ubiquitous computing mean that external information search is faster, and easier than ever before. Moreover, your 'internal' search will have left traces on the web or purchase sites if you have left reviews for your last TV; these are then reflected back at you.
- *Evaluation of alternatives*. Evaluation now tends to happen as information search is occurring (and in reality always did). Reviews and assessments of other users' experiences facilitate evaluation. Prior to the digital revolution only friends, family and co-workers were typically consulted, probably in

conjunction with specialist traditional print media. We will tend to trust other customers more than the company selling the product for reasons explored in Chapter 6.

- *Decision.* Technology augments decision making and can even make decisions on our behalf by initiating re-purchase if sanctioned for low involvement goods.
- *Post-purchase evaluation.* Is readily enacted through posting reviews or through other forms of online feedback; this is often enacted via social media.

The interventions facilitated by ubiquitous computing and smart devices via analytics and data processing are described here as Exogenous Cognition (EC). This is a key concept in *CB&A*. It leans on some work in human computer interaction and some previously more obscure notions about the externalized manifestation of cognition. Here it is conceptualized as a distinct concept driven by marketing activity.

What is exogenous cognition?

Exogenous cognition describes the intervention and interaction of an external not human source to the cognitive decision making of a consumer (beyond person but contributing to person). An external cognitive system has been described '… as an external object that serves to accomplish a function that would otherwise be attained via the action of internal cognitive processes' (Barr et al. 2015, p. 473). The roots of the notion of an external cognitive system lie in the philosophical discussion regarding the boundaries of cognition and the idea of 'extended mind' (Clark and Chalmers 1998; Menary 2010). This work explores how cognition and thinking manifest beyond the human mind.

Now we all have two brains: our primary brain, the one in our cranium, and the external 'brain' tagged with our ID, the one that manifests in our smartphone and browser and the distributed system of computing beyond. Figure 4.3 and Figure 4.4 depict the core structure and manifestation of the exogenous cognitive system specific to marketing subsequently referred to as exogenous cognition (EC). These figures need to be considered in conjunction with each other.

The selves that we help to create in the digital realm are a reflection of us, but not necessarily an accurate reflection. EC is therefore not entirely positive but a full discussion of the potential negative and positive effects on decision making and consumer well-being is dealt with in a following section. Table 4.1 provides a review of its essential nature and elemental features.

How has EC come about? Pervasive technology, the distributed system that seeks to record and analyse our behaviour and sentiment, is marketing-driven but built on recent advances in artificial intelligence (AI), machine learning

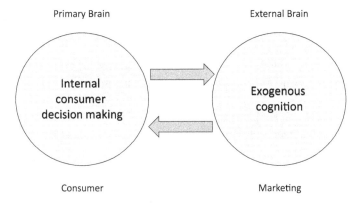

Primary Brain

External Brain

Consumer

Marketing

Figure 4.3 The basic ecosystem of exogenous cognition

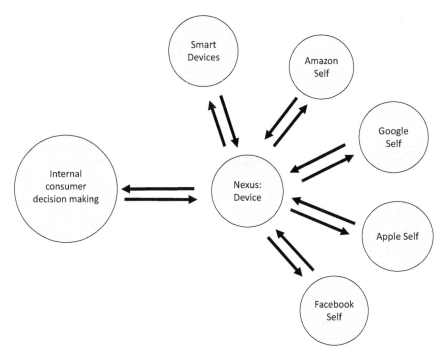

Figure 4.4 Examples of 'the selves' embedded within a distributed system of computing/ analytics

and mobile technology. Consumers have eagerly adopted these innovations because they bring many benefits to our lives, nonetheless they also enable a huge exercise in consumer surveillance. We have surrendered ourselves readily to these devices and the system behind them, but the benefits/utility inherent

Table 4.1 Elements of exogenous cognition

Element of exogenous cognition	Description and implications
Intelligent	The initial information source of EC is the individual. EC will tend to reflect and augment the decision and cognitive expressions of the individual. The source is therefore a sentient and intelligent being; this intelligence will be manifest in the distributed system that enables EC to occur. Moreover, the system of analytics is driven by artificial intelligence (AI). AI has its limits; the implications of these limitations are biases and fallacious inferences (discussed below) – but it does represent a form of intelligence in its own right. It is a form of stupid intelligence. We can train machines to recognize a giraffe in a photograph but the machine does not know what a giraffe is.
Autonomous	The structures that facilitate EC are not entirely or even nominally under the control of the consumer. The consumer provides inputs and interacts with the system that feeds EC, but the control is diffuse. A variety of sources distribute and process this data; some of these elements interact with each other but the consumer does not have control over the system (in fact no one actor does).
Interactive	As depicted above, EC is interactive. The nexus is the device and app/platform in use at any one time. The consumer and the external 'brain' feed each other information.
Diffuse and opaque	The distributed system of computational analytics infrastructure is complex and determined by consumer preferences for interfaces and apps (e.g. Apple vs. Android operating system on a phone).
Unrelenting	The processing of data and targeting of communications is unremitting and cumulative. It is ceaseless because it is mechanized.
Morally neutral	Machines have no morals. They might inherit some biases from their designers but they have no moral sense.

in this adoption is only one explanation of the normalization of EC. Cognitive miserliness (e.g. Taylor 1981; Barr et al. 2015) refers to the tendency for people to find an easy way out or follow a path of least resistance when it comes to an information-based decision. Essentially we have an innate tendency to make life easy for ourselves. Decisions can be stimulating and we might even seek them as a distraction (e.g. a crossword puzzle); however the flip side to this is the fact that necessary decision making and the plethora of decisions facing us in a cluttered and cognitively demanding world tend to make us seek easy solutions. The Cognitive Reflection Test (CRT) (e.g. Frederick 2005) exemplifies this tendency. Consider the following problem:

> *A cricket bat and a ball cost £1.10 in total. The bat costs £1 more than the ball. How much does the cricket ball cost?*

Too many answer 10p assuming the bat is £1. If the ball was 10p then the bat at £1 would only be 90p more not £1 more. So one of the conditions, the second, is not met. The answer is 5p for the ball and £1.05 for the bat. The maths are not complex here but we tend to glance at the problem and find the 'easy' but wrong solution. There is ample evidence that we opt for less burdensome forms of processing information when we can (e.g. Baron 1998). Extant consumer research has tended to neglect this cognitive laziness (the relative neglect of the role of heuristic processing being a case in point; see Chapter 6). Marketing analytics plays upon this tendency and seeks to make information search as efficient as possible and, as already stated, fast-track our decision making or even make recommendations and decisions for us. The smartphone has provided us with the perfect way of contracting out our cognition (Barr et al. 2015). In fact, emerging research even suggests that the mere presence of a smartphone affects thinking (Ward et al. 2017; Gazzaley and Rosen 2016).

Managerial and ethical implications of EC

The emergence of analytics-driven marketing and the pervasiveness of EC has some very profound implications for the management of marketing and for managerial ethics:

I. Funnelling, reinforcement and bias

Algorithms underpin search and targeting technology and data determines them. Data is often biased and so the analytic outputs will often have biases; moreover the algorithm might reinforce those biases. For example, if, in a given market, men are the principal buyers of beer online then MC regarding beer will tend to target men. There is a strong element of self-fulfilling prophecy here. If men drink more beer, then target men with beer MC. Surely this will make men more likely to continue to be the principal drinkers of beer if the MC is at all effective? Women (or those online thought not to be men) will not be subject to the MC and will only switch from other alcoholic drinks if other stimuli prompts them. Female beer drinkers might not receive the MC for beer or might even be classified as men because they drink beer. Either way the automated marketing will often tend to reinforce biases when the inferences from the data are 'accurate'. Loyal/frequent consumers will be encouraged to re-purchase. Conversely, someone with a high entropy score is more likely to be classified as such and to be sent more varied offers as a derived variety seeker.

Algorithms draw conclusions about you which might be wrong; they will only revise their inferences when contrary evidence mounts up (they are arch deployers of abductive reasoning, reaching the most obvious conclusion). Ultimately, probability drives algorithms. Your ISP or browser will order, rank and filter/bias the results of your search according to your search history and the profile of your browsing behaviour and the probability that you will sustain that trajectory. An algorithm can suggest things we might like or might want to try for a change but more often than not it will tend to suggest things that we have bought before or have a higher probability of buying (or have already searched for). Even when it suggests things 'for a change' intentionally or not then another form of influence is happening.

2. Disruption and entropy

Automated marketing will either disrupt or change our behaviour intentionally (to get us to switch from our favourite brand) or by accident (an online offer targeted at the person who last used our device that makes us change behaviour nonetheless). Whether intended or not the potential exists to disrupt behaviour in ways that are to our aggregate/individual benefit/welfare or not.

3. Consumer welfare: reinforcement and disruption effects

Points 1 and 2 above outline the potential for analytics-driven marketing to either channel and funnel behaviour (potentially to compromise choice and therefore consumer sovereignty) or disrupt behaviour. Figure 4.5 summarizes the basic outcomes of these potential effects on welfare. Welfare is a subjective

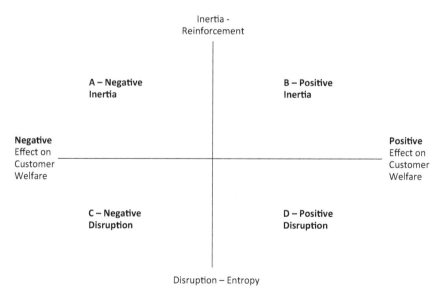

Figure 4.5 Classification of the positive and negative effects of exogenous cognition, analytics and automated marketing

condition: determined by value judgements and views. These will vary. So, ideas on what is good or bad for welfare and well-being will depend on individual and social perspectives. This point should be borne in mind.

A. *Negative inertia.* A consumer is encouraged to continue a course of action that is detrimental to their welfare or collective welfare (e.g. to keep drinking large quantities of high sugar drinks). Negative effects will typically relate to health, over-spending and debt, vulnerability or anti-social actions.

B. *Positive inertia.* A consumer is encouraged to sustain behaviour that is enhancing or self-improving or prosocial (e.g. an app encourages you to learn a foreign language over an extended period of time). Positive effects will typically relate to health, financial prudence, prosocial or life enhancing actions (such as education).

C. *Negative disruption.* A consumer is encouraged to change their normal behaviour in a way that is to their detriment or the detriment of society. For example, marketing communications that encourage someone who has maintained a diet to control type 2 diabetes to go on a pizza blowout. This one event then leads to longer-term negative behaviour change.

D. *Positive disruption.* A consumer is encouraged to change their normal behaviour in a way that is to their benefit (or to the benefit of society or the collective). For example targeted marketing communications that offers nicotine substitutes at a discount provoking a given consumer to attempt to kick a smoking habit.

There is a third dimension. Whether the disruption (be it positive or negative) or inertia (be it positive or negative) is intended or not. Analytics makes mistakes. Your exogenized cognition can result in outcomes that might be due to errors or inaccuracy. Table 4.2 provides examples to illustrate the incorporation of intention/accident with the dimensions outlined above in Figure 4.5. This accounts for eight categories of impact according to these three dimensions.

4. Real-time marketing

Marketing is increasingly real-time, adapting to what we are doing, buying and searching for now (Chapter 1 introduced this crucial theme and it will not be rehearsed here in full). Real-time and reflexive communications will tend to be more effective than those subject to lead times and delays (e.g. TV advertising).

5. Direct to device/consumer – individualized

Traditional advertising is like artillery bombardment. It is targeted but over large areas rather than individual combatants. Direct marketing and personalized

Table 4.2 Examples of unintentional and intentional impacts

	Intentional negative	Intentional positive	Unintentional negative	Unintentional positive
Inertia	Encouraging you to gamble online to levels above your income score in full knowledge of your likely income level.	Encouraging you to keep to a low-salt diet.	Your liking for cake results in offers from various sources that collectively undermines your attempts to lose weight.	Continual and unwanted offers for beer (one you don't even like) hardens your resolve to keep off alcohol.
Disruption	Encouraging you to start smoking when you do not.	Encouraging you to start a low-salt diet based on information that you have high blood pressure.	A poorly targeted offer introduces you to something 'bad' you never even thought of.	A poorly targeted offer introduces you to something 'good' you never even thought of.

advertising is more akin to sniping; individuals targeted ruthlessly through a cross hair. A party political broadcast will have less effect on you than a private chat with the premier of your nation.

6. Ethics of persuasion

Real-time and direct forms of persuasion are more likely to be effective. The offer of a free doughnut with your coffee sent because you are in close proximity to your favourite coffee outlet in a city you're unfamiliar with is more likely to affect behaviour than the advert for the offer you saw last night on TV (thanks to your GPS tracked life). If marketing is becoming more effective and 'personal' then ethics become even more acute. There's a good chance you'll have that doughnut (and the sugar and fat). Moulding behaviour has become more likely under conditions of EC and automated marketing.

EC and the 'lens' through which we view extant consumer research

This chapter serves as a link between the 'revealed consumer', the consumer we see via data (Chapters 1, 2 and 3) and the large body of work that has sought to understand the various processes that underpin consumer decision making (Chapters 5, 6 and 7). The rest of the book explores what might be termed meta-themes and their components. The following chapters provide a parsimonious tour of key concepts, research and ideas – those deemed to be relevant in the age of EC and the associated analytics structure that defines contemporary consumer marketing; to reiterate:

Marketing and consumers have fundamentally changed by virtue of the digital revolution and this necessitates a fresh approach to understanding the anatomy of consumption.

CB&A concludes with a method for intelligently considering the importance of the diverse range of influences on the consumer. A 'structure' or format is required that is cognizant of the complexity discussed in the first sections of this chapter. This format needs to be able to account for complexity and be applicable to account for various contexts (including temporal dynamics/variations). It must also allow each of the 'traditions' of consumer research to 'speak' or be heard; but it must also acknowledge the fundamental changes and issues outlined above, specifically the existence of EC.

The proposed format/solution was derived via the input of analytics practitioners and scholars with a knowledge of analytics and consumer behaviour. It is called MADS – the Modular, Adaptive, Dynamic, Schematic. It is modular because each element or feature represents a discrete theme. It is adaptive because it can be changed in order to account for different consumption and purchase contexts or for different consumers/segments etc. It is dynamic because it can be used to explore the temporal realm – i.e. it can be used to explore the dynamics of various features or elements, pre, during or post consumption or at different consumer life stages. It is a schematic because it is based on a network premise; not a linear premise. It is a dynamic apparatus for thinking about consumer choice and behaviour. However, before it can be used and applied, the various features, themes and elements that underpin it need to be understood. This is the function of the next three chapters. Figure 4.6 might not make a great deal of sense to you at this particular point, but it will do by the time you reach the end of the book.

Conclusion

Many seminal models of consumer choice did incorporate feedback loops and were not entirely linear in nature. However, many did envisage and promote a dominant or salient linear sequential element exemplified by Figure 4.2. Decision making is a 'messy' and often non-linear process. The subsequent chapters account for the essential/temporal linearity of choice and events and the fuzzy nature of determinants and antecedents.

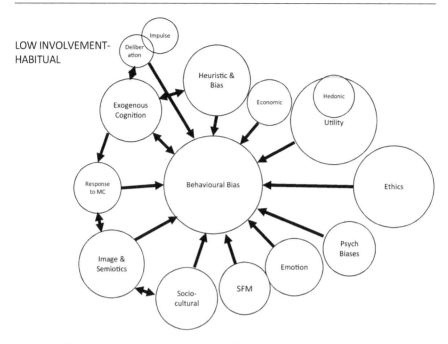

Figure 4.6 Example visualization of the MADS format

EC, analytics and ubiquitous computing have changed marketing and the enactment of choice in various ways. This chapter has outlined the principal effects. The world of the consumer and the practice of marketing is now more interactive, more mechanized, more instantaneous and more data-driven. This requires a re-appraisal and review of the most pertinent extant consumer research. The following chapters contain that (parsimonious) review.

References

Barr, N., Pennycook, G., Stolz, J.A. and Fugelsang, J.A. 2015. The brain in your pocket: Evidence that smartphones are used to supplant thinking. *Computers in Human Behavior*, 48, pp. 473–480.

Baron, J. 1998. *Judgment misguided: Intuition and error in public decision making*. New York: Oxford University Press.

Clark, A. and Chalmers, D. 1998. The extended mind. *Analysis*, 58(1), pp. 7–19.

Estrin, D. and Thompson, C.W. 2015. Internet of you: Data big and small [guest editors' introduction]. *IEEE Internet Computing*, 19(6), pp. 8–10.

Foxall, G.R. 1995. Science and interpretation in consumer research: A radical behaviourist perspective. *European Journal of Marketing*, 29(9), pp. 3–99.

Frederick, S. 2005. Cognitive reflection and decision making. *Journal of Economic Perspectives*, 19(4), pp. 25–42.

Gazzaley, A. and Rosen, L.D. 2016. *The distracted mind: Ancient brains in a high-tech world*. Cambridge, MA: MIT Press.

Howard, J.A. and Sheth, J.N. 1969. *The theory of buyer behavior*. New York: John Wiley & Sons.

Lancaster, K.J. 1966. A new approach to consumer theory. *Journal of Political Economy*, 74(2), pp. 132–157.

Menary, R. ed. 2010. *The extended mind*. Cambridge, MA: MIT Press.

Taylor, S.E. 1981. The interface of cognitive and social psychology. In J.H. Harvey (Ed.), *Cognition, social behavior, and the environment* (pp. 189–211). Hillsdale, NJ: Erlbaum.

Tversky, A. and Kahneman, D. 1986. Rational choice and the framing of decisions. *Journal of Business*, 59(4), pp. S251–S278.

Veblen, T. 1899. *The theory of the leisure class*. Project Gutenberg.

Ward, A.F., Duke, K., Gneezy, A. and Bos, M.W. 2017. Brain drain: The mere presence of one's own smartphone reduces available cognitive capacity. *Journal of the Association for Consumer Research*, 2(2), pp. 140–154.

Chapter 5

Elemental features of consumer choice

Needs, economics, deliberation and impulse

Introduction

Humans have needs. These needs are a conflation of basic evolutional and physiological needs and the perceived needs stemming from being an agent in a complex socio-cultural structure. The range of needs that we attempt to satiate in a given day are myriad; enormously varied. The following everyday example readily illustrates the inherent complexity of need.

Susan and the sushi bar

Dr Susan Tench leaves the hospital with her friend Naomi for a well-earned lunch. Both of them agree that they are starving, but they have a great deal to talk about; the hospital is undergoing a major re-organization. Susan suggests that they don't just grab something and eat on the hoof. She asserts that she would appreciate a more leisurely lunch, Naomi agrees. Susan suggests a local pub, it does a range of food and they have eaten there a number of times. It's a short walk and the service is swift. Naomi mentions her health kick, she's trying to avoid certain foods in an attempt to improve her diet and well-being. Naomi suggests the new sushi bar at the end of the high street – she shows Susan the reviews on her smartphone. Susan isn't keen on sushi; it's ok but not her preferred option, especially for lunch on a busy shift. She was hoping for something more filling to see her through to nightfall. Naomi seems very keen – she persists in reading out the reviews. Susan relents, why not – the reviews are good? Perhaps she should give sushi another chance. They head for the sushi bar deep in conversation…

How can we describe the needs of these two friends? The meal is serving a fundamental need; the need for food. It is also serving various other functions;

a break from work, pleasure or a hedonic function, relaxation, social bonding and friendship, possibly even conflict avoidance, and in Naomi's case the quest for a healthier lifestyle. These needs are discrete but some are related. Together they form a complex of needs serving a variety of motivations and goals. Some instances of purchase and consumption have a self-evident and overriding need (Chapter 4 reviewed the 'problem recognition' conceptualization of need). For example filling your car up with fuel. This is an entirely utilitarian act on the face of it. The petroleum is required to drive the car. However, what the fuel facilitates is more complex; it opens the door to work, leisure and favours. There are often a plethora of needs behind many everyday acts of purchase and consumption. However, some classification of need is useful in order to understand and define an anatomy of need that we can use to explore consumer behaviour more systematically.

Utility and needs

There is some disagreement over the efficacy and validity of Maslow's hierarchy of needs – it has been challenged, supported and adapted (e.g. Kenrick et al. 2010). But it does serve as some kind of basis for moving forward; it does provide a language or brief lexicon of need that we can adapt. Maslow suggested the following need typology (these are in reverse order in terms of the hierarchy):

- Physiological Needs – Biologically-driven, food and reproduction.
- Safety – Shelter, warmth and sanctuary from the dangers of nature.
- Social – The requirement for human interaction and kinship.
- Esteem – The requirement for standing, power and recognition.
- Self-actualization – Full realization of one's human potential in terms of creative, intellectual and social ambitions.

He ordered these in a hierarchy, suggesting that satiation of one level would lead to fixation on the higher-order need (in reality needs occur as conflations, as the example above illustrates). We can therefore see needs as layers of a sphere with a core, mantle and crust (see Figure 5.1). Each is a part of the morphology, each is distinct but together they form a more complex whole. We cannot readily separate them or understand them in isolation; we must consider them in unison. This simple conceptualization also helps us understand products as layered entities e.g. conflations of intrinsic and extrinsic elements from the practical to the relational and symbolic.

The <u>Core Need</u> is the elemental need, and will tend to be the fundamental function of the product or service; context will also dictate it. For example,

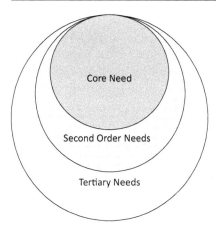

Figure 5.1 Embedded needs

the elemental need in a ball gown purchase will not be the standard requirement for clothes (warmth, practicality etc.). It is more likely to be display and
self-esteem. For winter clothes, then, the core function will be warmth and
comfort and practical function but this will invariably be mediated by the
requirement for something fashionable and/or aesthetically appropriate for
the usage context; or the need to identify with a particular group. Branding
might also be an element of this layer if the product is conspicuously consumed
(not for everyone though – once again context and individual variance must
be considered). <u>Second-order Needs</u> will be distinct from the core need but
still influential. They will still determine a great deal about the actual item
purchased; however they are secondary to the elemental aim. <u>Tertiary Needs</u>
are more ephemeral but might also be very influential; for example the need
for variety in an FMCG market (e.g. soft drinks). The core need is the need to
quench thirst, a secondary need might relate to the requirement for a low sugar
option, whilst the tertiary need is the requirement for variety. Marketers can
employ purposive research to require consumers to identify and rank needs.

Neo-classical economics also attempted to provide an underlying theory of
preference, need and choice from the 1960s onwards. The framework was initially influential but is essentially void of any concession to psychological or
socio-cultural variables and does not give a managerially useful account of consumer choice in the real world. Nonetheless, a very quick review and appraisal
is given here for the sake of completeness and because it does provide some
useful elements for a consideration of need (even if the whole approach has
issues). Utility theory and Lancaster's consumer theory (Lancaster 1966) suggest
the following:

a.　People seek attributes rather than goods.
b.　People seek bundles of attributes and trade-off preferences between goods in order to acquire these attributes.
c.　People have the ability to rank their preferences for attributes/products.

These are not controversial in such a reduced form. The problem in the theory lies in the assumptions and the specifics of the theory as alluded to above. They assume that rationality drives people (sometimes referred to as the *homo economicus* or economic human paradigm). It also promotes an idea of the consumer as an accountant; mentally ranking and scoring products in terms of attributes with relative scores ascribed. This is an abstraction of reality, clearly people assess things according to certain criteria and these might be differentially 'weighted' but the idea that they systematically indulge this form of accounting autonomously is questionable (and the approach has been thoroughly interrogated). However people can often rank needs and utility if a researcher requires it (see perceived use value below). Moreover, the reality is that people often buy things for 'irrational' reasons, they act on a sense of fun, impulse and many essentially emotional drivers. A primary function of neoclassical economic theory is to support other theory not to universally describe the genesis and mechanics of choice as they happen in the real world (behavioural economics eschews this charge since it does not turn a blind eye to psychological drivers). The following example (alluded to in Chapter 4) exemplifies the core constraint:

> If Person X buys cat food even though they don't have a cat (or anyone they know; they live in an entirely catless world) then utility theory would merely assert that they must derive some utility from it; otherwise they would not buy it. It does not equip us to determine what that utility is based on. Perhaps they eat the cat food. Perhaps they use the food for making pies for human consumption. Both of these rather alarming possibilities are viable under the basic tenets of the bald utility theory.

Thankfully we have already gone further in the section above. We have already conceptualized need (with utility embedded within it) as a blend or cocktail of elements that cannot be readily or easily separated in all circumstances or contexts. But a useful delineation of need requires the imposition of some kind of structure beyond this initial notion of a complex of factors.

Table 5.1 provides some examples of specific needs or outcomes of consumption and purchase. It promotes the idea that utilitarian drivers and hedonic drivers often overlap or are aspects of the same object. It incorporates the notion of core, secondary and tertiary needs outlined above but delineates between

Table 5.1 Utility and hedonic needs: mobility example

Needs	Mobility needs	Description/commentary
UTILITY		
Use Value	Transport	The ability to get from place to place is a relatively straightforward requirement for many of us. If the choice leads to a mode of transport that is not the cheapest or even more efficient but perhaps the most enjoyable then that need or requirement is expressing itself. So a more rounded view of the need in that case is a requirement to get places in an enjoyable way. In this case the core need is the requirement for transportation and the second-order need is the requirement to do so in an enjoyable manner.
	Safety	A woman might require a car that is safe but also stylish (among other things). Safety is self-evidently a function of the need to avoid danger and risk to yourself and others and is fundamental in many need hierarchies and typologies.
	Esteem	The overriding need for an automobile purchase might be the requirement for a car that exudes and communicates esteem or status. Perhaps the individual in question isn't massively concerned with the other more common elements of functionality; their core need is for something that is congruent with their perceived or aspirational status. Luxury goods often perform a similar function to alternatives; the real gain is their announcement of status through acquisition and ownership (and often their aesthetics). Esteem also has an underlying hedonic element but it is a common core need and relates to Maslow's strata.
HEDONIC		
Pleasure and enjoyment	Fun	Fun can be a primary determinant of consumption. A person may go on a train ride for the hell of it, they may buy a motorbike just for leisure and ride it because they enjoy it. The core utility they derive is therefore hedonic – it is still utility but we distinguish this from the forms of utility outlined above which are more readily related to the seminal hierarchies and typologies and taxonomies of needs.
	Experience	The acquisition of experiences has become increasingly important (the section below explores the reasons for the increasing profile of experiential consumption). The extrapolation in this case has a relationship with the commentary above for 'fun'. If a journey is undertaken for the sake of the journey – to say that you have done it – to savour the journey as a thing in itself, then the need satiated is experiential.

(continued)

Table 5.1 (Cont.)

Needs	Mobility needs	Description/commentary
	Gratification	This element potentially relates to esteem but not necessarily. Gratification explains the effect of satiation of desires. Something that is gratifying can be enriching (life enhancing) and/or pleasurable. The act of gratification is satisfying in itself – it is a tautology and emotions stem from it (emotions are crucial to understanding need and choice but are dealt with in Chapter 7). For example, a stylish car can make you feel good and can enforce ideas about you in social contexts.

those that are essentially utilitarian and those that are essentially hedonic. So, the table identifies six specific needs under the utility and hedonic headings respectively (i.e. transport, safety and esteem; fun, experience, gratification). The core, secondary and tertiary needs can be any combination of these six sub-elements and will vary from person to person.

As the discussion above illustrates and as a point of re-emphasis these elements are inextricably linked; they tend to overlap and interrelate. More concerted attempts to neatly divide the antecedents and features of need run the risk of descending into increasingly nuanced semantics. For example it is quite possible to describe a situation (a journey or instance of car purchase) engendered by the requirement for all of the examples of need outlined above. A car purchase could require transport, safety, esteem, fun. The act of acquisition of a new car can be gratifying in itself. Can these needs really be ordered or ranked as per economic theory? The short answer is yes; consumers will tend to have necessary (highly ranked or primary) needs and more subordinate needs. They won't consciously score these (in most cases) but they will tend to have notional priorities.

Whilst we can attempt to order these the order will vary between individual consumers or groups of consumers bound together by significant commonalities. Purposive research and analytics can attempt to identify patterns or segments in terms of need (requirements). Any attempt to provoke consumers into ranking and scoring their needs is imposing the task upon them; it does not necessarily follow that they actually indulge this form of accounting in any systematic way in their lives when safe from contact with market researchers. It is far more likely that they operate rules of thumb or heuristics (see Chapter 6). Faulkner's concept of Perceived Use Value (PUV – Faulkner 1995) usefully provides a method for quantifying the needs and features of products and can be used to inform purposive research (people approximate this in their heads but we can ask them to rank and quantify their priorities and perceived utility).

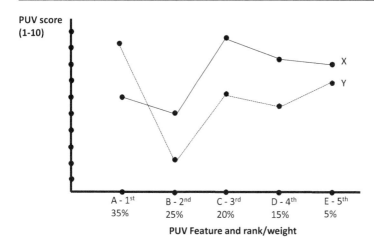

PUV score
(1-10)

| | A - 1ˢᵗ | B - 2ⁿᵈ | C - 3ʳᵈ | D - 4ᵗʰ | E - 5ᵗʰ |
| | 35% | 25% | 20% | 15% | 5% |

PUV Feature and rank/weight

Figure 5.2 Perceived use value – holiday/vacation destination
Legend:
A = Relaxation
B = Activity
C = Fun
D = Companionship (friendship and social)
E = Romance/Sex

Envisage a scenario where analysis and market research has established that older singletons from a given country appraise potential holiday/vacation destinations according to five overriding requirements (on average/in aggregate) as outlined in the legend for Figure 5.2. Scores are derived from people from the relevant population. Each need (and associated product attribute) is ranked and weighted (higher weight reflecting the importance people attach to the item) on a ten point Likert scale. The scenario further illustrates the contextual and variant nature of needs and requirements.

Once again the delineation should not be allowed to obscure the fact that needs overlap, for example, relaxation is pleasurable and so is fun. Destination X scores slightly better in terms of the overall PUV. In terms of requirement B neither do well, so the 'ideal' destination would score higher. The profile for each need is different and self-evident in Figure 5.2. Marketers can employ this form of analysis in order to match destinations with the needs and expectations of given segments, sub-segments or individuals; clearly it can inform positioning strategy. The results of such purposive analysis can also be merged with/inform analysis of transactional data revealed via sites like booking.com (although any purposive study data will have to be renewed and updated as destinations and needs evolve). A person or segment might always tend to holiday in a destination close to Type X; a reasonable inference being their preference for the

Table 5.2 Destination scores – PUV

Need/attribute	Formula and rounded totals (score x by weight)	
	Destination X	*Destination Y*
A	6 × 0.35 = 2.1	9.3 × 0.35 = 3.26
B	5 × 0.25 = 1.25	2 × 0.25 = 0.5
C	9.5 × 0.20 = 1.9	6 × 0.20 = 1.2
D	8.5 × 0.15 = 1.3	5.3 × 0.15 = 0.80
E	7 × 0.05 = 0.35	6.9 × 0.05 = 0.35
PUV score/total	6.9	6.1

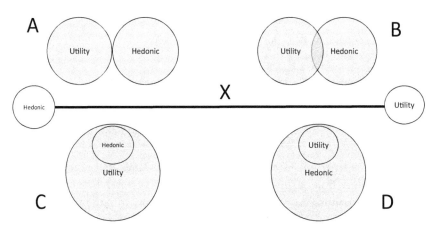

Figure 5.3 Towards an enhanced conceptualization of the anatomy of need

needs addressed by Type X; this equates to retrofitting the market research to the analytics (behaviour).

Once we have indulged or satiated necessity then we indulge pleasure and other 'higher-order' needs. Hedonic and experiential-driven consumer behaviour are increasingly important, especially under conditions of higher discretionary incomes. The blended nature of need is exemplified by the conceptualization below; a utility–hedonic blend. The two are embedded within each other; this notion is explored and elaborated on in Figure 5.3.

The PUV logic encapsulates the idea that utility (use value) is multifaceted. The term utility is subsequently used to represent a variant blend of needs dependent on the market, product and consumers in question. Hedonic requirements are seen as distinct but embedded within the overall notion of use value (or vice versa). Situation A is not consistent with this assertion. B is to some

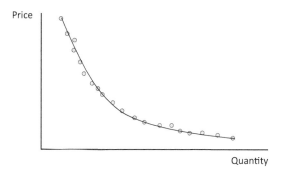

Figure 5.4 The simple demand curve

extent and X is not. A continuum (as in X) naturally suggests that the two are polar opposites and that something can be entirely hedonic with no other use value. Embedding the two as depicted by C and D acknowledges the assertion that they are facets of each other and appropriates some benefits of a continua-based conceptualization. C depicts a scenario where primarily non-hedonic elements dominate (e.g. choice of writing instrument) – hedonic elements are not entirely excluded (e.g. the pleasure of owning and using a well-designed and aesthetically pleasing pen). D depicts a scenario where hedonistic drivers lead the need impetus (e.g. a trip to a theme park) – other use value elements are not entirely excluded (e.g. social or family bonding, distraction from stress).

We cannot clear up need in this section entirely. Indeed many of the following pages return to the notion of need directly or indirectly and Chapter 4 has dealt with it already in terms of problem recognition. Likewise, subsequent chapters cannot eschew it. Needs and utility permeate consumption entirely.

The economic psychology of price and value

Elementary economic theory suggests the simple (generally non-linear) rela-tionship in Figure 5.4. This equates to higher sales the lower the price. Clearly this basic model of demand holds for many situations and it also provides a touchstone for situations and scenarios that contradict the basic logic.

Sometimes, in marketing terms, high prices are desirable. We, as consumers, expect them, they can become a feature or even a part of the product's utility. Price is not just an amount: it is a cue. It indicates something about the product. We expect premium brands to be expensive and they oblige. Premium brands do often cost more to produce but sometimes they are produced on quite low-cost bases with high margins; the price is also designed to feed notions of desirability and aspiration (Rolex brand value would collapse if it offered a buy one get one free sales promotion). The buyer wants the association with luxury and premium. Heuristics, mental rules of thumb (see Chapter 6), are very important when it comes to pricing cues. Low price means lower quality, higher price means better quality (of course, this is often not the case; we often pay premium prices for brands that are more desirable but not necessarily better by any rational measure of utility or quality). Or, low price means good value (but not necessarily, if the product mark-up is 500%, then the margin dictates that it is not). Consumer minds are full of ideas about fair and reasonable prices for various things; consumers learn these heuristics, but not formally. Rather, they come from a hotchpotch of ideas and experience.

What follows is a review of some of the more common pricing strategies. Their supply-side logic is reviewed here as well as the essential demand-side (consumer) psychology:

1. *Absorption pricing.* The aim in absorption pricing is to ensure that all costs are absorbed, or recovered. Thus, the price of the product includes the variable cost of production and distribution (wages, power, materials, etc.) of each item plus a proportionate amount of the fixed costs (real estate, plant, normal profit etc.). This is entirely supply-side driven and the price setter is at the mercy of consumer perception.

2. *Contribution margin-based pricing.* This is sometimes called cost-plus pricing. A company determines its break-even price for the product by working out all the costs involved in the production, marketing and distribution. Then a 'mark-up' or 'margin' is set for each unit of production, this being based on the profit the company desires, its sales objectives and the price it thinks the market will take. If the margin is substantial then this is also called 'rip-off' pricing. The margin can be maximized by investing in a premium or intermediate brand image and outsourcing production to low-cost locations. The danger here is consumer perception or knowledge of the margin. Brands can and have been damaged by press reports and leaks. If product image perceptions wander too far away from the 'reality' of production then this dissonance can manifest itself in the consumer's mind (this will challenge the overall perceived utility of the product).

3. *Creaming or skimming.* In many skimming scenarios goods are offered at higher prices so that fewer sales are needed to break even. Skimming is usually employed to reimburse the cost of investment of the original research into the product and so is commonly used for tech goods. The 'early adopter' (see Chapter 7) consumers pay a high price so the rest of us can get it cheaper later. The company is getting us to pay for the R&D to reduce its risks.

4. *Decoy pricing.* A company offers you three products (e.g. mobile phones). 'A' is very cheap and very basic but reasonable value, 'B' is better and costs much more than 'A', whilst 'C' is discernibly better still and only slightly

more to buy than 'B'. You compare them on your trip to the shop or your browse of the website and you buy the best one ('C') because its features are great value for that little bit more than 'B'. You have been nudged into this situation. The 'B' is a decoy, produced only to get you to buy the superior one with the highest margin. 'C' has also been priced according to a 'cost-plus' strategy (its extra features cost very little per unit to install). If you were only faced with 'A' and 'B' you might have chosen 'A' (many will buy 'A' anyway). This has cost implications to the producer but it must make sense in money terms or companies wouldn't bother. 'B' will eventually be sold off at a lower cost when stocks of 'A' are depleted. This final sales promotion tactic is built into the marketing plan and the revenue schedule.

5. *Freemium.* The word 'freemium' obviously reflects the fact that the service is free to some and others pay up cash. A company offers a basic product or service free of charge (typically digital things like software, apps and games) while charging a premium for advanced features, functionality or freedom from excessive marketing communications (ads). It is never truly free. You usually let them have your data; that data opens up a world of targeted marketing (and exogenous cognition).

6. *High–low pricing.* The company offers a product at a higher price than the competition but bundles it up with offers and promotions and extras that make you think that it is even better value than the competition.

7. *Limit pricing.* A company can only pull this one off if it has a monopoly (or at least a large market share) or is first to market. It pitches the price below cost so that no one can compete with it in any way that is economically rational (placing itself to the extremes of the demand curve). The danger is the cue/heuristic in terms of quality as discussed above (low price = low quality); the consumer may also react to other companies being undercut and possibly driven out of business (via media coverage of 'unfair' competition).

8. *Loss leader.* A brand offers a cheap version in order to stimulate the overall demand for the brand. For example a good value entry-level version that can mean that one day you will buy the premium or deluxe version at a later time (by inducing loyalty or through tying you into a payment plan).

9. *Odd pricing or so-called psychological pricing.* £9.99 or £9.95 sounds less than £10; it is less but we will tend to perceive it as better value (out of proportion to the amount).

10. *Pay what you want.* For example for a downloaded album.

11. *Penetration pricing.* This is a simple conditioning tactic (see Chapter 6) whereby the product is offered to you at a low price at first to lure you into a longer cycle of purchase. Sales promotion like this can work and can fail. A subsequent section explores this in more detail.

12. *Predatory pricing.* This is undercutting to drive out the opposition. Again, this can lead to bad press and affect consumer perception of a brand.
13. *Premium pricing.* We assume that better things are more expensive as discussed above.
14. *Price discrimination.* Travel to London from York at 7:00 am and you will pay twice the price paid by the person who goes at 10:00 am. There have been examples of online real-time price discrimination based on the fact that the retailer has used an algorithm that suggests Person Z will pay more for a given product or have a higher disposable income. This has clear ethical and perceptual dangers as pricing is individualized in a form of automated blind auction.
15. *Time-based pricing.* Budget airlines like this. The price varies according to when you buy not just when you travel.
16. *Subscription.* It's worth noting that this has become increasingly common as a result of the digital revolution (mobile phones, apps etc). Companies like it because it provides for a steady and more predictable income stream underpinned by a contract and the <u>Inertia Effect</u>; the tendency not to change provider due to the perception of hassle or disruption. Notions of 'time poverty' mean that many of us don't review and change our contracts as often as we could.

Subscription leads us back into a consideration of the forms of utility and ownership in the digital economy in particular. Ownership is increasingly contingent when it comes to digital and virtual goods (see Watkins, Denegri-Knott and Molesworth 2016). With DVGs we have less control than the tangible product such as the kitchen table. We can use the table when we want (right to use), paint it or burn it (right to transform), sell it on eBay (right to income), give it away (right to transfer), it's ours until we die (right of continuity) and the law enforces these rights. DVGs emphasize how products and tangible elements of offerings have been replaced by service-based models facilitated by technological change. For example, Spotify vs. CDs, Netflix vs. DVDs. As we move from the physical to the virtual many of these rights are restricted or denied. Now, that's not a problem in itself since we must consider that these services are better value for money or provide other benefits (or utility) such as the elimination of the need for storage of CDs. At the very least it demonstrates changes in utility, value and means of exchange and pricing. Many DVGs are supplied via freemium or through subscription, they tie us in because they induce dependency (Spotify 'has' your music collection).

Individual responses to these strategies of pricing and charging (and ownership and utility) will vary. The underlying psychological biases of the individual will determine many of these (e.g. risk aversion) and these are dealt with in detail in Chapter 7. A useful concept to try and encapsulate consumer responses is Value Consciousness – VC. A consumer can be value (bargain) conscious overall or within given markets. They may have product groups where they are less likely to compromise on quality. Once again we have a context dependent variable or feature, it is not fixed (a US dollar billionaire can still be value-conscious, just from a higher baseline). Value consciousness can also be enforced or innate or a function of the two. Enforced VC can occur through limited income or discretionary income or relative/absolute poverty. This is enforced or imposed; VC may rise for a large number of consumers if the prevailing economic conditions dictate (e.g. in the 2008 banking crisis). Innate VC is a psychological tendency. It is quite possible that the two occur in unison and therefore reinforce each other. Innate VC is a possible driver of more pronounced forms of bargain hunting behaviour. Bargain hunting for its own sake is referred to as the 'thrill of the hunt'. The consumer derives hedonic feedback and satisfaction from achieving perceived savings for their own sake (irrespective of the actual utility derived from the product). Here the utility resides largely in the act of acquisition. Bargain hunting is the mirror image of a susceptibility to indulge premium pricing. The Louis Vuitton bag is likely to be acquired for what it announces about the owner as well as the perceived value and quality. The seeker of luxury goods (at full price) is not value-conscious in the true or reduced meaning of the term. They are conscious of the premium value of owning such a thing, they are not seeking a bargain or averse to paying higher prices. Oddly enough the 'logic' of the counterfeit luxury good buyer encapsulates a great deal about contemporary perceptions of utility and value (Bian et al. 2016):

- Counterfeit goods are cheaper than the originals; this attracts VC consumers and bargain hunters.
- They are desirable (if they are convincing copies) because they also bring the benefits associated with the premium price seeker (image, esteem etc.).

The objective here is not to promote the purchase of counterfeit goods (obviously); the aim is to emphasize how counterfeits powerfully (and often irresistibly) combine or conflate different elements of the universe of value and utility.

In many economies value and utility perceptions are being changed by higher levels of discretionary income; the real or perceived surplus income once all 'essentials' have been accounted for (however, perceptions of what is essential are also changing). For example, Hong Kong has a justified reputation for the purchase of luxury and premium consumer goods, increases in discretionary income partly explain this. Freely and readily available credit (the ubiquitous credit card) has also made purchase easier; credit offers an extension of discretionary income (at a price of course). Arguably this increases the like-lihood of impulse purchase as well (see section below).

Digital platforms also have big impacts on our ability to compare prices in very short time frames. On the web, comparison is easier. It is likely that this can increase VC in many instances and might have helped to increase it overall. It is highly likely that it has lowered price expectations for many goods; branded and generic. Digitization of consumption will also lead to a greater and more direct exposure to targeted offers. Offers distort and disrupt notions of value and price perception. The following section deals with the psychology of offers and sales promotion explicitly.

Sales promotion effects

Sales Promotion (SP) has always been important, arguably even more important in the era of real-time analytics where prices and inducements can adjust almost instantaneously according to browsing and online search behaviour (via the state of exogenous cognition). SP uses various temporary manipulations including price reductions, gifts and redeemed rewards. SP therefore refers to bundle tactics that offer you 'extra'; it appeals to our sense of a bargain. Buy one get one free (the so-called BOGOF), 30% extra free, three for two, half price, 50% off, save £10, 'comes with a free gift'. All these devices work for self-evident reasons relating to VC. Sales promotion can be a form of operant conditioning (see Chapter 6); it reinforces or encourages behaviour via reward (or punishment can figure too; punitive charges for leaving a contract early for example). The longer the sustenance of the reward the more likely it is to endure even if there is a gradual reduction in the reward (e.g. your first year with the satellite TV company is the cheapest, the second year less so and the third year it's doubled). Consider the two time series in Figure 5.5.

In Case A the SP for an FMCG achieves an uplift in sales that diminishes (this could be done as part of a product launch or as part of the normal dynamics

Figure 5.5 Sales promotion time signatures

of competition for an established product). The sales return to their pre-SP level. This is quite typical of certain types of SP in FMCG markets all over the world. The SP is either an actual reduction in price (50% off) or the provision of extra value (25% extra free, BOGOF etc.). If this is how consumers respond then what is the point? The point at a product launch is to try to condition and induce some loyalty or if the product is established the SP can be used to disrupt competition (e.g. drawing consumers away from a rivals' new product). Online, in real-time it can be used to nudge someone towards a product they have just browsed, perhaps they have looked several times, a small inducement might be enough to convert this interest to purchase. There are many complex drivers of consumer choice but the basic rules of the demand curve underpin one key determinant of choice as the basic dynamics of SP demonstrate; people like cheap(er) stuff (notwithstanding the point about price as a quality cue).

In Case B something more enduring is happening. The SP has provoked a more sustained change in behaviour. The following reasons can account for this:

1. The conditioning has worked, consumers have been habituated to buying a product that is quite similar (a close substitute) to the competition. This is one form of loyalty (see Chapter 3).
2. Consumers are sticking with the product subject to the SP because they have come to appreciate that it has certain attributes that make it superior in terms of utility (from image to practical superiority). Sales (behavioural) data alone will not allow you to discriminate between this explanation and number 1. Purposive research is required to do that.
3. The consumer is tied into a subscription or another supply-side factor creating an inertia effect. This could include a loyalty scheme like a frequent flyer scheme. Retail loyalty cards tend to be adopted by people who are already loyal to the retailer (they are as much about data collection as inducing loyalty by linking purchases to individuals).

Clearly Case B is the preferred outcome. If SP becomes a norm, this is akin to a continuous price war that erodes profits. It becomes an expectation in some categories (some products like beer and shampoo are perennially on offer in UK superstores). This can encourage switching behaviour as the norm (if the product attributes are not valued by the consumer; i.e. if they are quite similar). This will diminish loyalty effects and will further emphasize variety seeking tendencies in fast-moving markets (e.g. snack food). Analytics should allow marketers to identify the people most susceptible or conversely those who are impervious to SP. It should also identify those people likely to 'exploit' the offer and return to previous purchase preferences as opposed to those likely to switch for longer (based on their past responses to SP). This allows an augmentation of measures of behavioural biases (Chapter 3).

Research into sales promotion and price perception in general has generated findings that are sometimes inconclusive, however the following concepts are useful and the findings below tend to hold for many scenarios (see Devlin et al. 2007 and 2013; McKechnie et al. 2012 for detail):

- People often have vague notions about the 'market price' for many products. The accuracy will depend on how often they buy it. Responses to discounts tend to be 'of the moment'. We do not walk round with price lists in our head. 'How much is a pint of beer'? If we ask this question then we should expect the following questions in response: 'Supermarket or pub? Which supermarket or pub? Which beer? Happy hour?' Price varies in short time frames, and as *CB&A* has already highlighted, this temporal variance has increased in the digital era and it will not mysteriously disappear. The Internal Reference Price (IRP) is a concept that suggests that we do have a price in our head. If we do then the IRP is often vague or inaccurate. Once again we rely on heuristics (mental rules of thumb).
- The pre-SP price is often referred to as the Advertised Reference Price (ARP). 'Was $100, now $79!'. The ARP is $100 and the sales price is $79. It is useful to have a clear name for this.
- Believability is a key factor in discounts. Discounts that are too large or not contextualized will score lower in terms of believability. We expect them on Black Friday – they will be more believable. A half price holiday in peak season will arouse suspicion. If the ARP is inflated then the offer can be framed as bigger, but this runs the risk of undermining believability. Research has suggested that the presence of an ARP does not make an offer more believable than one that simply says '10% off' (as opposed to '10% off was £20'). Believability varies according to the product. We know that some things get discounted to manage inventory (to fill up a half booked hotel, to get rid of end of line computers etc.). Who would not be suspicious if one new car at one dealer was half price ('what's wrong with it?')? Too good to be true? This adage rings true when it comes to the psychology of SP. They can also encourage people to believe that they were being ripped off prior to the promotion.
- Time limits work ('For one week only!'). eBay sellers know this, it plays on our sense that the opportunity might pass and to act today not tomorrow.
- Percentages work better for low price products, whilst monetary (or absolute values) do better for high priced items. So if the SP is for FMCG then go for % (because we don't tend to store prices for these things very accurately) – if it's a holiday remind the consumer how much they are saving in money (e.g. ¥100,000) – we also tend to remember how much our holidays cost (it's high involvement).

ROOM WITH A VIEW?

ROOM WITH A VIEW?

Save £500

50% off!

**Was £1,000 for a family of four –
one week full board, now £500!**

**Was £1,500 for a family of four –
one week full board – now £750!**

Book today and save a further £50!

**Travel insurance worth £50
included**

Figure 5.6 Framing prices and discounts

With the above in mind, which of the examples in Figure 5.6 are more believable?

Deliberation and impulse

Do we plan purchases or do we tend to act on impulse? Of course we do both. In fact, one purchase scenario can readily contain elements of planning and impulse or spontaneity. For example you might plan to buy a new smartphone and in the store or on the web page you may make an impulsive decision to spend more than you intended. From the outset *CB&A* contends that impulse and deliberation co-exist; they are embedded in the same way that utilitarian and hedonic elements are. They are discrete concepts but they co-habit; in other words a purchase scenario cannot necessarily be seen as *either or* (utterly planned or entirely impulsive). Even impulsive acts involve thinking – the temporal frame is compressed. It might seem perverse therefore to divorce them in this section (initially at any rate). This separation is required to understand the seminal ideas that can lead to a more blended view of how purchase actually happens in the age of the smart device.

Involvement is a core concept here and has been mentioned before. Involvement can be high, low or somewhere in between. Higher involvement implies a purchase that is not routine, that requires conscious choice, cognitive effort and might occur over an extended temporal frame. Low involvement purchases imply less presence of these elements.

Deliberation

As the previous chapter outlines, the genesis of consumer research gave rise to an approach which concentrated on cognitive elements – this was exemplified by the information processing models pioneered by Howard and Sheth (1969) among others. These models provided a language or lexicon to understand consumer choice and many of the core elements of these approaches echo in the MADS structure; they are embedded in the approach adopted here and are not rehearsed in full (they have been superseded by a seismic shift in marketing and consumer behaviour outlined previously). The various models provide a flow diagram approach to understanding consumer thinking and action, very much based on an input-output paradigm. They tend to privilege cognitive processes but do consider factors such as the symbolic value of goods. One other commonly occurring element to the various models (from those designed to address advertising effectiveness to those addressing purchase dynamics) is the linear sequential element depicted in Figure 5.7.

This essential logic lies at the heart of more complex behavioural theories (such as the Theory of Planned Behaviour – TPB – reviewed below). Attitudes (can) lead to intentions and these intentions are then enacted or not. For example:

- Attitude – 'My car is damaging the environment'.
- Intention – To buy a hybrid car.
- Behaviour – Purchase of a hybrid car.

There are many potential problems with adhering to this logic too religiously (purchase and consumption are circular activities subject to feedback and they can be 'fast and dirty'). It is applicable and it does have value but it is not the inevitable sequence of events. Intentions might not be enacted, for example. Moreover, attitudes are not the only things in our heads (emotions are also

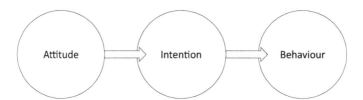

Figure 5.7 Basic linear sequential logic

powerful drivers of behaviour in their own right – attitude dominated theory suggests that emotions are subordinate to attitude). <u>Cognitive dissonance (CD)</u> is another case in point; attitudes don't always point the same way. It is possible to hold attitudes that are in conflict (e.g. 'Smoking is bad for me' vs. 'Smoking helps me relax after a stressful day at work'). This leads to internal dialogue.

Attitudes are important. They are the subject of much research; in fact, a bewildering array of research, ideas, theories and findings. This section reduces these insights radically in order to provide an actionable, managerially relevant and accessible tour of the most salient concepts. Attitudes are crucial to understanding how and why people make decisions about the things that they buy and consume and how they dispose of stuff; they are an essential element of deliberative decision making. Attitudes serve various functions. They allow us to store opinions, ideas, beliefs and feelings. Specifically, they have a:

- *Knowledge function*: they allow us to store learning – e.g. 'Airline A is unreliable'.
- *Value expression function*: they allow us to express our views and ethics – e.g. 'Airline B exploits their workers through their use of zero-hours contracts'.
- *Emotional manifestation*: they allow us to make sense of emotions and convert emotions into knowledge and values.

Attitudes are not innate, spontaneous or random; they are derived and manufactured. They are the product of myriad social and internal processes and interactions. Various other sections in *CB&A* add layers of understanding to attitude and its role in the consumer's life (a notable example being the section in Chapter 6 regarding cognitive processes in reaction to MC – marketing communications). The principal determinants from a marketing point of view are:

- *Experience*. We convert our experiences into attitudes via memory. This process is continuous and unceasing. We are sentient sponges.
- *Others*. We glean insight from hearing other people's accounts of life (particularly those we trust) whether face-to-face or via social media.
- *Media*. The media in all its forms is a machine practically designed to shape and engender attitudes.
- *MC*. Marketing communications is almost entirely about changing the way we think and act. Many of our ideas about products originate or are reinforced via MC.

The Theory of Reasoned Action (TRA), or Theory of Planned Behaviour (TPB), provides a framework that builds on the simple logic in Figure 5.7 (see

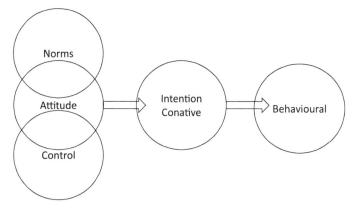

Figure 5.8 Simplification of TPB (reasoned action)

Madden, Ellen and Ajzen 1992 for a review; also Fishbein and Ajzen 1975). The full-blown model describes various determining and moderating effects. It has been operationalized and empirically tested and is often robust. The account below is a somewhat reduced account/version – it provides for a level of detail that is sufficient to mesh with the overall approach and scope of this book. The approach has some limitations in marketing applications and *CB&A* contends that its effect will also be challenged under conditions of exogenous cognition. For example it has historically been quite successful at accounting for people's approach to more salient life decisions; an instance might be the desire to lose weight. This will likely loom large in a person's mind, it will require and provoke 'internal dialogue' to quite a high order. The theory is more likely to fit when the scenario is for a higher involvement purchase although its component parts will also emerge in lower involvement situations. Figure 5.8 provides the essential structure of the model/s.

Within the model attitudes conflate and are formed and enabled or inhibited by (social) norms and the individual's ability to control the behaviour. Attitudes are assigned to these three categories – the core attitude towards the behaviour, attitudes relating to norms and those relating to control. These are elaborated below:

1. *Core attitude function*. <u>Behavioural beliefs</u> produce a favourable or unfavourable attitude towards the behaviour and lead to <u>attitudes towards the behaviour</u> – 'eating pizza makes me fat and leads to regret'.
2. *Normative function*. <u>Normative beliefs</u> are an individual's perception of social normative pressures, or associates' beliefs that they should or should not perform such behaviour. E.g. 'My friends think eating pizza

is unhealthy'. This leads to a <u>subjective norm</u>, an individual's perception about the particular behaviour, influenced by the judgement of significant others (e.g. parents, partner, friends, teachers). E.g. 'Pizza eaters are fat, lazy and unhealthy people'.

3. *Control function.* <u>Control beliefs</u> are an individual's beliefs about the presence of factors that may facilitate or hinder performance of the behaviour. E.g. 'If I go out with Naomi tonight – she likes to share pizza, she also likes a few drinks beforehand but I will not succumb to pizza – I will eat salad!' This leads to <u>perceived behavioural control</u>, an individual's perceived ease or difficulty of performing the particular behaviour. It is assumed that perceived behavioural control is determined by the total set of accessible control beliefs. E.g. 'This will be a challenge, given the presence of Naomi, alcohol and the fact that it is a Friday night and we are going to an Italian restaurant that does great pizza…'. <u>Actual behavioural control</u> is the true determinant of the successful conversion from intention to behaviour. If Susan gets drunk then she may succumb to pizza (whatever her intentions).

    <u>Behavioural intention</u> is quite simply the individual's readiness to enact behaviour. It is based on attitude towards the behaviour, subjective norms and perceived behavioural control, with each predictor weighted for its importance in relation to the behaviour and population of interest (e.g. 'I intend to order salad with Naomi').

    <u>Behaviour</u> is self-evident, but for the sake of completeness is an individual's observable response in a given situation with respect to a given target. Ajzen (1991) states that a behaviour is a function of compatible intentions and perceptions of behavioural control in that perceived behavioural control is expected to moderate the effect of intention on behaviour, such that a favourable intention produces the behaviour only when perceived behavioural control is strong (e.g. 'Oh dear – I got drunk and ordered a 24" meat feast pizza all to myself… again').

The essential linear sequential logic and its offspring, such as TPB and the modules of the information processing models (that pretty much started coherent consumer research), are useful and have some traction if applied and deployed intelligently. The speed of real-time marketing and the effect of exogenous cognition and analytic structures doesn't entirely undermine the idea and logic of the linear sequential approach – it does mean that decisions are expedited (hence the case for heuristics). Decision making used to take more time; it used to take more effort. Online reviews, social media and forums mean that it is syndicated and faster (possibly more biased too). <u>Information Search</u> is a term coined by the originators of the information processing school and it is still relevant. Consumers still search for information (particularly for higher involvement purchases); <u>Internal Search</u> still occurs (recall of attitudes, knowledge and experience of the brand or product); External Search has changed radically as asserted in Chapter 4; technology has transformed that element.

Satisfaction and disconfirmation

Satisfaction underpins and reinforces attitudes about products and provides powerful feedback for future deliberation. The expectancy disconfirmation model is simple, elegant and neat. It asserts that you will be satisfied with something (a flight, a film, a book) if it meets your expectations; you will not be satiated if it falls short of your expectations. If it exceeds your expectations then you will achieve a state beyond satisfaction. Satisfaction is committed to memory and has powerful feedback effects on future purchases, social media and many aspects of consumption. The fact that it is readily encapsulated should not diminish its importance. Measuring satisfaction is either achieved through some form of survey (asking the hotel guest to answer some questions) or can be gleaned from behavioural data by implication. Repeat patronage or buying might indicate that the consumer is satisfied; this would be classed as *derived* satisfaction as opposed to *true* satisfaction since it cannot be proven that they buy again because they are satisfied; they may be 'specious loyals' (see Chapter 2).

Impulse

Exploring impulse purchase affords an opportunity to explore some other aspects of consumer decision making, in particular it allows us to explore how emotion can drive purchase (this is expanded in Chapter 7). Impulse is not a difficult concept and it can be dealt with in a relatively short section; however it is very important. The schematic in Figure 5.9 derives from a synthesis of extant research on impulse purchase but it is also a useful touchstone for other manifestations of purchase (Smith and Green 2002).

   Impulse is not a deliberative process in essence but nothing we do is void of thinking. Impulse purchase is often triggered by emotional responses to everyday life (as purchase is in general). This can come in the form of compensatory consumption. Compensatory consumption refers to a situation in which we buy things in order to compensate for something negative. For example we might buy an item to cheer ourselves up after an admonishment from a co-worker or an argument with a friend. The trigger is a negative emotion. Equally we might buy something because we are in a good mood or to reward ourselves (for a great grade in a consumer behaviour assignment for example). This is what we call a self-gift. Social context also helps to encourage; the friend encouraging you to treat yourself is a powerful driver of impulse enactment. Once an impulse is manifested we will often tend to indulge internal dialogue

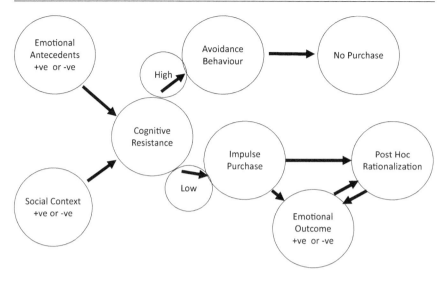

Figure 5.9 A model of impulse purchase episodes

or debate and this will lead to weak/low or strong <u>cognitive resistance</u> ('That's too much to spend on myself' – 'I deserve this' – 'It's less than the price of a meal out'). If we are with someone then they can affect this process by speaking on our behalf ('That's expensive' – 'You deserve it' – 'It's only the price of a couple of pizzas'). We can talk ourselves out of it and we will put it back on the rack, leave the shop to kill temptation or switch off the device (<u>avoidance behaviour</u>). If resistance is weak then we will indulge the impulse and buy. This can lead to regret or enable self-satisfaction, these are essentially emotional outcomes and underline the hedonic nature of impulse. <u>Post hoc rationalization (PHR)</u> will result ('I shouldn't have spent that much') and this can even lead to us returning the item and reinforce the emotional fallout. On the other hand the PHR might be essentially positive and reinforce the positive emotional reaction and confirm the purchase as justified ('I'm glad I treated myself for a change, it's about time I had a new watch, even though it was on the pricey side…'). Cognition and emotion are utterly intertwined. PHR occurs for planned purchases too. Purchase is not the end point of consumption it is merely a stage (with responses to present purchase echoing in future actions and thoughts).

Marketing tries to encourage impulse purchase. Sales promotion and marketing communications will play on the emotional triggers. Items are placed near point-of-sale terminals to tempt us. Ads pop up to encourage us. Much of this is benign although there is a dark side to impulse purchase. It can encourage us to get into debt, and buy things that will gather dust in the garage (because we haven't thought through the actual PUV). Impulse disorders are real. <u>Compulsive and addictive purchase</u> gets people into financial problems and has a range of negative emotional and relational consequences. Transactional data might give you some clues but once again 'excessive' purchase is simply signalled or derived within behavioural data; to know that is truly the result of a disorder requires purposive research although abductive inference is possible. For example, the person who buys high-end pens from your stationary web shop every day could be: selling them on or a pen collector. The latter is fine if they can afford it, they can indulge their passion for pens. If you have data (postcode/zip code or other data) suggesting that they are a vulnerable consumer (e.g. elderly, a minor, poor) then you should cross-reference that with their spending. Having data on people comes with burdens and responsibilities. Outlier purchase behaviour can mean a loyal or affluent customer or someone with a problem.

As stated earlier, impulse and deliberative decision making are not entirely discrete and depending on the temporal span of the purchase can be equally as powerful (as Figure 5.9 demonstrates impulse is not devoid of thinking either, whether pre, during or post purchase). You can plan to buy a new car, go on an extensive information search and once you enter the dealership you might spend much more than you intended because the shiny new car looks so good and the deal was just too attractive to miss (and was only on for another day). Impulse and deliberation are embedded within each other. Impulse stalks deliberation and vice versa. The final chapter of this book explores various scenarios where the two forces coalesce.

Conclusion

This chapter has summarized the processes of and influences on decision making that have powerful and definitive effects. These influences are not necessarily overriding but they will often have strident and discernible impacts. The perceived worth/utility of things, the perceived value of things, what we think about things and whether we think a great deal about the purchase or not are all self-evidently potent determinants of consumer choice and behaviour. However, they are elemental but not necessarily the principal drivers. The following two chapters review other effects and processes that have the potential to govern and direct decision making for a number of instances and contexts.

References

Ajzen, I. 1991. The theory of planned behavior. *Organizational Behavior and Human Decision Processes*, 50(2), pp. 179–211.

Bian, X., Wang, K.Y., Smith, A. and Yannopoulou, N. 2016. New insights into unethical counterfeit consumption. *Journal of Business Research*, 69(10), pp. 4249–4258.

Devlin, J., Ennew, C., McKechnie, S. and Smith, A. 2007. A study of comparison price advertising incorporating a time-limited offer. *Journal of Product and Brand Management*, 16(4), pp. 280–285.

Devlin, J., Ennew, C., McKechnie, S. and Smith, A. 2013. Would you believe it? A detailed investigation of believability in comparative price advertising. *Journal of Marketing Management*, 29(7/8), pp. 793–811.

Faulkner, D. 1995. The customer matrix. In D. Faulkner (Ed.), *The essence of competitive strategy* (pp. 7–22). London: Pearson Education.

Fishbein, M. and Ajzen, I. 1975. *Belief, attitude, intention, and behavior: An introduction to theory and research.* Reading, MA: Addison-Wesley.

Green, S. and Smith, A. 2002. Impulse purchase: A qualitative study of female shoppers, *Proceedings of the 31st European Marketing Academy Conference. Braga, Portugal.*

Howard, J.A. and Sheth, J.N. 1969. *The theory of buyer behavior.* New York: John Wiley & Sons.

Kenrick, D.T., Griskevicius, V., Neuberg, S.L. and Schaller, M. 2010. Renovating the pyramid of needs: Contemporary extensions built upon ancient foundations. *Perspectives on Psychological Science*, 5(3), pp. 292–314.

Lancaster, K.J. 1966. A new approach to consumer theory. *Journal of Political Economy*, 74(2), pp. 132–157.

McKechnie, S., Devlin, J., Ennew, C. and Smith, A. 2012. Effects of discount framing in comparative price advertising. *European Journal of Marketing*, 46(11/12), pp. 1501–1522.

Madden, T.J., Ellen, P.S. and Ajzen, I. 1992. A comparison of the theory of planned behavior and the theory of reasoned action. *Personality and Social Psychology Bulletin*, 18(1), pp. 3–9.

Watkins, R.D., Denegri-Knott, J. and Molesworth, M. 2016. The relationship between ownership and possession: Observations from the context of digital virtual goods. *Journal of Marketing Management*, 32(1–2), pp. 44–70.

Chapter 6

Perceptual and communicative features of consumer choice

Introduction

This chapter explores the role of semiotics and signs, learning, memory, trust and persuasion in terms of consumers' interpretation and decision making. These are all crucial in an age when there is more marketing communication than ever before (much of it direct). The chapter also considers the role of heuristics, perceptual biases and framing; and more generally considers how consumers respond to MC in the age of analytics.

Brands and marketing communications as signs

Brands and companies are often anonymous or dehumanized to us unless we have direct service contact (like going out to eat or travelling on a plane). Have you ever met anyone from Google? Unlikely that many of their users have. The digitization of the economy has led to an even greater role for signifiers; the dehumanization of exchange has increased the need for effective signs, signifiers and messages.

The previous chapter characterized need as a layered or embedded concept. That conceptualization links directly with how we can describe and explain the way that products and especially brands are perceived by the consumer and how marketing communications works (in fact, marketing communications is a tautology, marketing is all about communication). Needs are multifaceted and complex and needs are reflected in the composition of products and brands. Products are the offspring of our needs. Products satisfy practical requirements and subtle requirements such as symbolic interaction. For example, the Rolex watch tells the time but the buyer is investing in something far more nuanced, something that communicates. These nuances and the structures and drivers behind them form the basis of coverage in this chapter.

The linear sequential approach is commonly employed to understand how marketing communications and other signals such as branding work; this approach (among others) will be revisited later in the chapter. However we

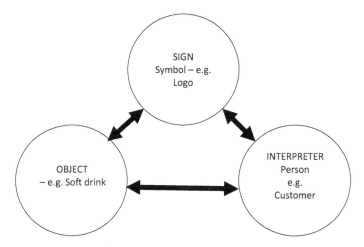

Figure 6.1 The basic semiotic triad

start with a review of the elementary aspects of the theory of semiotics; attributable in large part to Swiss linguist Ferdinand de Saussure and his early 20th century 'Theory of Meaning'. At the extreme end, every form of cultural artefact can be seen as a form of communication. However, the essential theory of semiotics is elegant and actually very simple, once understood it is quite a powerful way of dissecting and constructing meaning (coding and encoding ads for example). MCs do not happen by accident, they are constructs. If we know how to deconstruct them then we are better placed to construct them. Figure 6.1 encapsulates the core premise.

According to semiotic theory there are three types of sign:

1. Iconic signs – a non-abstract sign that represents the object e.g. a statue of a famous person.
2. Indexical signs – an object or event with a connection or causal relationship with the object e.g. smoke from a fire.
3. Symbolic signs – essentially arbitrary signs only related to the object based on an agreement, convention or learned association. This is the form of sign most common and relevant to marketing. Brands, logos and product names are assigned and are arbitrary; we have to learn the association since it is not based on resemblance or resonance (as in 1) or causal link (as in 2).

The theory separates the thing, the object, item or represented artefact, from the thing that signifies it or represents it. The word cat and your pet cat are not the same thing. The word is the sign, symbol or signifier, the cat is the object, and you are the interpreter. In marketing brands represent a physical object or a service or a conflation of the two; a logo represents an object, it is not the same thing as the object. Seeing the sign, the logo will trigger an association with the object/product (these associations are learned and conditioned and this aspect is dealt with below). In Figure 6.1 the interpreter may be exposed to the sign and the object, just the object or just the sign. Seeing the object may trigger recall of the logo and even the more complex signifiers received and stored via marketing communications (designed to give a positive image and network of desirable associations). This network of associations will stimulate memory. Equally the performance and the appearance of the thing itself will feed our response to the logo, ad or other sign (if we hate cats then the word itself will trigger negative thoughts). The key point is to appreciate and understand that symbolic signs are arbitrary and discrete from the thing they represent. We could decide to refer to cats as sneets. This would not change the intrinsic nature of cats; it simply replaces the key signifier. In short, brands and other MC signs are made-up, they can morph and change even if the thing they represent does not (e.g. change the logo on the can but don't change the drink). However, they are imbued with meaning, sometimes the process of imbuing them with meaning is the consequence of relentless, expansive and expensive MC; think NIKE. NIKE is a brand management and product development company essentially, much of the rest of its activity is outsourced. It spends most of its time reinforcing the meaning of its brand (its sign) and the development of the object (the products). Sometimes the lines can seem blurred from a utility perspective; sometimes we desire the signifier/the logo on the clothing as much or more than the intrinsic thing; they become entwined. Symbolic value can be monetized as is the case with luxury, mid-range and high-end brands alike (if all products spoke for themselves why bother with brands?).

Signs in marketing are myriad and numerous and often conflated together: logos, ads, brand names, tag lines, celebrity endorsers. All of these are signs and they can be marshalled to give a product associations that the marketer hopes will stimulate positive recall and association.

In order to become familiar with other basic but useful terms of semiotic theory; these two concepts allow us to deconstruct an ad or logo, to decode them in a more systematic way than an intuitive response.

Look at the image in Figure 6.2 carefully and write down any associations or thoughts that come into your mind, however trivial or random they might seem.

Now we can order and categorize these. Let's assume you wrote the following (you might well have gone much further but that will be dealt with below) –

Tree, countryside, hillside, dead tree, cloud, sky, bushes and grass.

These are all examples of denotation. Denotation is the first order of understanding meaning in an image or a piece of text. Denotation simply identifies what is in

Figure 6.2 Monochrome tree

the image; its essential terms of reference. Denotation is an objective stage in deconstructing the image, but all of us have biases in perception and this can even affect denotation (what we see or don't see as salient in the composition of the image). If you were asked to think about why someone would show you that image or what meaning or message they might try to convey by showing this to you then you will tend to look more carefully at the image and with a more emotional lens. Connotation is the second order of decoding and thinking about meaning. You might note the following connotations:

> *Death, decay, solitude, beauty in decay, cycle of life, cloud as halo/virtual leaves – mirroring death etc.*

Connotation and meaning would change if this image was in full colour. If this image was contextualized by being the central image of an ad raising awareness about global warming with a tag line 'One day all trees will look like this' then the interplay between the image and the text will determine and bias our interpretation of the connotations. Connotations are derived from learned responses and are culturally and socially determined. A subsequent section explores the role of conditioning in this process of appropriation.

Figure 6.3 The N/LAB logo

The following example reinforces and elaborates the initial exposition above and provides for a more detailed deconstruction based on a logo as opposed to a more abstract artefact (semiotic theory has filled numerous books – the treatment here is brief but adequate for the purposes of informing analytics-driven marketing).

Once again, spend some time looking at the image in Figure 6.3 and write down as accurately as you can what it <u>denotes</u>. You will likely record something like the following:

> *NLAB spelt, N is in heavier font, LAB in less bold font, N and L divided by diagonal line that cuts off/obscures lower left portion of N and upper portion of L. Image is monochrome.*

Now we can consider the potential connotation of each denotation, bearing in mind that connotation is subjective and variant between individuals and groups. However, groups of people are often bound together by commonalities in the way they interpret signs and the way in which they derive meaning. Many people who share certain common ethics, culture, geography and values might well view a brand's signifiers in a similar way.

- *N/LAB spelt, N is in heavier font, LAB in less bold font.* NLAB means nothing in English but lab infers a laboratory with all the associations of experimentation and scientific endeavour. The use of capitals suggests an acronym. The juxtaposition of an N and L seems wilfully challenging or even antagonistic bearing in mind the conventions of language. The N is emphasized but the meaning remains ambiguous, perhaps intentionally, it arouses curiosity. This might be the intention and could link with the connotation of inquiry above.

- *N and L divided by diagonal line that cuts off/obscures lower left portion of N and upper portion of L.* This serves to emphasize the separation between the N and LAB as alluded above. It also suggests increase as depicted on graphs, this could also indicate improvement and/or aspiration and also has connotations of quantitative inquiry and the representation of data. The fact that both letters are missing a portion at the margin suggests they are 'tucked-in' to something beyond the foreground; this could indicate a 'dimension' beyond or behind – a secreted link. This could link with the allusions to ambiguity outlined above.
- *Image is monochrome.* The monochrome theme suggests boldness and clarity.

The overall connotation-based analysis suggests various elements of reinforcement and contradiction or more likely challenge. It will work at a subconscious level for the reader who wrote the account above but, unconsciously or not, it will impact perception of the object (entity) in question – the N/LAB. Frankly the analysis of connotation could go deeper and further. There is a parallel here with the inference from data highlighted in Chapter 1. The further we go from those inferences that are 'closer' to the image (data) and the target audience or cultural context then the more we have to be wary of those inferences. The person/people who coded (designed) the image may have consciously or unconsciously done/intended all of the things above or none of them. They cannot be entirely arbitrary though – they cannot be random. In a sense it doesn't matter what the coders or originators of the message meant: it is more important what the audience thinks they mean. Adding a tag line might help as depicted in Figure 6.4.

Transformative Analytics

Figure 6.4 The N/LAB logo with tag line

Once again, the inclusion of words to interplay and interact with the image makes a huge contribution to meaning. Marketers instinctively know the power of the image alone as well as the combined power of images underlined with text. The inclusion of the words under the logo plays towards information. Words are signs but they are often less ambiguous or variant in meaning (in marketing) than images. The word 'Transformative' immediately connects with some of the observations on the image above and clarifies and reinforces them. 'Analytics' equally connects with many of the proposed connotations outlined.

How is this useful in terms of analytics-driven marketing? You can use customer data to inform the construction of the message; semiotics is a way of understanding meaning, if you don't have a method or protocol to construct an image for a reasonable commonality in terms of decoding/understanding (i.e. how to manufacture meaning), then you are much less likely to be able to convert insights from analytics into messages, brands and other signifiers that will work for your target audience. In short, if you have no idea at all about how meaning is constructed then how can you hope to use data/analytics to inform how you do analytics designed to inform marketing communications and branding decisions?

Learning and memory

We learn things and these are stored and recalled as attitudes, beliefs, heuristics and emotion. Various cognitive aspects of learning have already been covered. Learning is a complex subject but there are some simple concepts that allow us to make sense of it. Conditioning theory is one of those concepts. Conditioning is associated with the behaviourist psychology which seeks to explore the stimulus–response relationship and then construct theory to explain the behaviour. Its greatest exponent and advocate in consumer research is Gordon Foxall; he contends that marketing is primarily about stimulus and response and we should treat speculative attempts to determine cognitive processes with caution (e.g. Foxall 1995).

Figure 6.5 demonstrates the very simple relationship. Things (signifiers like logos and brand names) trigger responses. Marketing is a voracious generator of stimuli. All communication can be conceptualized as stimuli; these lead to responses; we are not inert, we react. Classical conditioning (CC) refers to a situation where the response to the stimulus is learned or conditioned over time, the association is not innate but constructed and often arbitrary (as is the case with semiotics). The conditioned stimulus (CS) is learned (the logo for a fast food chain). It becomes associated with the unconditioned stimulus (UC); presence and sight of food provokes hunger. So we see the golden arches and we suddenly feel more hungry and might just pull into the outlet and order a burger.

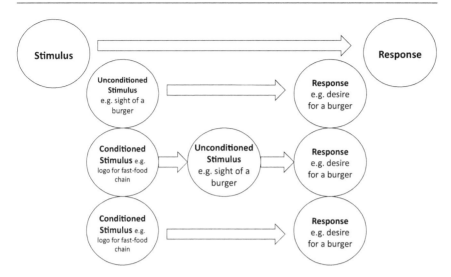

Figure 6.5 Stimulus–response and classical conditioning

It is difficult to identify many truly innate or unconditioned stimuli in marketing contexts. If seeing a burger is partly a learned or conditioned association; the original Pavlovian example cites the dogs' salivation at mealtime as the UC; but one can argue that many of our 'innate' UCs are at least partly socially constructed (e.g. is the response to perceived danger learned or innate?). Nonetheless, we can think about and apply the very simple stimulus–response paradigm very widely. For example we learn to associate the sound of the doorbell with someone being on the other side of it. If we lived in a world without doorbells and we visited the one house in the world with one then the sound will not provoke us to make for the door and let the person in. We would likely wander around the house looking for the source of the bell believing it to be some kind of alarm or a fatuous prank. After a few iterations we will learn to make the association. The doorbell will automatically ensure that we make for the door to the point that the associated stimuli represents someone being at the door. We don't think 'doorbell' we think 'someone has called round'. Marketers spend very large amounts of money teaching us to associate signifiers with positive ideas about the things they endeavour to sell us. Burberry wants you to think 'quality', 'Britishness', 'class', 'style' etc. It wants these associations to be automatic whenever you see the brand name. However, there is a problem here and it relates to the notion of <u>salience</u> (if an airline loses your bags you are unlikely to forget it; if the coffee was lukewarm on the flight, then you are unlikely to remember it five years on).

Imagine you're back in the house you've never been to before. You receive an SMS from the owner asking you to find their wallet. They left it in the study but they cannot recall where. The study is a mess, piles of books, clothes and various ephemera. You curse them as you rifle through the detritus in a futile attempt to locate the wallet. If they always leave it in the same place and you know that (learn it) it's easy. Marketing wants you to know 'where the wallet is'. However, marketers know that you are assailed by numerous marketing messages, cues and signals every hour of the day. You live in a world beset and cluttered with marketing communications; making or forming an association that is automatic requires repetition and consistency (and money and effort and data). Product launches are especially costly for various reasons, one being the need to educate the consumer what the product *is/does* and *means* in all that clutter and noise. Marketing is a fight for attention in a very noisy venue.

Operant conditioning (OC) is also important in marketing. Operant conditioning relies on stimuli (positive and/or negative) to reinforce behaviour or response. For example a shampoo brand offers seductively low prices initially at launch. The price gradually climbs, small increases that are not salient. This induces you to behave by a gradual reduction in the reward (in OC the positive reinforcement). Reinforcement can be negative and become punishment; for example punitive charges to prevent you going overdrawn on a current/ checking account (these might increase the more you do it). You learn not to do this (or maybe you don't…). The anatomy of OC in marketing is outlined in Figure 6.6.

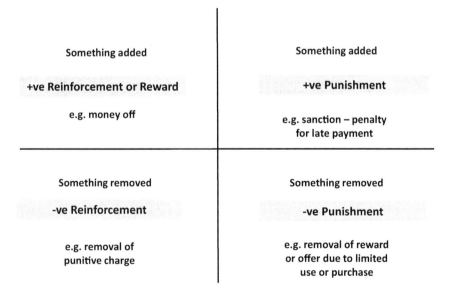

Something added	Something added
+ve Reinforcement or Reward	**+ve Punishment**
e.g. money off	e.g. sanction – penalty for late payment
Something removed	Something removed
-ve Reinforcement	**-ve Punishment**
e.g. removal of punitive charge	e.g. removal of reward or offer due to limited use or purchase

Figure 6.6 Operant conditioning in marketing

There are essentially four options when it comes to moulding or directing consumer behaviour via OC. You can add or increase something good (positive reward) or you can reduce or eliminate something bad (negative reinforcement); likewise you can add something bad or aversive to punish or remove something good (like a price concession). Marketing is primarily a positive activity. Continual punishment of customers isn't going to get you very far for very long but the examples illustrate that they do have a place and are employed. OC has really worked if the reward or punishment can be withdrawn and the behaviour or response is sustained. When this happens you have been trained. Repetition and exposure are not difficult concepts, but they are essential to the process of 'teaching' the consumer and reminding them i.e. to conditioning them. Marketers often object to this sort of terminology since it appears to sully what they do; this does not change the fact that it *is* what they aim to do.

Trust and persuasion

Who must you trust?

Felix goes to the refectory in the factory where he works and takes the sandwiches out of his lunchbox. Bernadette is sitting opposite him as usual. She wears her signature sullen expression but it breaks when she sees what's in Felix's sandwich.

'Oh my God! Is that chicken in your sandwich Felix?'

He takes it out of his mouth and inspects the sandwich but he already knows the answer. 'Yes'.

'It's not American chicken is it?' she asks.

'I don't know, probably, yes, I think it might be'.

'Don't eat it! Haven't you seen the news feeds? Apparently US chickens are all infected with a form of avian virus that can infect humans. I'm never going to eat chicken again'.

Felix forgoes his lunch. He checks his phone after Bernadette leaves and watches a video clip of a learned woman, the Professor of Food Hygiene at the University of Toronto, tell the CNN interviewer 'that the risk is less than being eaten by a shark, only a fraction of American chickens have the virus and cooked chicken is 100% safe'. Still, he leaves the sandwich and buys a corndog…

Trust is a complex concept and much researched, perhaps over-researched. Why would Felix trust the professor over Bernadette, or as it seems, vice versa? Various concepts and research allow us to understand why he might privilege one source over the other. The answer hinges around the concept of Source Credibility among many other things. Source credibility is built on:

- Perceived expertise.
- Proximity – this being a complex of relational dimensions.

We are programmed to trust someone with perceived authority or knowledge (this is why toothpaste ads employ dentists and why scientists endorse toilet cleaning agents). However, we also tend to trust those close or 'known' to us. In the digital era 'known' can mean someone we are familiar with or with a high centrality score in a social network. There are consumers known as Expert Consumers or other Opinion Leaders (such as journalists, celebrities or YouTubers with a conviction or interest regarding a product or diet etc.). The web has elevated the status and influence of these nodes (Chapter 3). Information and hence credibility flow to and from these nodes. An expert who is your friend has got all the credentials. If Bernadette was a friend and a Professor of Food Hygiene then Felix would never eat US chicken again.

Persuasion knowledge

As already stated there are numerous models but the Persuasion Knowledge Model – PKM (Friestad and Wright 1994 – see also Hibbert et al. 2007) allows us to draw various strands and elements together in a coherent and useful format. Figure 6.7 adapts the PKM for the context in question (i.e. analytics-driven marketing).

This adaptation of the PKM links the notion of conditioning directly. It also alludes to the role of emotion/affect (see Chapter 7). The PKM adds what we call intermediary variables or features and suggests what might happen as the stimulus is processed by our brains.

Persuasive Potential is a function of the following:

- *Credibility of the artefact.* Is the ad or message credible? Does it make claims that are believable? As viewers/interpreters we will tend to assess this and reach a judgement.
- *Scepticism.* This is a blend of our innate tendency to be sceptical (moderated by the actual message or sign in question).
- *Perception of manipulative intent.* Essentially encapsulates our ability to be advertising literate. We know that ads try to make us vote one way or another, to buy stuff, to change and switch. MC has a purpose and that purpose is not lost on us.

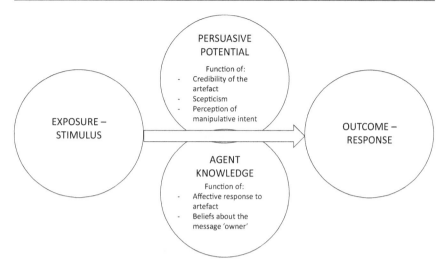

Figure 6.7 Truncated persuasion knowledge model

<u>Agent Knowledge</u> is the complex of ideas we have about the source of the message (the brand, the politician, the charity etc.). It is based on:

• *Affective response.* Our emotional response to the message. These emotional factors are often neglected in consumer research but they are very important and powerful. MC provokes emotions. Expose people to information and images and they cannot disengage their emotions.
• *Beliefs.* What we believe about the brand or person in question is self-evidently crucial in terms of their credibility and believability. If they have failed us or wronged us or if people we trust run them down then they are far less likely to believe the message from that source.

In short, a credible message, that we like, that doesn't feel overtly manipulative, from a trusted and known source, requiring that we do something achievable and believable is more likely to work than the opposite. Obvious really, but theory adds structure and format to these intuitive ideas – some of the best social and behavioural science research has confirmed what we already 'know' or what might seem obvious.

Social and observational learning

Social and observational learning are also important. Chapter 7 deals with the social dimensions around consumption in full, but they require some exposition here. We learn from observing others, from watching, witnessing and observing their use of products and things. We learn by simply being in the world. We are naturally inquisitive and acquisitive beings and programmed to watch, observe, adopt and adapt.

There are various concepts and theories to draw on here but Bandura's social cognitive learning theory (SCLT) is representative and emblematic (Bandura 2001). It states that there are four stages involved in observational learning. The theory refers to the party/group or person observed as 'the model'. This can be confusing for obvious reasons, so the explanation below refers to the model/object:

1. *Attention.* Attention is self-evidently essential for learning to occur. SCLT states that the characteristics of the model/object determine the level and nature of attention. So, does the observer like or identify with the model/object? Attention is also a function of the characteristics of the observer, their expectations or level of emotional arousal. If you like the model/object, or aspire to be them (for example a favoured celebrity or someone you perceive to be a higher achiever or more socially successful than yourself) then you will be predisposed to pay more attention to them. The intensity of attention will tend to determine how likely you are to remember the behaviour observed.

2. *Retention/memory.* Can the observer 'code' or structure the information in an easily remembered form or to mentally (or actually) replicate the model/object's actions? Emulation begins with a deconstruction and reconstruction of the behaviour in question. How does that model/object achieve the behaviour? Can that be understood and replicated? The observer will likely think about the behaviour consciously and subconsciously re-enact it. We might well emulate someone without a great deal of conscious effort.

3. *Initiation.* Observers must be able to emulate the behaviour in question – without descending into pantomime or caricature. It is one thing to watch and admire how someone perceived to be socially confident and influential dresses, deports and conducts themselves at a mutual friend's house party; it is another entirely to replicate or mirror that behaviour without looking like we are making fun of them or making a fool of ourselves. Many behaviours we seek to copy have more subtle or nuanced behavioural rituals or traits. These carry less of a risk.

4. *Motivation.* The observer clearly needs to be motivated to emulate. Motivation will often be based on the desire to be 'better'; healthier, more likeable, more confident, more attractive to potential sexual partners, command greater respect at work.

This is clearly another example of the linear sequential logic that is echoed in the theory of planned behaviour and the seminal information processing models of consumer choice already reviewed. In reality the process is messier and is not necessarily conducted in the manner of 'casual ethnography'; much of the process will be done at a subconscious level. For example we might start to dress like a friend without consciously making a decision to do so; this will happen in part because they may even intervene or be present during purchase decisions (i.e. on a shopping trip). Nonetheless, SCLT provides another layer of structure and language to understand how we learn, how we develop behaviours and how we interact with a complex world.

Heuristics and perceptual biases

Heuristics have been mentioned before but are dealt with here more fully and thoroughly and within the context of bias in perception. The effect of cognitive miserliness and our willingness to adopt tactics and behaviours to reduce cognitive effort and load were introduced and discussed in Chapter 4 during the introduction of the notion of <u>Exogenous Cognition</u>. However, cognitive miserliness is equally relevant and pertinent here as an explanation of the power and (arguably) the increased importance of heuristics in the age of pervasive social media and analytics. The contention that consumer-informed algorithms will tend to funnel and reinforce attitudes and behaviour has already been made as well. For example:

> *Existing Heuristic: 'Brand X pollutes the environment';*
> *Reinforcement Stimuli: Membership of a social media grouping or forum that directs and exposes the consumer to stories that reinforce the existing heuristic.*
> *Reinforced Heuristic: 'Brand X pollutes the environment'.*

The reinforced heuristic is the same but it is likely to have increased in intensity, power and salience. In short, heuristics will effectively have different cognitive 'weights'.

We buy, use and consume numerous things every day. The heuristic, the mental rule of thumb, that gets us out of numerous tricky decisions by means of short-circuitry: 'Italians are passionate'; 'French food is good'; 'Carbohydrates are bad'; 'Rolex watches are good'; 'German engineering is good'; 'German beer is good'; 'German food is bad'; 'Australian barbeques are best'; 'Anything hand-reared, organic or free-range is good'; 'Cheaper must be lower quality than expensive'. Crucially, heuristics have dangers – they can be wrong and they can be based on poor information, stereotypes and misconceptions and other forms of <u>Biased Perception</u>. We all see the world through a distorted lens, a lens coloured by our views, ethics, culture, beliefs and psychological biases (e.g. personality – Chapter 7). Nonetheless, heuristics save us a lot of time. They're quick and easy and we can use them for both spontaneous and planned decisions.

Schema theory

Schema Theory describes a heuristic technique that provides another scenario for how we encode and retrieve information; how we structure our thoughts about the world. Schemata/schemas are abstractions of networks of associations in our mind, they are semantic maps or concept networks.

Person Y has a network of heuristic associations for healthy living; the central and therefore defining node and the node in the network with the highest centrality score (see Chapter 3). Closer inspection suggests that there are also sub-schemas: 'Happier', 'Exercise' and 'Self-Control'. 'Dietary supplements' are out on a limb comparatively. Various nodes have direct links with others.

A 'Happiness' schema might well link with similar elements but the structure would likely change (e.g. with elements such as family, friends, nights out etc.). Likewise the schema in Figure 6.8 could link with another via 'Outdoors' perhaps to 'Holiday/Vacation'.

Marketers will seek to explore if schemas are common or shared (though they will never be entirely homogeneous) for a given segment or target group; they will also seek to construct them at the individual level. In reality this will mean inference from social media data, transactional data or purposive research (for example via a word association task). In reality the only reasonable way to explore schema structure for a group is by identifying the key nodes or topics; unless network analysis based on associated topics in social media is undertaken. Schemas are abstractions, an individual will only construct one consciously if required to by a researcher; the fact that we can construct these semantic

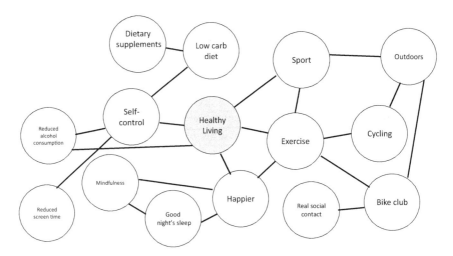

Figure 6.8 Example schema for healthy lifestyle associations for Person Y

networks suggests that they reside in some form in our heads even if they are in reality abstractions of highly complex and opaque neurological processes.

Marketers and others seeking to influence the way we perceive things will also seek to influence the structure of the schema; in other words to bias and promote certain associations. Most obviously by ensuring that a certain brand is associated with a healthy lifestyle for example. Schemas can shift; the lens through which you organize your thoughts on the world can alter, sometimes over short time frames. For example, a recent and affecting documentary on pollution of aquatic ecosystems might change your associations with certain forms of packaging and this can lead to an adjustment and change in behaviour and preferences.

The notion of a <u>Self-Schema</u> (Figure 6.9) refers specifically to how the individual might conceptualize the self – their own view of themselves. There is a clear link here with the various manifestations and dimensions of self-image and the impact on consumption and purchase (see Chapter 7). There is also a link between how we might see ourselves and the groups that we identify with or are aversive to (Chapter 7). These connections will be explored in due course; they are potentially powerful in social media oriented analysis (or at least in explaining the underlying processes of that form of social interaction).

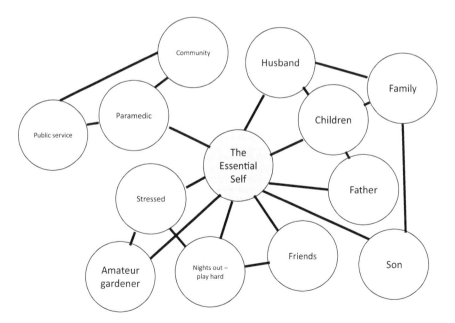

Figure 6.9 A simplified self-schema

The self-schema suggests that this individual primarily sees themselves as a family-oriented individual and public servant. Their perception of themselves as stressed is also a key node. A sub-schema is derived via their employment. Once again, the schema will manifest itself in how this person communicates online and there will be clues/traces in purchase and transactional data.

Framing

Framing is a central notion in what is referred to as Nudging and therefore to the much hyped movement of Behavioural Economics. The basis of framing is actually quite straightforward and the concept has been referred to previously. Daniel Kahneman and Amos Tversky (e.g. 1986) developed the idea through their application of prospect theory (Kahneman received the Nobel Prize in Economics Science for his efforts; Tversky died prior to the award and a laureate is not awarded posthumously). The nuances of prospect theory are required to understand the basis of framing and its wider significance in marketing since prospect theory is based on perceptions of risk when a subject is presented with a loss or gain based problem and 'gambling scenario' under conditions of risk. This application is only of relevance to some sales promotion frames (a fairly rare sub-type) and there is limited evidence that consumers approach purchase decisions as gambles as such, although they will tend to weigh the positive and potential negatives of a purchase and the frame of the problem. If the decision is provoked by marketing communications, i.e. where the frame is externally controlled and determined, then framing is even more relevant.

Framing relies on the formation of heuristics based on the interpretation of the information provided to the subject. The fundamental finding in framing research is that the same factual information presented in a different format or 'frame' will affect the decision made based on that information. So, the same facts are presented in a differential manner:

- FRAME A:
  'Edwina scored 50% in the Consumer Behaviour module class test. This is the average score for the class. Edwina performs consistently'.
- FRAME B:
  'Edwina scored five out of ten in the Consumer Behaviour module class test. This is a marginal pass. Edwina shows no signs of improvement'.

Edwina will likely be happier with her tutor's feedback if it comes in the form of Frame A. She is at least average, she's consistent and somehow 50% sounds better than five out of ten, which sounds more like a bad score for a dance contest (if you rate a film five out of ten then the glass feels half empty not half full). Frame B is negatively framed.

In reality many communications that might influence the consumer (via social media or other person-to-person contact) will likely combine the positive and negative and be more complex to decode since they will not be contrived (are not 'premediated' and are often more spontaneous). Marketing communications will tend to use framing in a more consistent and essentially predictable way but will not necessarily be void of nuance and subtlety (see Figure 5.6, Chapter 5 – Sales promotion). Positive framing protocols will typically be used to describe the brand's own offers and products e.g. favourable comparisons, attractive offers, positive adjectives and adverbs etc. Negative protocols and devices are deployed to describe competitor's products or to describe a problem that can be resolved by purchase of the product. For example:

Positively Framed Text:

1.   *Fast acting Avamol is the bestselling over-the-counter painkiller in Europe. Ninety million customers can't be wrong. Don't trust us, check out the online reviews here.*

Negatively Framed Text:

(Competitor)
2.   *Rotavo watches are twice the price of our watches; are they twice as good? Not according to whichwatch.com – the leading watch review site. Think what you could do with the money saved…*

(Problem to be resolved)
3.   *Dressed to kill? You might think so but dandruff has killed your chances tonight. Flaked shoulders are the biggest turn-off, not to mention the incessant scratching and itching.*

In 1 the frame is almost entirely positive. In 2 it is negative save for the positioning of the review site. Example 3 is entirely negative and this form of problem frame is usually juxtaposed with a positive frame asserting the ability of the product in question to resolve the negative/problem.

A-B tests can be used to test the efficacy of differently framed online ads for example (simultaneously on two comparable groups). Analytics can readily identify the frame with the superior click rate, the other can then be withdrawn from service. It is possible to do this in very short time frames and at comparatively low cost compared to changes or field experiments with traditional advertising and marketing communications.

A basic knowledge of framing enhances deconstruction or construction of a piece of marketing communications (often a combination of image and text in interplay). When combined with an elementary semiotic analysis then the potential to construct and deconstruct intelligently rather than instinctively is exponentially increased. Semiotics and basic framing analysis can be undertaken as 'armchair' exercises – they simply amount to thinking about words and images in a more structured and deliberative fashion. The other concepts such as conditioning and PKM allow us to appreciate how marketing communication works. Fact is, how it works is a hugely complex process that encompasses almost all of the material covered in this book (and many other volumes besides). We conclude with a consideration of communication effectiveness directly.

Responses to and effectiveness of MC

Much of this chapter has referred to the various ways in which we can try to understand and influence how consumers respond to pieces of communication. The old adage still holds true for traditional media-based advertising (through TV for example) – 'Half the money I spend on advertising is wasted; the trouble is I don't know which half'. This remark is attributed to John Wanamaker (1838–1922) and rings true for the kind of advertising he was talking about (print-based – targeted to groups through channels/specific publications). Not so for communications in the age of exogenous cognition and analytics. The web and social media has not changed the basic lessons of communication inherent in semiotics, framing and conditioning theory and the myriad other attempts to explore how we make sense of the world, *but* response to MC has become real-time – even if an artefact (e.g. an SMS message) is ignored then the sender knows this and they know who has ignored it. Nowadays the consumer is tracked.

The traditional ways of understanding how effective marketing communications are still have some value, not least in acting as a starting point or touchstone to a more contemporary and holistic understanding of how effectiveness can be achieved in the age of direct/individually targeted 'ads' and MC. A common and elementary example is depicted in Figure 6.10.

Even a cursory glance at Figure 6.10 is enough to determine that, once again, the employment of a linear sequential logic has occurred; this element and sequence is reflected in many more complex models of ad and MC effectiveness. The notion of moving the consumer along a hierarchical or incremental is ubiquitous (particularly in practice-based models) and is not entirely fallacious. However, if the aim is repeat purchase (for FMCG or even products or brands with a slower moving cycle of renewal) then this sequence is a module in a feedback loop. Scholten's (1996) model contains the following echo of the AIDA sequence:

Exposure – Reception – Persuasion – Retention – Behaviour

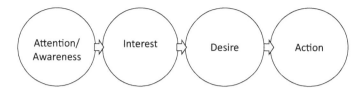

Figure 6.10 The AIDA mnemonic

In turn this echoes the basic attitude to behaviour sequence: Thinking (cognitive); Intention (conative); Behaviour. The stages identified are useful as categories for managing marketing communications but due to the chaotic, cluttered and recursive nature of the message reception and the nature of consumption things are not as simple as that. The linear sequential process has to be repeated and rehearsed every time the consumer is exposed to any message connected with the product and exposure, reception and persuasion will happen concurrently. Moreover, behaviour is not an inevitable outcome. We will be exposed to numerous ads for cars that we may never buy; this fact does not make this communication pointless since any recognition or positive views resulting might be shared or influence others and we have the potential to move from a 'constrained loyal' to a 'composite loyal' (Chapter 2).

Much of the debate around the effectiveness and the reception of marketing communications essentially amounts to a confrontation between the process (e.g. PKM) versus meaning schools (e.g. semiotics). These approaches are not incompatible. Both of them have been mined for this chapter and when blended they allow for a useful holistic understanding of communication.

The strong theory (e.g. Jones 1999) suggests that advertising has a strong element of persuasion which works by: creating and building brands, differentiating between brands and increasing sales. However, studies do not reveal that people rush out to buy products after seeing advertisements. Many purchase propensities are habitual, steady and predictable. Advertising can shift perceptions but this is not easy and is often achieved over long time frames. Ehrenberg et al. (1988) maintain that advertising primarily reinforces customer/consumer decisions to buy and use brands; the so-called weak theory. Ads simply reinforce values, maintain brands and help to defend market share. The strong and weak theories are not incompatible; ads and MC in general have strong and weak effects. The strength of the effect relies on the quality of the message and the efficacy of delivery. It is possible and common to have bad marketing communications. Good marketing communications will more likely have a stronger effect. It logically follows that we require some way of assessing the quality of messages. As Chapter 3 highlighted, marketing is fond of quantitative measures and 'counts' (likes, hits etc.). The digitization of marketing has made the generation of quantitative measures even easier; these measures have their place but they should not be allowed to obscure the fact that MC requires qualitative assessment. A-B tests will tell you which online ad or message is superior but this is a comparative assessment of quality. The A-B test will not tell you that your message is optimal, i.e. the best you can do; it will simply confirm that A is less bad than B.

Message research comes in various forms beyond the boundaries of what is possible via analytics. Messages can be pre-tested via focus groups or consumer juries. Readability tests can be conducted to see if meaning transfer is effective. However, pre-tests struggle to replicate the clutter and white noise of reality. Post exposure tests of recognition and recall are still common for ads delivered via offline media. Emotional measurement systems and physiological arousal, eye tracking and even neuroscience can be deployed but are only viable/cost-effective for large and expansive campaigns over longer time frames. The ultimate test remains the maintenance or uplift in sales. However, as observed previously, isolating the effect of communications from other variables can be problematic. Ultimately, the assessment of effectiveness and the method employed to achieve that assessment depends on your objectives. Communications might seek to increase awareness, influence attitudes, create emotional responses, enhance brand values, change behaviour, among many other things. Multiple objectives are common and require multiple forms of assessment.

Conclusion

Ritson and Elliott (1995 and 1999) delineate a model of advertising literacy that asserts that meaning is co-created. Co-creation questions, or more accurately augments, the process-based approaches exemplified in the AIDA flow concept and cognitive-based models of communication. It leans on the observation that meaning is not fixed, it varies from individual to individual and is not hypodermic. Messages are not crossword puzzles with only one common solution, they are fuzzier than that. Ritson and Elliott were also among the first to highlight the role of MC in the construction of self *and* group identity. Communication connects the individual and social realm; it is a crucial nexus for the two. Adverts and MC affect the conscious, the subconscious and the collective conscious. The social realm represents a core focus for the next chapter.

References

Bandura, A. 2001. Social cognitive theory: An agentic perspective. *Annual Review of Psychology*, 52(1), pp. 1–26.

Ehrenberg, A.1988. *Repeat-buying: Facts, theory and applications.* Oxford: Oxford University Press.

Foxall, G.R. 1995. Science and interpretation in consumer research: A radical behaviourist perspective. *European Journal of Marketing*, 29(9), pp. 3–99.

Friestad, M. and Wright, P. 1994. The persuasion knowledge model: How people cope with persuasion attempts. *Journal of Consumer Research*, 21(1), pp. 1–31.

Hibbert, S., Smith, A., Davies, A. and Ireland, F. 2007. Guilt appeals: Persuasion knowledge and charitable giving. *Psychology and Marketing*, 24(8), pp. 723–742.

Jones, J.P. ed. 1999. *How to use advertising to build strong brands.* Thousand Oaks, CA: Sage.

Ritson, M. and Elliott, R. 1995. A model of advertising literacy: The praxiology and co-creation of advertising meaning. *Proceedings of the 24th Annual Conference of the European Marketing Academy. Cergy-Pontoise, France: Imprimerie Basuyau.*

Ritson, M. and Elliott, R. 1999. The social uses of advertising: An ethnographic study of adolescent advertising audiences. *Journal of Consumer Research*, 26(3), pp. 260–277.

Scholten, M. 1996. Lost and found: The information-processing model of advertising effectiveness. *Journal of Business Research*, 37(2), pp. 97–104.

Tversky, A. and Kahneman, D. 1986. Rational choice and the framing of decisions. *Journal of Business*, 59(4), pp. S251–S278.

Chapter 7

Individual and social features of consumption

Introduction

This chapter explores the links between various aspects of the social and private self. In fact, the chapter raises questions about the efficacy of this bifurcated view of the consumer. The individual and social realm link inextricably. They 'converse'; the social realm nourishes the self and the self nourishes social interaction. They are not entirely discrete. Specifically the chapter deals with a variety of related concepts and topics; for example socio-cultural determinants, norms, group effects, the socio-familial milieu, ethics, emotions and 'innate' or underlying psychological traits.

Nature vs. nurture?

The social and behavioural sciences have expended an enormous amount of effort trying to establish rules or structures of human behaviour, whether in the social realm or the individual realm. The division between the 'inside' (the mind) and the outside (the world of others) is best seen as an interface rather than a barrier. People are physiologically, physically self-contained but 'the world of others' is providing inputs and provoking action or 'outputs' from the individual continually; this notion lies at the heart of the exogenous cognition concept. Human life is the manifestation of continual interaction and since consumption is merely a domain of human existence then any attempt to understand it holistically must reside within the existing structures of knowledge.

This chapter ostensibly splits them up but the chapter as a whole is about understanding the individual in the world. The 'Nature vs. Nurture' question exemplifies this ongoing meta-debate in social and behavioural science; genes vs. environment; innate traits vs. identities; prenatally determined personality vs. socially constructed 'personality'. However we couch or position the specific debate common themes emerge. What programmes the mind?

Consider the following examples.

Example 1

Two twins are separated at birth. One twin (A) is confined to a room almost entirely void of stimuli save for one window overlooking a lawn where no one is ever seen. They are educated via a computer interface and learn to read, speak and function intellectually to a high level. They are well fed and only interact with the person who provides them food – this interaction is not verbal. The room is warm and comfortable but amounts to a cell, to prison. The other (B) is brought up in a family of three other well-balanced children, two highly successful parents with even temperaments and boundless material wealth. When they are ten years old an eminent psychologist subjects them to a behavioural test and this determines that they have significantly different orientations in terms of personality, empathy and emotional response.

Example 2

A neuroscience study determines that men and women have different cognitive capabilities and strengths. Men seem to be better suited to problem solving tasks whilst women display superior empathy and what we might call emotional intelligence. Since biological gender, as opposed to gender orientation, is determined prenatally by chromosomes they conclude that these traits are evidence that the genders have different, predetermined cognitive structures. That we are biologically determined to think in a different way. During an interview, the lead researcher, who is a man, suggests that the study proves that women are more suited to the caring professions and men will always make better astronauts. This results in a social media backlash.

What has Example 1 really demonstrated? On the face of it, the inhumane and entirely unethical experiment seems to provide substantive evidence for the nurture side of the see-saw. Example 2 on the other hand seems to provide evidence that nature determines key attributes. The real lesson is that when it comes to trying to understand people the method employed can sometimes bias the inferences from the outcome. We know that people can be trained to think differently (cognitive behavioural therapy being a case in point) and this can result in neurological changes. It is possible that women and men are socialized to behave in certain ways from an early age in the same way that Twin A is being socialized (or not) to behave and think in a certain way (not in exactly the same way of course). There is no definitive answer here. We are not born the same, we are not cloned from one source code. If Twin A and B had been brought up in the same circumstances then the outcome of the study when they were ten years old would likely reveal that they were more similar than the outcome in Example 1. There might still be differences, some of these might be innate, but their experience of life would have been different too (see Guo 2005 and Sacerdote 2011). No two hominids can experience life in exactly the same way.

Now, the examples above might seem a little fanciful and obliquely related to the core function of *CB&A*. The reverse is true. We can adopt extreme positions. Essentially these two extremes could be characterized as pure <u>social constructivist</u> vs. a pure <u>evolutionary-biological</u> understanding of the human world. In other words, pure nurture vs. pure nature. This chapter cannot hope to resolve this debate; it continues and ultimately it is fruitful because it makes us examine the subject in hand in a more intelligent and balanced manner. The rest of this chapter will explore the 'innate' and the 'constructed' and where pertinent, the interplay between the two. However, we should keep the essential controversy and ambiguity that lies at the heart of the focus; visualize the nature–nurture see-saw in mind at every turn.

The socio-cultural realm

Me, myself and us

Roberto is getting ready for a big night out. The office where he works is holding an evening welcome event for the new CEO. Naturally he wants to make a good impression on her. He is trying on various combinations of clothes but nothing seems to work. He enlists his daughter's help, he trusts her eye for style and colour but she dismisses ensemble after ensemble:

'No, too preppy, it's not you.'

'Too formal, makes you look like the company stiff, you're a marketer not an accountant!'

'Too young, don't announce a midlife crisis.'

'Too casual, looks like you don't care.'

Roberto runs out of ideas. 'Perhaps I should go in fancy dress, at least she'll remember me.'

'Not a good idea dad.'

'I don't want to feel like I'm trying to be someone else, I always feel uptight in clothes that aren't err... me. You know what I mean? I'm worried about being out of step with my co-workers, what does "smart casual" even mean? Perhaps I should phone Ines and ask what she knows about what anyone else is wearing?'

The short scenario above encapsulates various points that echo throughout this chapter. What we wear projects an image, clothes are signifiers but they have an impact on how we feel. The two are inextricably linked. The scenario also illustrates how friends and family can influence our decisions. Some decisions are co-created explicitly; they have the direct input of others. The scenario above contains *explicit* intervention via Roberto's daughter and *implicit* intervention through his concern about what others might think of what he wears and how he will fit with the pervasive style of the evening (the norms or conventions of such an event and how one should dress).

Consumer culture theory (CCT) asserts that this process or phenomenon is best understood through a cultural analysis or lens. Social theory, sociology and anthropology constitute the primary base disciplines of CCT. However, social psychology provides us with a number of powerful concepts too. This chapter will explore various ideas from all of these perspectives.

Many words are difficult to pin down, we know what they mean when we hear them, they trigger thoughts that are often consistent at the individual level, but they do mean different things to different people; they are polysemic or, at the very least, fuzzy. Culture is one of those words. There are numerous definitions out there, this is as good as any: a shared set of values, beliefs that influence and determine behaviour which are expressed via various rituals and symbols and actions. This definition alludes to a number of factors that have already been covered (i.e. attitudes and beliefs, reactions to stimuli and symbols/signs). The definition is wide in scope. Rituals are essential to any comprehensive understanding.

Rituals

Rituals are sets of symbolic behaviours that occur in a fixed sequence and tend to be repeated periodically. They are not enacted solely for practical reasons. Roberto's CEO welcome party is a case in point from the scenario above. It is a ritual. It is one way of welcoming someone to a group. A social event allows various other rituals to be indulged; the welcome speech for example; the mirror image is the leaving party. For the purposes of understanding consumer behaviour, Table 7.1 provides some illustrative examples.

A number of rituals are primarily consumption rituals. Black Friday is the starkest example of this. It has no cultural or valid commercial significance outside of the US but it has become a pure consumption ritual in the UK and elsewhere. People will queue and jostle to get the best offline bargains. Other rituals and celebrations have become increasingly consumption and buying oriented; purchase has become a very significant element in the ritual. In the UK, back in the 1980s, Halloween and 'trick or treat' in its modern form was not widely practised (although the practice does have its origins in European

Table 7.1 Ritual typology and examples

Ritual type	Examples
Exchange rituals	Gift giving, dowries
Possession rituals	Housewarming parties
Appearance rituals	Routine before a night out
Religious rituals	Christmas, Passover, Ramadan
Life stage rituals	Marriage, graduation, birthdays
Family rituals	Mealtime, bedtime, holidays
Friendship rituals	Days/nights out, sleepovers
Public celebration rituals	Guy Fawkes Night, Independence Day, Halloween, Bastille Day, New Year
Consumer ritual	Black Friday, January sales

traditions going back some hundreds of years). Now, Halloween in the UK is all about costumes (a buying ritual), acquiring confectionary from neighbours (sharing ritual); certainly from a child's point of view. For parents it subsequently becomes an acquisition ritual and a family ritual based around consumption, purchase and familial sub-rituals.

Many widely practised rituals have some very obvious impacts on consumer behaviour (see Figure 7.1) and also determine the configuration and resource deployment for analytics. For example 'Christmas Analysts' are employed within retailer analytics teams; it is not uncommon. That period of the year is so crucial to many retailers (on and offline) that it is worth dedicating significant resources to the analysis of past sales promotions and spending dynamics during that period. In terms of analytics a predictable and regular/seasonal event is an opportunity given that so much about consumer behaviour is variant and problematic to predict.

Consider the following account of the conventions and norms of the Valentine's Day ritual as practised in many Western cultures:

> *Presents and cards are bought in advance. Red roses are purchased. A meal out is booked. The evening is spent as a couple.*

Consider where these come from. Valentine's Day is entirely socially constructed. Consider what they enforce (also the sanctions for not indulging in the ritual; an argument, break-up etc.). Various cultural norms are being appropriated on Valentine's Day; gift giving, the notion of love and romance etc. Now, consider their impact on marketing. Marketing has a vested interest in re-enforcing and reminding people about pervasive norms and rituals. An advert warning of the potentially negative consequences of forgetting or neglecting Valentine's

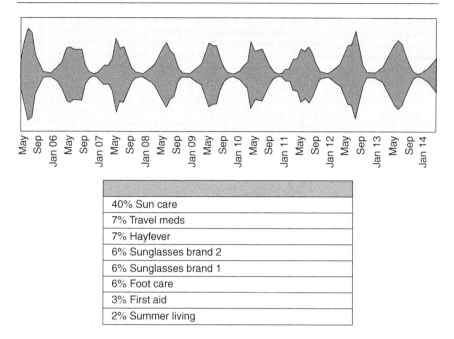

| 40% Sun care |
| 7% Travel meds |
| 7% Hayfever |
| 6% Sunglasses brand 2 |
| 6% Sunglasses brand 1 |
| 6% Foot care |
| 3% First aid |
| 2% Summer living |

Figure 7.1 Topic pulse for summer holiday/vacation product associations

Day will have persuasive impact because it is drawing on the pervasive cultural <u>norms</u> and <u>myths</u>.

Myths

Myths are socio-cultural narratives and are elementally related to beliefs and values. For example the myth of the underdog who comes good in the end is reflected in many cultures and is reinforced via various cultural artefacts. For example: David and Goliath; Aladdin; the notion of the 'American Dream'; Charlie Chaplain's film *The Tramp*; the movie *Kung Fu Panda*; the movie *Slumdog Millionaire*.

All of these underpin the idea. Myths don't have to be true, they are not empirical. They influence behaviour via their impact on our beliefs; we might reject them or adopt them enthusiastically, either way they will have an influence as a positive or negative for ensuring we conform or react. Myths serve a value expressive function. They are exemplified by the sayings that still have some cultural capital. Most myths have an opposing myth, and all have an underlying narrative that chimes with ideas that are enmeshed in our culture and therefore ourselves; see Table 7.2.

Table 7.2 Myth, counter narrative and underlying values

Myth and underlying value	Counter myth and underlying value
'hard work pays off' (The narrative of industry and productivity)	'take it easy' (The narrative of the lotus eater)
'good things come to those who wait', 'patience is a virtue' (The narrative of restraint)	'just do it', 'seize the day' (The narrative of action)

These stories and cultural touchstones are used in marketing communications all the time. They are a form of heuristic for the message transmitter (the marketer; social media poster) and the receiver (consumer). Ads can readily appropriate them (indeed we might recognize the tag line inserted within the table). Marketing communications helps to shape, challenge and reflect the culture that it draws on. Advertising has often been accused of reinforcing the prevailing cultural and social norms: the so-called unintended consequence of advertising (Pollay 1986). Consider the issue of its perceived effect on body image perceptions. Advertising has been accused of reinforcing unrealistic and even harmful ideas around body image (Dittmar 2009). The argument runs something like this:

> *Adverts promote an ideal. Ads will tend to use people perceived to be desirable and they are also prone to exaggeration or puffery in order to get their message across. They don't have much time to communicate and will do so in a manner that is arresting (in terms of visual images as well as text). Sexiness and desirability are therefore appropriated in order to create associations with the product. However, this appropriation has unintended consequences ('externalities'). It's not simply the effect of an ad on its own it is the aggregate effect of the ads that mine a similar ideal of sexual attraction and body image. So, whether it intends to or not, MC reinforces potentially harmful and pernicious and prescriptive ideas that might have impacts and outcomes that are socially undesirable (e.g. encouraging anxiety about body image, eating disorders etc.).*

The subversive ad simply turns this on its head and presents people with 'sub-optimal' physiques in order to suggest that they are in tune with another narrative ('it is what's inside that matters' – 'we present real people; therefore we are authentic too…'). These ads are still playing the same game, they just appropriate the counter narrative instead. The key point is that ads are playing games in a cultural landscape; they are contributors and miners of *culture* and *myths* are a key part of this process of symbolic exchange.

Look at the following:

Love is the answer – all you need is love – love changes everything – I'm loving it – love actually…

One is a tag line, one is a quotation, two are refrains from songs and song titles and another is a film. All of them help to reinforce the notion of the power and desirability of love. Romance/love myths and narratives are favourite appropriations in MC and can have powerful psychological impacts on consumer decision making (especially on Valentine's Day) for self-evident reasons.

Norms

Myths can reinforce norms but norms have a vigour and anatomy of their own in the life and decisions of the consumer. Norms are rules that are socially constructed and absorbed. They have already been referred to in Chapter 5 in terms of their role in decision making (specifically in the theory of planned behaviour/ theory of reasoned action). Norms can have their root in myths but they are also derived from law, vicarious learning and various forms of social interaction. They are learned and conditioned.

If Roberto did go to the welcome party for the new CEO dressed as a chicken then he would transgress various norms. It is a sobering thought. We might like to think of ourselves as autonomous free-thinking beings, but very often our decisions are expressions of constraint as much as they are expressions of freedom and unfettered thinking. Rules are more specific than values and to some extent are the operationalization of values.

There are two essential forms of norm:

- *Enacted norms.* These are explicit and well understood and are sometimes expressed via legislation. Traffic lights are a global norm. Unless you are colour blind then you will tend to obey this norm; there are legal sanctions if you jump a red light. These are most relevant to consumer misbehaviour; for example stealing the hotel bathrobe. That act is illegal and can have consequences that might involve a law enforcement officer.
- *Crescive norms.* These are more widely applicable and relevant to active consumer decision making and the practice of marketing (norms are referred to and navigated in various stages of marketing from product development to marketing communications).
  - *Customs.* Customs are basic rules that govern actions. For example greeting conventions.

- *Mores.* Mores are customs that emphasize moral aspects of behaviour, e.g. monogamy.
- *Conventions.* Conventions are more subtle and weave their way into various practices in everyday life – e.g. types of gardens, drinks served to visitors, shiny clean hair, reciprocation in gift giving. These are arguably the most fertile area to incorporate and 'play with' during the construction of marketing communications.

Normalization describes the process by which practices and behaviour become norms. This associates with learned behaviour (Chapter 6). Released in 1979, the Sony Walkman was the first portable method of listening to music. It caused a stir. The early adopters were stared at and subject to questions and curiosity. Walking or skating round with something clipped to your belt and wires coming out of your ears was not normal. Marketing communications, celebrity usage, press coverage and vicarious learning ensured that this practice and product usage became normalized. Decades later we are not remotely surprised or interested by someone walking around with headphones; we aren't even worried, shocked or bothered if they appear to be talking to themselves. Normalization is powerful.

Conformity is an associated but equally powerful social force. A great deal of consumption and purchase behaviour (and marketing) can be understood by the metaphor of two opposing personas or voices continually trying to provoke the consumer to act according to their prejudice. One voice advocates autonomy, self-expression and individuality; the other advocates conformity and compliance. Many of us possess these two instincts and their weight varies from situation to situation. Wearing a flamboyant costume for a funeral service will not meet with approval (unless sanctioned by the group dynamic); it is imbued with social and relational risks. Most of us will eschew this behaviour because of this. On the other hand, we also like to express ourselves through consumption. Our perceived individuality is enacted through what we buy and consume (this is comprehensively dealt with below).

A simple psychological experiment called the conformity test (e.g Asch 1951) emphatically demonstrates the power of conformity. A group of people are given an exhibit like that depicted in Figure 7.2. In the control group the individuals are left to make their own assessment during the course of normal group interaction of which line out of A, B, C or D is the same length as X. In the other groups a plant or stooge is present with the express objective of dominating and influencing the decision. They confidently assert that the wrong line is the answer and a significant number of people conform and convince themselves that it is A and not B. In the control groups more people give the correct answer. This is a more sophisticated manifestation of the fable called *The Emperor's New Clothes.* It is also a powerful illustration of perceptual bias; but bias induced by social interaction.

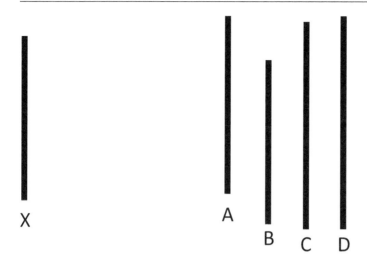

Figure 7.2 Conformity test exhibit

Group influence and sub-culture

Norms and conformity lie at the heart of how groups operate on and offline and lead us on to the topic of sub-cultures (groupings within or even opposed to the overriding culture e.g. national cultural norms). Real or imagined group pressure (due to cohesion and perceived expertise/source credibility of the group) often results in a change in behaviour or beliefs or the reinforcement and sustenance of behaviour or beliefs. This can happen in two ways:

- *Compliance.* We conform to group norms without really accepting them. For example student binge drinking might be undertaken simply to help bond with a group. Similarly we might wear a brand or style that allows us to associate with a group even though we can feel some dissonance or discomfort doing so.
- *Internalization.* Conformity is more profound and probably more sustainable if we indulge a private acceptance of group norms. Essentially we have made a 'leap of faith'; internalization implies that we conform to the groups' behaviour, values and beliefs because we have adopted them as our own, or perhaps they were always our own and we have simply found a home for them e.g. an online enthusiasts group for a particular car brand.

Group association often leads to a *social comparison process*. This is the process by which people evaluate the 'correctness' of their actions, beliefs and attitudes; in a sense this is a form of self-policing or self-censorship. There are two key ways in which this appraisal process is enacted:

1. Reflected appraisal

The conscious self-judgement about the appropriateness and congruence of your speech, behaviour and appearance, i.e. how are people responding to me? I must be behaving/dressing (in)correctly for this event. In the scenario above, Roberto is likely to undertake this form of appraisal at the welcome event for the new CEO. This form of appraisal is also relevant to online interactions – for any given group there are things that you should not say/post. The notion of *crescive norms* is particularly pertinent here; indeed, norms are the triggers for reflected appraisal and comparative appraisal.

2. Comparative appraisal

This is a form of self-rating (not quantitative as such) against the perceived hierarchy of behaviour or individuals. Essentially this equates to the observation of how well you are doing compared to others (see Venkat and Ogden 2002 for ad-induced social comparison). For example we will tend to judge and appraise others according to their possessions in various ways (not just in terms of social standing or achievement, we may also judge them by ethical beliefs). Again, this relates directly back to norms. It would be a brave CEO who drives to work in a beaten up camper van. This would be an essentially subversive act and might cause various co-workers to question their judgement or even conclude that they are squandering their substantive earnings on some other pursuits. It might also be judged as self-consciously 'rebellious' or crassly announcing what an 'individual' they are. Whatever, there is a norm that is adhered to in many office car parks the world over; the CEO drives a car that symbolizes their position in the hierarchy. Comparative appraisal is often more subtle and involves self-assessment of more ephemeral attributes than social status/achievement. For example, 'How popular am I in the group?' – 'How fashionably am I dressed?' – 'Why don't people ever 'like' my posts as much as Linda's?' This in turn relates to perceived social self and ideal social self (see section below) as well as the dynamics of a given *reference group*.

Reference groups

A reference group (RG) is a straightforward construct. An RG is constituted by two or more people who share a common purpose, identity or ethos. A reference group is used by its members as a point of reference to evaluate the correctness of actions, beliefs and attitudes. RGs are groups that you can be associated with or identify with and this might be due to your lifestyle, demographics, politics, ethics, taste in music or many other things. Your membership may well be implied rather than formal. Marketers like to know or infer your potential RGs because it helps them to do segmentation and target products at you. You reveal your reference groups to them by your use of social media and your purchases, browsing etc.

RGs can be negatively valenced ('Out Groups') or positive ('In Groups'). Think of them as matter and anti-matter. Out groups are groups that help you to define and delineate your own identity and beliefs via your non-membership. A consumer who chooses to become vegan on the basis of ethics and concern for the environment will undoubtedly tend to identify less with meat-eating consumers. They *are* as much a vegan as they *aren't* an omnivore. The negative social spaces for the individual are as powerful as the positive ones in many respects. If you are young you will tend to feel self-conscious about dressing 'old'; if you are poor then you might aspire to acquire brands that belie your true position. If you are a fashionista then you will tend to avoid brands associated with groups perceived to be 'out of touch'. RGs can lead to *othering*: the self-conscious or conscious activation of exclusion in which those who don't conform or are opposed to your RG are identified as different, not compliant or even a threat. For example, social media discussions of the use of an idealized body image depiction in a high-profile ad campaign might 'other' those who actually conform to that image. Social media has tended to reinforce and polarize opinion around many subjects. The so-called 'echo chamber effect', where likeminded people simply reinforce each other's ideas and debate is stifled. This process of 'cleansing' and exclusion is not new and also happens with offline groups, the old notion of 'preaching to the converted'. Groups tend to select more extreme positions than individuals because of these processes and dynamics – i.e. the groups' attitude will be more extreme than the average individuals' initial attitude.

Another way of delineating between in and out RGs is by applying two dimensions; membership and non-membership, and whether the motivation or identification is positive or negatively valenced. Figure 7.3 provides four types of RG interaction on the basis of these two dimensions.

Category A – *Aspirational* RGs are characterized by positive disposition towards the group but via non-membership. This is a group that you aspire to join or would ideally like to join but are not yet able to. You might aspire to be a successful musician or sportsperson. This aspirational association may still affect your contemporary purchase and consumption behaviour. You may be more prone to emulate the lifestyle of the aspirant RG.

Category B – *Contactual* RGs represent groups that you have a positive association with and that you are a member of. Contact could be virtual, however. Examples would include sports clubs, social groups, religious or political groups.

Category C – *Avoidance* RGs are simply groups that are your core 'out groups'; people who don't share your politics, lifestyle, origins or outlook. You

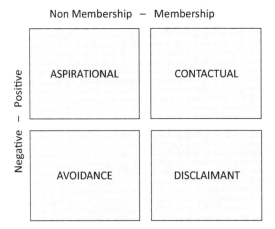

Figure 7.3 Positive and negative RG membership and non-membership

have negative association with them (this doesn't necessarily mean you hate them, it just means you have a negative identification with them).

Category D – *Disclaimant* RGs are groupings for which you have a negative association, one that you are not comfortable with but an RG to which you belong. Perhaps you are overweight because you eat to excess, perhaps you do not want to do this but cannot achieve this end. Membership of such a group can mean the members are stigmatized.

'In groups' come in many forms whether they are offline or online. Forms, degree and the intimacy of contact will vary accordingly. An RG might simply be a group you identify with but have no contact with. Table 7.3 summarizes types and examples.

So, a group can be primary and informal or secondary and informal or primary/secondary and formal. For example, your employment RGs are likely to be formal and primary. The more important the RG or the more influential the more likely it impacts on your purchase and consumption. Impact is also determined by the other features of the RG, for example the distinctiveness of the RG and the relevance and proximity of the RG to the person's lifestyle (these are best thought of as continuums rather than binaries).

A person's RGs can be organized as a schema (see also Chapter 6). In this abstracted example (Figure 7.4) only the positive and relatively primary groups are represented along with their core interrelationships with each other. Three sub-schemas emerge – a family/parent cluster, a social/leisure cluster and an employment/community cluster. These are likely to emerge in a number of individuals' RG schemas and can be used to target and communicate more effectively to the individual or segment in question. How can marketers

Table 7.3 Reference group manifestations

RG Type	Characteristics
Primary	Interact with them relatively often and consider it important to follow their opinions or norms (family, close friends, religious groups).
Secondary	Less frequent contact and norms less binding/obliging (religious groups, professional associations).
Formal	Conduct and behaviour tend to be highly codified (religion, work, country club).
Informal	Few explicit rules about appropriate behaviour (volunteer groups, friends).

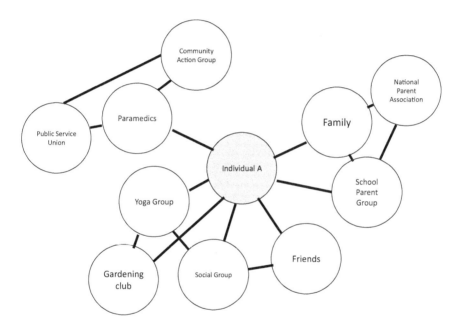

Figure 7.4 Positive and principal RGs for given individual

establish a person's/segment's RGs? The answers should now come naturally to you but bear repeating:

- Inference from transaction data.
- Inference from social media or browsing (non-transactional online data).
- Directly from purposive research (e.g. survey).

Role within groups will dictate various things about the individual and will in turn affect your consumer behaviour. Group roles vary e.g. leader, follower, opinion leader, gatekeeper etc. Identifying opinion leaders and influential individuals is obviously expedient from a marketing point of view; they will give you a route to influencing others. Social network analysis (SNA) is one powerful way of doing this (see Chapter 3); i.e. centrality scores for nodes (people or groups). A short circuit of a full-blown SNA would involve identifying heavy posters on review sites/functions for example; though this is less sophisticated and can be unreliable. The fact that they've posted lots of reviews doesn't mean they are influential (even if lots of people said they found the review helpful). Simple counts can be dangerous and exemplify the problem with some of the more elementary forms of online analytics.

Types of contributions on and offline will tend to fall into the following categories, although things can be far more nuanced in reality. Nonetheless, the following classification is useful and the terminology is commonly employed:

1. *Pure contributors.* Give lots of time, effort, advice and don't ask for much in return. They will always get something out of the interaction in the RG but it can be more ephemeral (esteem, status, praise, friendship, a disinterested fulfilment from helping people etc.).
2. *Reciprocal contributors.* They commit resources and receive as per 1.
3. *Pure askers.* Commit few resources and benefit from membership of the group (be it advice, other people's time and concern, money, help etc.).
4. *Lurkers.* This is almost exclusively an online manifestation. They are voyeurs, not asking explicitly for anything but gleaning from their membership of the forum or community.

Brand communities

RGs can be very product and brand focused. For example on and offline owners' clubs, fan clubs and other groupings of enthusiasts. Some people get very excited about cars, Lego, football teams and all sorts of other stuff, and when they do and self-identify as owners, fans and enthusiasts then there are clear opportunities for the brands they connect with – don't treat your owners' club or authorized discussion group with contempt. The group can manifest itself digitally and physically to varying degrees (see Chapter 3). They will interact online via use of various virtual interaction and communication tools: electronic discussion forums, social networks, blogs, bulletin boards, chat rooms, newsgroups, email and personal web pages.

In some sectors (e.g. electronics goods, software, games) this can lead to consumers becoming collaborative innovators and co-creators (a Marxist would see this as free labour). Again this can involve online interaction or meet-ups. They can fulfil various roles for the brand in question by providing new product ideas and suggestions. This can elevate them to the status of 'co-producers' providing input on product features and design trade-offs. There are self-evident opportunities to use them as 'product testers' assisting in the identification of product design flaws and 'product users' (Sawhney et al. 2000; Nambisan and Baron 2007). It is often a challenge for many manufacturers to reliably track how the use and functionality of the product pans out post release. Scanning forums or purposive research has its drawbacks so getting users to provide continuous feedback, effectively 'diaries of usage and experience', provides very rich and valuable data streams; high-depth data that drills into real customer experiences and can be used to triangulate with cross-sectional data.

There are various motives to become involved in such communities. There can be social benefits, the experience can provide self-enhancement and opportunities to seek valued expert advice. Even economic benefits can accrue (e.g. cost savings) from tips and tricks or even free samples. Motivation might be disinterested or altruistic; a function of a desire to help the company or assist other consumers.

The socio-familial milieu

Family are often a primary reference group, even if we hate them or are alienated from them and they're effectively an 'out group'. For most of us, family and certainly friends are primary RGs. As highlighted in Chapter 6, proximity and intimacy are linked to source credibility and influence. Friends and family will tend to influence us in positive and negative ways when it comes to purchase decisions. For example a valued friend raves about a new shampoo and this encourages you to try it; your parent/carer buys the same shoes as you, encouraging you to never wear them again.

The term preferred here is the *Socio-Familial Milieu* (SFM). Family and friends often interconnect. Moreover, in many societies (by no means all) the challenge to traditional roles (mid-20th century gender roles and gender identity), the increase in monogamous relationship breakdown and broader social flux means that the following life cycle is more of a touchstone than a 'norm':

Infant – Teen – Single – Partnership – Parent – Empty Nester – Corpse

However, it is still very common and should not be eschewed, indeed it is not eschewed by marketers as a means to categorize and associate. If you are a parent then you are a parent and this role will affect your behaviour. Many people will end up in more than one relationship and have distributed families with half-siblings and act as step-parents, many will never have children. The following definitions are as useful as any others to delineate:

- Familial Household = The persons within a private or instituted household who are related as partners, as parents, or never-married child, or child by blood or adoption.
- Household = 'Shared residence and common housekeeping arrangements' (EU household panel).

Whatever the composition of a household they are what we term 'decision making units'. A consumer can make many decisions on their own volition but many decisions are made and influenced by households even if the individuals within it aren't related (e.g. roommates/flatmates). A crucial feature is role designation in decision making (typically this will vary according to product category and perceived expertise) or the degree of shared decision making. These are labelled as either:

A. *Syncratic or joint.* Decisions made by a group or coalition in the household [with information flows between household members]. Typical examples will often be holidays/vacations and other high involvement products and/or products with shared use and utility. However, neither high involvement nor shared use are necessary or sufficient conditions for syncratic decisions. A dominant or sanctioned adult may well appropriate the decision (e.g. for the family car).
B. *Autonomic.* Decisions made by a single household member. Again this can be sanctioned by others or appropriated by the individual. The key is to identify the decision maker.

Children's buying power has increased dramatically. Syncratic and autonomic decision styles can occur for spending by children and teens. Many will have a small allowance to spend on FMCGs and sundries. However, a ten-year-old will likely not autonomously buy their own clothes, though they will have a say; this is unlikely for the choice of home insurance. *The Influence Triangle* in Figure 7.5 illustrates some scenarios in a fictional household.

A. *Grocery.* The regular bulk grocery shop is the responsibility of Adult 1. Once preferences are established for Child and Adult 2 then the in-store decisions are made entirely by Adult 1. The other two can still influence the decision but the principal decision maker is Adult 1.
B. *Family automobile.* Adults 1 and 2 have a joint and equal influence. The child has some say and if the child accompanies them to the showroom on the final decision day they may exert some influence on certain factors.
C. *Gardening equipment.* Adult 2 is the gardener in the household and the other two have little interest or influence over the choice of tools for this task.
D. *Child clothing.* This is a joint decision between Adult 2 and Child. Child influence tactics include:

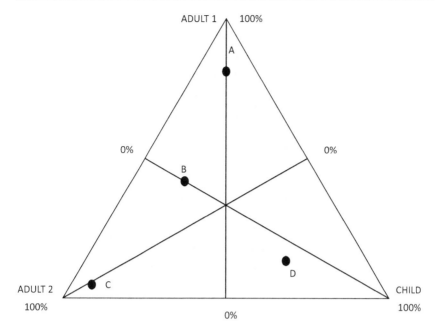

Figure 7.5 The influence triangle

- Bargaining: making deals, seeking a compromise.
- Impression management: misrepresenting facts in order to win.
- Use of authority: claiming superior expertise.
- Reasoning: using logical arguments.
- Emotional appeals: using emotions to get what they want.
- Additional information: obtaining further information or a third party opinion.

Status, gender roles and protocols will vary from household to household. Labour is one factor, whether it is labour within the home or outside. How much money the adult brings into the house is known to affect their influence over decisions. Kirchler (1990 and 1995) provides an insightful breakdown of inter-adult influence tactics. These are summarized and elaborated in Table 7.4. These are relevant to many forms of family and household.

Other issues also influence family and household decisions. Role overload can occur where someone is tasked with too many functions outwith and within the household. Role conflict can also affect individuals within the house (e.g. mother vs. CEO). One result is greater conflict avoidance or delegating decisions, or using exogenous cognition (EC) to make decisions

Table 7.4 Observed inter-adult influence tactics

Tactic	Manifestation and elaboration
Persuasion	Positive emotion; Negative emotion; Helplessness (including tears and pretending to be ill); Aggression; Rewards and inducements; Punishment (e.g. domestic labour withdrawal); Insistence and intransigence; Leaving the scene; Distorted information; Overt information (open demands about one's goals regarding the purchase); Indirect coalition (indicating the needs of another e.g. child); Direct coalition (discussing while 'allies' are present).
Conflict avoidance	Deciding and acting without discussion; Role assignment (decisions are delegated according to expertise, interests and roles); Yielding or giving up.
Bargaining	Trade-off and ledger management (past concessions and favours aired); Integrative bargaining (rational inclusive search of joint-optimization of the decision).
Reasoned argumentation	Reason and logic used in an oppositional discussion without undue emotion.

less time greedy. Multiple roles are common and reflected in the RG schema in Figure 7.4. Time poverty, limited income and busyness will often mean that the decision process is less deliberative, less syncratic and pressured. The 'winner' is EC and the distributed system of analytics as discussed in Chapter 4.

Consumers and ethics

Ethics and morals are powerful drivers of human behaviour and are inherently complex. The reduced treatment of this topic in this section is not aimed at providing a comprehensive review of the anatomy of ethics (this is yet another topic that can and has filled numerous volumes of work). It *is* designed to contextualize ethics in terms of the decision making process for products in the age of exogenous cognition.

Ethics relate to values and attitudes; indeed, this is where they are 'stored'. They are an excellent example of a behavioural influence and motivation co-created by the individual and the social realm. They are a product of experience and thought, the influence of others and norms and conformity (dealt with earlier in the chapter). There is also an important link with emotion (see section below).

One important distinction is required. The two topics below are related but discrete and should not be confused or conflated:

- *Consumer ethics.* Research in this area has been concerned with good behaviour (e.g. telling the waiter that they missed the bottle of wine off the bill) *and* bad behaviour (e.g. 'borrowing' a dress for a charity ball and returning it to the store the following day having re-attached the label insisting that said dress didn't fit). Consumers do bad things and this can affect the quality of data acquired. They can lie on forms, use other people's identities and say something wasn't delivered when it was. Analytics needs to detect such behaviour for self-evident reasons.
- *Ethical consumers.* They are consumers who make certain decisions (usually biased towards certain categories) based in part or primarily because of their ethical stance on an issue e.g. animal rights, environmental destruction or labour exploitation. Social media has made consumer boycotts and other protest action easier to engender and more concerted and co-ordinated.

Ethical consumers will tend to follow the following sequential model prior to any behaviour change: Problem Recognition → Resolution Strategy → Outcome/Action/Inaction → Appraisal. You cannot make an ethical decision if you don't acknowledge a problem, issue or dilemma (plastic bottles cause harm and waste). You may then choose to ignore it or decide how you intend to address the problem (stop buying plastic bottles and encourage others to do so). You will appraise the effectiveness of this and this might lead to abandoning the strategy or changing or augmenting it (you spend one weekend afternoon every week picking up discarded plastic bottles and start a community action group that becomes a world movement via social media after a local celebrity reposts your tweets).

People who act on their ethical concerns to a high order are described as AMÉLIEs in Figure 7.6 – i.e. Amélie (after the eponymous movie character) – a virtuous person with a reliable moral compass intent on improving the world around her. In other words an AMÉLIE has a high order of consistency between her ethics and actions; her actions are enacted to a high order (she goes to great lengths to impose her stance). *Voluntary simplifiers* (Shaw and Newholm 2002) are examples of this kind of behaviour. They eschew various things that they can afford in order to reduce their negative impact on humanity and the planet. If you don't have a strong ethical concern and don't act then you are a SNOLLYGOSTER; self-evidently someone who does not care about an issue (such as plastic bottles) and acts accordingly (happily throws them into the river on the way to work). A BANDWAGONER is someone who doesn't really care about the issues but seeks social approval or wants to avoid social sanction of a norm violation. They conform without conviction. Social media pressure has

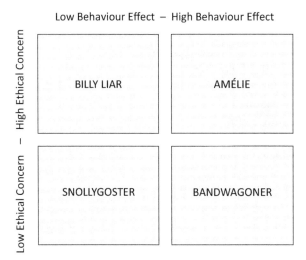

Low Behaviour Effect − High Behaviour Effect

High Ethical Concern

BILLY LIAR   AMÉLIE

Low Ethical Concern

SNOLLYGOSTER   BANDWAGONER

Figure 7.6 Typology of ethical behaviour

driven much virtue signalling behaviour but BANDWAGONERS have always lived among us. Many of us are BILLY LIARS (after the character in the novel of the same name who cannot enact his ambitions and leave his small town for London). We are concerned and we often fail to act on that concern (the explanations for membership of this category are explored below). In reality our membership of these groups is not fixed; we can move between these categories depending on the timing, situation or product category or the intensity of our feelings on the issue in question. So you might be all four within a given day; a snollygoster when it comes to foie gras, a bandwagoner when it comes to organic food, a Billy Liar when it comes to an apparel brand whose products you know are made by poorly paid people in Bangladesh who work in shoddy conditions and an Amélie when it comes to littering. Otherwise, you simply move between groups as your values change over time (sometimes over short time frames if awareness of an issue is raised by the media/social media).

Much has been made of the so-called <u>attitude-behaviour gap</u> (ABG) as an explanation for Billy Liars; this is a concept that highlights the need for an explanation of dissonance between attitudes or values held and behaviour (or specifically the failure to behave according to ethics). The ABG might not even exist or be as large as some research has suggested. Methodological shortcomings can account for it in part; we care when the researcher asks the question because that increased awareness provokes us; alternatively we indulge social desirability bias (SDB) and answer according to norms. Another explanation of the ABG is denial. Denial (the suppression of dissonance) enables us to sustain behaviour that we believe is unethical but it is equally powerful in terms of explaining how we sustain behaviour that is harmful to ourselves (e.g. smoking cigarettes).

The following denial strategies are relevant to the consumer ethics of good and bad behaviour, specifically failing to do things you or others regard as good (e.g. recycling) or things that are regarded as bad according to prevailing social norms (e.g. stealing restaurant cutlery). These strategies are called <u>neutralization</u> <u>techniques</u> and were originally outlined by the sociologists Sykes and Matza (1957) via their investigation of delinquency and have been developed and applied in consumer research by Chatzidakis, Hibbert and Smith (2007). There are five techniques:

1. *Denial of responsibility.* A circumstance in which one argues that one is not personally accountable for the social-norm-violating behaviour because factors 'beyond one's control' were afoot. 'It's not my fault I don't recycle. The local government should make it easier'.
2. *Denial of injury.* A circumstance in which one contends that personal misconduct is not really serious because the other party did not directly suffer significantly as a result. 'What's the big deal? Nobody's going to miss one hotel towel…'
3. *Denial of victim.* A circumstance in which one counters the blame for personal actions by arguing that the violated party deserved whatever happened. 'It's their fault; if the waiter had been more civil with me I would have told them they'd not charged me for the Dom Pérignon 2004'.
4. *Condemning the condemners.* A circumstance in which one deflects accusations of misconduct by pointing out that those who would condemn engage in similarly disapproved activities. 'Why are you giving me a hard time about the hotel towel, Emilia? What about the dress you "borrowed" from the store for Malay's party?'
5. *Appeal to higher loyalties.* A circumstance in which one argues that norm-violating behaviour is the result of an attempt to actualize some higher-order ideal or value. 'I'd like to buy more environmentally friendly furniture that isn't made of endangered hard woods but I'm really into design. I suppose I'm an aesthete first and foremost'. (Here the 'higher loyalty' is the quest for beauty/optimal aesthetics but it could be low order life convenience of a plastic bottle of water over the bother of filling a reusable one from a tap.)

There is also a hidden number six. It's the 'law of the ledger'. Put simply, 'I've done some good stuff so I can now do bad stuff'. This is common in ethical choice and even dietary/health choice (e.g. 'I had a salad for lunch so I'm going to have the meat feast pizza all to myself for my evening meal'). An ethical example would be exemplified by taking a holiday that increases your carbon footprint by consoling yourself that you were good because you bought an electric vehicle. Emotions are also powerful drivers of ethics (Gregory-Smith, Smith and Winklhofer 2013) and also govern other aspects of consumer choice.

Emotion

Emotions are transient but also enduring manifestations (we can recall them or they might persist over long time frames). They have been the subject of research in consumer behaviour but the attitude-based models tend to position emotions (or affect) as a function of attitude (reinforcing the attitude for example; with emotions stored as attitudes; nonetheless with a life of their own). Emotions are difficult to research; difficult for a third party to access and 'know' because of their essential qualities (i.e. transient, subjective, inherently personal, feeling not word based). They are very important but elusive. Analytics-driven attempts to understand consumer behaviour have a particular challenge. Purposive research is best placed to access emotions, but this requires psychographics; interactive research and direct contact with the consumer on or offline via interview or survey. Such surveys can be very brief; a couple of questions about how you 'feel' when you check out of the hotel. Analytics often relies on sentiment-based gleaning of emotions or proxy measures based on language used (linguistic and semantic assessments of online feedback). These are reduced and can give false signals as Chapter 3 highlights. So, emotions present a variety of challenges to the analytic marketer; this should not obscure their importance; something difficult to find but hugely influential. This section provides a review of emotions in terms of their structure (and fluidity), features and potential effects on consumption and purchase.

Emotions can be defined/understood according to the following features/ dimensions:

- *Cognitive salience.* Emotions are not easily repressed or invalidated, they are experienced and potentially potent.
- *Physiological expression.* Emotions can raise our blood pressure, make us go red, and provoke various other physical reactions. This is why lie detectors exist.
- *Action and activation tendencies.* Their potency and salience make for a motivational driver which can be overwhelming or subtle (depending on the emotion in question and the intensity of it).
- *Expression and communication.* We are emotional beings and betray our emotions via facial expressions, body language and vocal expression.

They also display the following qualities and these account for their power in terms of consumer decision making, reaction to MC and behaviour:

1. *Memory and recall*. Emotions have powerful memory effects. Imagine that you are being shown an image provoking an emotional response, for example a brand associated with a close relative or time in your childhood, then it will trigger memories and various feelings and images. Our memories of our experiences of certain brands or products will have an emotional dimension (positive or negative) that will affect how we recall; this in turn will influence future purchase decisions unless there are other overriding factors (e.g. continuing to fly with the budget airline you hate because you're on a tight budget).

2. *Intensity*. Emotions have an intensity. They are 'felt' not 'thought' as such. They can be low to high in intensity. In MC, understanding the optimal level you need to provoke is important. For example for charity 'guilt appeals', provoking too much guilt can be counterproductive and provoke avoidance behaviour (turning the TV off) or an aversive response.

3. *Immediacy*. Emotions are immediate. They can provoke a profound change in our psychological state within a very short time frame. If a sales assistant is rude to you ('would look okay on someone slimmer…'), then it will likely provoke an emotional response. The immediacy and intensity combined might be powerful enough for you to walk out the store leaving behind an item you had intended to purchase prior to their ill-thought remark.

An understanding and appreciation of emotion in consumer research relies on being able to distinguish between the following widely employed concepts. These terms appear in various models and papers:

- *Feeling*. The subjective experience of something, this is not exclusive to emotions (e.g. feeling of having been somewhere before); in other words feelings describe the private experience of emotion but are not exclusively a manifestation of emotion.
- *Mood*. Moods are diffuse and enduring and can present a cocktail of discrete emotions over a longer temporal frame (e.g. nervousness, sadness and embarrassment expressed over a whole day or more after an event provoking them).
- *Affect*. The experience of moods or feelings is often described as 'affect' – i.e. affective response to an event.

The words used to describe, label and classify emotions bound and to some extent constrain our understanding of them. These words pre-date concerted

Table 7.5 Examples of basic and self-conscious emotions

Emotion core type	Positive	Neutral	Negative
Basic	Amusement; Contentment	Surprise	Anger; Fear; Disgust; Sadness; Awe (surprise with fear)
Self-conscious	Pride; Triumph		Shame; Guilt; Embarrassment; Envy

research into emotions; the labels existed prior to the systematic deployment of those words to classify emotion. The question of how semantically distinct emotions are is an interesting, even vexing question; can we really delineate between shame and guilt? The short answer is yes, at least research has indicated that we can. Table 7.5 classifies emotions according to whether they are *basic* (elemental and recognized across cultural boundaries) or *self-conscious* (relating to our sense of ourselves or self-image and/or our consciousness/sensitivity to other people's reaction to us or view of us). Additionally, Table 7.5 also delineates according to whether an emotion is *negative, neutral* or *positive*. Typically you will want to provoke positive emotions in the consumer (basic or self-conscious); exceptions being the responses you may wish to provoke via political, charity or social marketing campaigns designed to challenge anti-social or unhealthy behaviour (i.e. 'de-marketing' something). However, MC will use the depiction of negative emotions to reinforce a message (e.g. the embarrassment felt by the friend told he has dandruff flakes on his jacket on a night out; the fear felt by the neighbour unmasked as a cheapskate for valuing/using a malfunctioning 'bargain' over a 'quality' brand). As 'Awe' indicates in the table, emotions can conflate and combine and be felt simultaneously; for example anger and disgust to form contempt.

Figure 7.7 provides an alternative classification based on the positive or negative valance/feeling (pleasant; unpleasant) and the activation effect (high or low). Once again marketers will wish to avoid provoking unpleasant emotions but may depict them in MC as described above (in order to illustrate how a product might resolve the negative feeling). The desirable or optimal level of activation depends on the context/market. A retail environment could aim at being relaxed or more engaging and exciting. What is being sold and who it is being sold to determines the optimum blend. For example retail demonstration of a virtual reality entertainment system for children versus a furniture store for adults. Likewise the product might sell itself based on low or high activation; for example a holiday/vacation resort could position itself as high or low depending on the target market (think Ibiza vs. Lake Constance).

Low Activation Effect — High Activation Effect

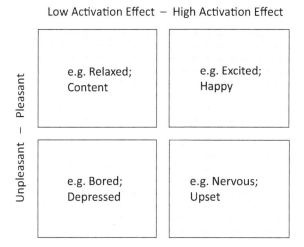

Figure 7.7 Emotion activation and valence in consumption

Underlying psychological factors

The chapter concludes with an exposition of one final element. The previous section dealt with the more transient, but potentially enduring role of emotion. Previous sections have dealt with many aspects that are arguably socially constructed and enforced (and explicitly in terms of how the process of conformity and normalization unfolds). This section is concerned with the 'hard-wired' or more innate or enduring elements. However, even these cannot escape the accusation of being socially constructed, learned, conditioned and enforced.

Risk and innovation

Levels of risk aversion and the propensity to try a new product or concept out, and certainly to embed it in your lifestyle, is one key factor in defining the *Innovator* and *Early Adopter* consumers in Figure 7.8 (see Mahajan, Muller and Bass 1993). These consumers are vanguard consumers and identifying them is a key challenge in analytics-driven marketing. Transactional data will tend to indicate the consumers who will try out new products in the target category and this can help guide targeting but the features in the data may hide/reveal more complex determinants (e.g. life stage, tendency to impulse). Most consumers are followers and fall into the *Early and Late Majority* categories, having witnessed the consumption of *Innovators* and *Early Adopters* or through exposure via social media and other social interactions as well as MC.

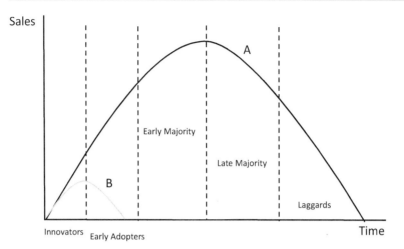

Figure 7.8 Consumer adoption of innovation

Risk in terms of innovation adoption comes in various forms but distils to the following key elements:

- *Resources (time and money).* The first buyers of a new product concept (e.g. new wearable technology for everyday use) will pay more for it unless it is promoted/subsidized. If it doesn't work/address the problem sufficiently or is deemed to be inferior to alternative existing solutions then money and time (acquiring and learning about the product) have been wasted.
- *Social and psychological.* If the product is not proven then it may not solve the 'problem' that the supplier has identified and envisaged. Google Glass was a case in point. People felt uncomfortable in the presence of *Innovators/ Early Adopters.* They felt observed. This anxiety and the sluggish take up prevented it from following curve 'A' and its evolution in the market more closely resembled curve 'B'. Many new product concepts fail even after extensive pre-testing and market research. A new wearable will bring attention to the user; they may be an extrovert and enjoy the attention (see section below), however the converse may be true. In the case of Google Glass some wearers were subject to abuse and unwanted attention. This encapsulates the social and psychological risk. You can face derision, attention and ridicule and not all of us will address or confront such reaction robustly. If you adopt something that receives negative social media and media attention then it is likely to affect you psychologically. You may choose to stop using it and it may lead to very negative psychological fallout (e.g. negative emotions).

The determinants of whether we are classified as a *Risk Taker* or *Risk Avoider* essentially come down to our access to resources (disposable income and time) and personality and self-perception.

Personality and sense of self

Even personality is not fixed (according to some research). However, if it does evolve or change then it seems that it will do so over long time frames (or as the result of trauma – in which case change can occur swiftly). Generally, personality is a stable element; certainly in comparison to emotion. They can predict your income and achievement levels reasonably well, among many other things, but predicting your purchase behaviour is trickier.

Table 7.6 summarizes the potential attributes/inferences stemming from scores relating to the Big Five personality traits. These are widely used and the psychographics used to generate them are considered to be robust and valid by the majority of researchers. The five traits are largely self-explanatory; although the items relating to trait score negatives and positives in Table 7.6 they also serve as descriptors of the trait (they essentially explain what it is).

People are therefore blends or conflations of the five dimensions. Imagine a survey informs you that a cluster of consumers are:

high openness – low conscientiousness – low extroversion – high agreeableness – low neuroticism

Table 7.6 Personality types and valence interpretation

Trait	Potential interpretation /inference of score			
	High score +ve	High score -ve	Low score +ve	Low score -ve
Openness to experience	imaginative, curious, creative	unfocused, unpredictable	pragmatic, data-driven	dogmatic, closed minded
Conscientiousness	organized, dependable, disciplined	stubborn, over-focused	spontaneous, flexible	sloppy, unreliable
Extroversion	energetic, sociable, assertive	attention seeking, domineering	reflective	self-absorbed
Agreeableness	co-operative	submissive	competitive	unruly
Neuroticism	dynamic	insecure	stable, calm	dull

You also have some limited demographic data. You have an app that helps people organize their lives from smart devices to scheduling. You have two key questions:

1. Are they likely to adopt this app?
2. If so, how should you promote the app?

The fact that they are low conscientiousness and high openness suggests that they might be suitable as a target group, or does it? Low conscientiousness suggests that they may need organization in their life but this could also mean that they might find the notion of such an app aversive: perhaps this should inform the way you target them (question 2). Low neuroticism also suggests the app might be appropriate on the one hand (they won't fear it going wrong or turn on devices at random); however, perhaps their potential stability might conflict with their openness. MC will need to design a message that will fit with these findings. Perhaps you conclude the following:

• Emphasis on innovation of app (appealing to openness); amusing references or images of the perils of disorganization they can identify with (to address low conscientiousness in a disarming way); frame as a co-operative 'friend' in their life (to play on agreeableness); frame as their little secret (for low extroversion).

There are some key lessons here:

A. *The assumption that personality is the key determinant or overriding factor is a potential trap.* It's a seductive idea and is often not questioned because personality seems so fundamental it follows that 'it must explain behaviour'. The material covered elsewhere in *CB&A* suggests that this is a potentially insecure assumption. Personality insight should be used with extreme caution. Perhaps a partner gets the app and insists they mesh with it. Perhaps this happens a lot. If it does then your targeting will not be appropriate. You would have spent time researching personality with a costly survey when you could have been asking questions about household dynamics. On the other hand, personality insight can work. If we establish that the early adopters in a market have consistent personality traits then that could be very useful in MC.

B. *Psychographics surveys can raise as many questions as they answer.* They provide interesting insights but these aren't necessarily conclusive. You might have a personality profile for all your customers but when you cross-reference it with the transaction data there is no association that is salient, even when the most powerful methods to uncover non-linear or submerged relationships with other features/variables are used.

C.   *How do you operationalize and use the insight from personality surveys?* How you convert that insight into actual marketing; this is a key question that recurs throughout the book. How do you get from data-driven insight to good marketing?

There is another key issue. How personality scores are derived. There are two methods:

*   Active trait measurement (via survey-based psychographics).
*   Passive trait measurement (via web-scraped data relating to individuals' social media data – or sentiment data or a conflation of these).

Active measurement means that a respondent knows that they are being assessed even if they don't know how that insight will be deployed. Passive measurement occurs without the explicit knowledge or even consent of the subject (person in question). There is much hype around the potential of social media data and its ability to betray psychological insights. Apparently it can even determine the results of national elections – well, there is very little proof of this. Some academic research suggests that computers are marginally better at predicting personalities from Facebook data than the subject's friends (Youyou, Kosinski and Stillwell 2015); however, passive trait measures are susceptible to error whilst active measures are often robust. The web is replete with consultancy companies making very bold claims about the power of passive trait measurement, it is also replete with companies making bold claims about some weight loss products.

Another analytics option is the '*virtual survey*' or partial survey. This entails actively surveying some customers and then drawing robust links with transaction data. The assumption is then made that others (the people who did not take part in the survey) can be assigned to a personality cluster on the basis of their purchase behaviour if this aligns with people who were surveyed.

One other aspect of underlying psychology requires consideration. People have a sense of themselves, a view of themselves. This may not accurately reflect their actual personality. They may think they are imaginative, disciplined and competitive; whilst their boss sees them as unfocused, stubborn and unruly. The area of research is all about self-image. Self-image allows us to enact *social symbolism*, where we project outwardly, constructing an identity in the social world; and *self symbolism*, where we project inwardly, constructing and reinforcing a self-identity. There are variants of self-image and various ways in which it influences our purchase:

- *Actual self.* This is your own honest perception about who you actually are. It can be negative overall or positive. How you see yourself will tend to influence certain purchases, particularly higher involvement products – things that 'fit' with who you are.
- *Ideal self.* This is a view of who you would like to be, or what you aspire to be, and we can also extend this to the kind of lifestyle you consider ideal. Your ideal self might resemble someone famous or someone you admire. You might buy things that 'fit' with your aspirations rather than actual self.
- *Perceived social self.* This is how you think others see you (not how they actually do see you). This may or may not be consistent with your actual self. Perhaps you hide your actual self; perhaps you lead a double life. This too can influence your purchase in some categories and encourage you to buy things that you think fit with how people see you; conversely you might buy something to challenge people's perception of you. Or you may buy things that conform to how you think you are perceived, in what Sartre called 'bad faith'. ('I have to dress crazy because everyone has me down as a zany guy, but deep inside I just want to be taken seriously – I'm trapped'). You might like your social image or hate it and again it can be close to your actual self or far from it. Clearly this is pertinent in terms of social media.
- *Ideal social self.* This is how you desire to be perceived – an aspirational social self. You might use social media or purchase things in order to project this image.
- *Extended self.* This can be a sort of fantasy self or a weekend self that is enacted – for example the seemingly convention-bound accountant who becomes a 'biker' on days off (Belk 1988). Obviously this affects purchase (the accountant buys biker stuff). There is also a clear link with reference groups.

Psychographics are required to capture all this. They use rating scales on which you score yourself on attributes like these: appetite for daring and excitement, youthfulness, trendiness, technical orientation, level of achievement, confidence, outdoor or indoor oriented, masculine/feminine. These and other traits are often derived from or related to the 'big five' personality traits and psycho-demographics. How do we use insights into self-image? The potential applications are similar to applications relating to personality.

One concept takes the notion of 'fit' a stage further. The Image Congruence Hypothesis (ICH) suggests that products and brands have symbolic value for individuals who evaluate them on the basis of their consistency (congruence) with their personal picture of themselves (i.e. their self-concept – actual or ideal etc.). Consumers who perceive a product image to be consistent with a dimension of self-image are likely to feel motivated to purchase and consume that product (e.g. Heath and Scott 1998). In some cases your ideal self may dominate and in others your social self or actual self might. So the man who aspires to a James Bond lifestyle buys an Aston Martin or Tom Ford suit (if he has the disposable income). ICH research has led to the attempt to assess the 'personality' of brands to see if they are congruent with various self-image dimensions. There is some support for the idea, that certain self-dimensions are consistent with Aaker's idea that brands can have a personality (Aaker 1997). However there is some controversy around this idea; a controversy that provides a salutary lesson about the operationalization/extension of psychographic research. Can a car brand have a personality? It is after all a car. ICH research suggests it can and that this can explain some choices. Avis, Forbes and Ferguson (2014) suggest that people are capable of giving rocks a personality; if they are asked to by a researcher. This does not mean that they do this in real life. It also raises another, as yet, unproven possibility: people simply project their personality or image onto things if asked rather than actually. This could be giving false positive results for the ICH. This doesn't undermine the notion of 'fit' i.e. people have notional ideas about a product image and the fit with self-image (rather than personifying brands). Nonetheless, psychographics should be used with extreme caution; they are not a 'magic bullet'.

Conclusion

Clearly this chapter represents a parsimonious tour of various related concepts and topics. The life of the individual in the world is an enormous subject. Moreover, this chapter links with numerous sections in other chapters. The filter used to select and appraise the variety of research in this area is the relevance and applicability to the practice of marketing. The chapter is the last one to provide themes for the MADS structure first referred to in Chapter 4. The following chapter explores how the various determinants and features of consumer behaviour can be incorporated into a structure of understanding to inform and enrich analytics.

References

Aaker, J.L. 1997. Dimensions of brand personality. *Journal of Marketing Research*, 34(3), pp. 347–356.

Asch, S.E. 1951. Effects of group pressure on the modification and distortion of judgments. In H. Guetzkow (Ed.), *Groups, leadership and men* (pp. 177–190). Pittsburgh, PA: Carnegie Press.

Avis, M., Forbes, S. and Ferguson, S. 2014. The brand personality of rocks: A critical evaluation of a brand personality scale. *Marketing Theory*, 14(4), pp. 451–475.

Belk, R.W. 1988. Possessions and the extended self. *Journal of Consumer Research*, 15(2), pp. 139–168.

Chatzidakis, A., Hibbert, S. and Smith, A.P. 2007. Why people don't take their concerns about fair trade to the supermarket: The role of neutralisation. *Journal of Business Ethics*, 74(1), pp. 89–100.

Dittmar, H. 2009. How do "body perfect" ideals in the media have a negative impact on body image and behaviors? Factors and processes related to self and identity. *Journal of Social and Clinical Psychology*, 28(1), pp. 1–8.

Guo, G. 2005. Twin studies: What can they tell us about nature and nurture? *Contexts*, 4(3), pp. 43–47.

Gregory-Smith, D., Smith, A. and Winklhofer, H. 2013. Emotions and dissonance in 'ethical' consumption choices. *Journal of Marketing Management*, 29(11–12), pp. 1201–1223.

Heath, A.P. and Scott, D. 1998. The self-concept and image congruence hypothesis: An empirical evaluation in the motor vehicle market. *European Journal of Marketing*, 32(11/12), pp. 1110–1123.

Kirchler, E. 1990. Household decision making. In P.E. Earl and S. Kemp (Eds.), *Elgar companion to consumer research and economic psychology* (pp. 296–304). Cheltenham: Edward Elgar.

Kirchler, E. 1995. Studying economic decisions within private households: A critical review and design for a "couple experiences diary". *Journal of Economic Psychology*, 16(3), pp. 393–419.

Mahajan, V., Muller, E. and Bass, F.M. 1993. New-product diffusion models. *Handbooks in Operations Research and Management Science*, 5, pp. 349–408.

Nambisan, S. and Baron, R.A. 2007. Interactions in virtual customer environments: Implications for product support and customer relationship management. *Journal of Interactive Marketing*, 21(2), pp. 42–62.

Pollay, R.W. 1986. The distorted mirror: Reflections on the unintended consequences of advertising. *The Journal of Marketing*, 50(2), pp. 18–36.

Sacerdote, B. 2011. Nature and nurture effects on children's outcomes: What have we learned from studies of twins and adoptees? In J. Benhabib, M.O. Jackson and A. Bisin (Eds.), *Handbook of social economics* (Vol. 1, pp. 1–30). San Diego, CA: North-Holland.

Sawhney, M. and Prandelli, E. 2000. Communities of creation: Managing distributed innovation in turbulent markets. *California Management Review*, 42(4), pp. 24–54.

Shaw, D. and Newholm, T. 2002. Voluntary simplicity and the ethics of consumption. *Psychology & Marketing*, 19(2), pp. 167–185.

Sykes, G.M. and Matza, D. 1957. Techniques of neutralization: A theory of delinquency. *American Sociological Review*, 22(6), pp. 664–670.

Venkat, R. and Ogden, H. 2002. Advertising-induced social comparison and body-image satisfaction: The moderating role of gender, self-esteem and locus of control. *Journal of Consumer Satisfaction, Dissatisfaction and Complaining Behavior*, 15, pp. 51–67.

Youyou, W., Kosinski, M. and Stillwell, D. 2015. Computer-based personality judgments are more accurate than those made by humans. *Proceedings of the National Academy of Sciences*, 112(4), pp. 1036–1040.

Knowledge-driven marketing and the Modular Adaptive Dynamic Schematic

Introduction

Chapter 8 returns directly to the practice and enactment of analytics-driven marketing. It explores the processes that surround the enactment of predictive and descriptive analytics and the elements that can obstruct and facilitate knowledge-driven marketing. The Modular Adaptive Dynamic Schematic (MADS) is proposed as a solution to incorporating insight from extant consumer research (reviewed in the preceding chapters) to myriad contexts; MADS is then applied via various illustrative examples. Finally, the issue of ethics is revisited before some concluding thoughts.

Applying acquired and extant knowledge

CB&A is structured around the assertion that there are two core streams of knowledge and insight; (1) the insights from data and analytics (including purposive research) – the revealed consumer, (2) the insights from previous scholarly and generic research – the known consumer. This final chapter determines the various challenges in combining these streams into coherent managerial decision making. Ultimately managers rarely or never know if their decisions are optimal or not; the only way to do this is by employing an experimental method to compare one decision to another (like an A-B test), and this isn't always possible, economical or practical. Nonetheless, optimization remains the aim of sound managerial practice. Analytics does allow the assessment of performance (even if there is uncertainty over whether the practice/solution is optimal). The ability to predict determines the performance of predictive analytics. The ability to uplift and improve performance (e.g. a new segmentation structure coincides with improved targeting and appears to represent a crucial causal factor) determines the efficacy of descriptive analytics.

An equally troublesome issue is the incorporation of extant consumer research insights into marketing analytics given the issues raised in Chapter 4.

The proposed 'solution' is the Modular Adaptive Dynamic Schematic (MADS). Before MADS is described in full and demonstrated below, a review of the marketing analytics process is required (in the context of knowledge-driven marketing – KDM).

Knowledge-driven marketing

There is quite a lot emerging about 'prescriptive analytics'; a form of high order analytics or meta-analytics that determines a data-driven/analytics orientation within an organization. Much of this is quite vague. Deka (2014) states that this distils to two features: (1) the ability to be reflexive and determine new ways of working based on lessons/strategic implications stemming from the analytics; (2) an objective-driven mindset that is cognizant of constraints. Both are easier said than done. For managers and analysts alike, getting to data-driven decisions isn't easy. The journey from intelligently framed research questions to communicating outputs with end users via all the intervening analytical and communication stages is complex. Huge amounts of data ostensibly open a portal to better knowledge and business performance but high data dimensionality, fractured data sets, a deficiency in appropriate skills, organizational complexity and other factors act as inhibitors to effectiveness; this affects the efficacy of analytical output and how that output transforms into decisions; this ultimately leads to sub-optimal decision making and performance. Poor managerial structures and communication can affect performance at every stage. Each stage and each team leading each stage need to be able to speak to each other. The managerial structure and information flows need to be efficient and accessible.

Figures 8.1 and 8.2 summarize the process of marketing analytics in consumer markets. The dotted lines represent opportunities for feedback or stages that might require a repetition of a component part of the process. Once the data is available the range of analytic techniques and approaches are selected and configured in order to address a marketing issue or problem (e.g. identify reasons for excessive churn; assess effectiveness of marketing sales promotion targeting). The organization can employ a blend of predictive and descriptive elements. The results require validation and testing (against other samples or other related data, or through ground truths established through other data sets or purposive research). For example are the results intuitively questionable; do the clusters make sense? Do the results contradict previous insight? Is the cluster solution superior, in terms of reconstruction error, in comparison to previous iterations? If a predictive approach is adopted then testing and validation will be based on splitting the sample and seeing if the predictive algorithm performs equally as well on the alternate data (data not used in the development of feature/variable selection; that data being the 'training' data[1]). Results require

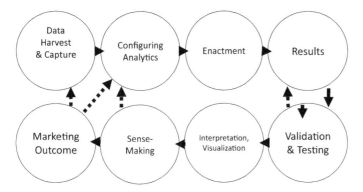

Figure 8.1 Analytics process for descriptive applications
Note: Dotted lines represent feedback.

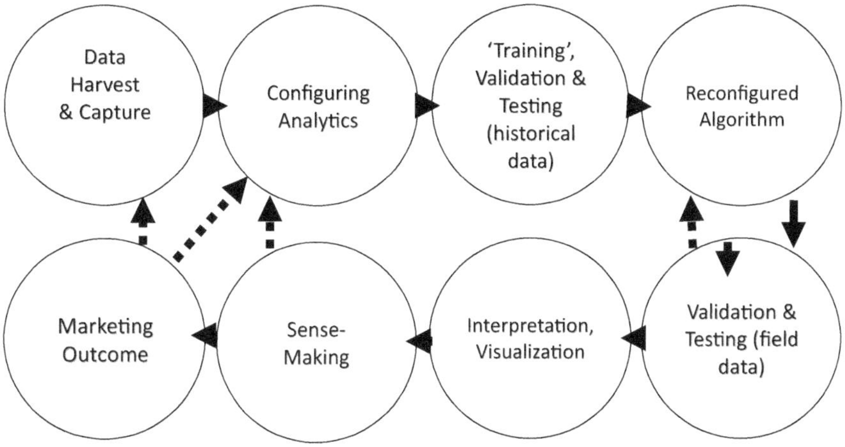

Figure 8.2 Analytics process for predictive applications
Note: Dotted lines represent feedback.

exposition and interpretation by a variety of individuals from various functions (analytics, marketing etc.). This stage is as complex as any other but crucial; it relies on human interaction. Sense-making is equally crucial. The process of converting quantitative results into qualitative decisions requires certain organizational qualities if it has any chance of being efficacious. For example, tolerance of new ideas, effective information exchange, a lack of rivalry or mistrust between analysts and marketers or senior decision makers. The more blurred the lines and skill sets the more likely this process will be co-operative and productive. If the senior decision maker is a blinkered and dogmatic accountant, the lead marketer reflects her/his team's skill set in being innumerate and vague about the analytics used and the analytics lead and team lack the skills to explain what they have done and why it is good then the likely outcome will be a sub-optimal decision. Prior and shared knowledge and expertise are crucial. *CB&A* is based on the logic that the greater the knowledge of consumer analytics and extant consumer research the more likely a positive outcome becomes. A sound knowledge of the subject matter of *CB&A* will enable an analyst or marketer to contribute more productively and intelligently to all of the stages in Figures 8.1 and 8.2.

Figures 8.1 and 8.2 are best understood and applied to a specific application (e.g. a segmentation exercise) rather than the management of the analytics function as a whole. Descriptive and predictive applications are often pursued simultaneously and this represents a further challenge; how do the insights from various analytics projects speak to each other? The danger is that in larger and more complex teams the insight from discrete functions/projects is siloed and discrete. Behavioural and sentiment insight requires audit and collation and this is not a trivial task. The various stages of Figures 8.1 and 8.2 are unpacked below.

1. Data harvest and capture

Data harvest is sometimes automatic and part of warehousing the transactional data required for operational imperatives. Purposive research will require bespoke methods of capture; these will need to be designed and deployed. Figures 8.1 and 8.2 depict the process for transactional data and other data harvested via the normal operation of the business rather than purposive research. One key point that often inhibits analytics is a data matrix design that is entirely driven or dominated by inventory management and other operational concerns and is not driven by analytics. Labelling and data categorization is often determined by the need for re-stocking and logistics management. For example various products will be classified according to where they are located in the store or website (e.g. 'long-life drinks'). This classification is likely to be sup-optimal for analytics purposes. The analytics team need to ensure that a column in the data classifies the products using a method informed by insights from prior analytics applications. The classification for inventory management is not meaningless in terms of analytics but it is unlikely to be optimized. Likewise the addition of other columns might be required for analytics purposes e.g. time in location not just local time; transaction ID is required to ensure that items bought together are associated. Moreover variables need to be measured in intervals that provide for as many possible interrogations of the data. Generally the more granular the better; record the day, hour and minutes and seconds.

Data flows need to be uninhibited and available to analytics applications in real-time otherwise one of the key advantages of digital marketing will be compromised.

2. Configuring analytics

Configuring a specific analytics project requires the marriage of marketing objectives with analytic design. This in turn requires close co-operation between analyst and marketers or teams and individuals with mixed/blended skill sets. If the organizational structure inhibits this co-operative and cross-functional approach then efficacy will suffer. Clear actionable aims and objectives are required (e.g. improved prediction of churn, improved customer segmentation). Feature/variable selection should be co-creative and could be seen as an intermediary stage between Configuring and Enactment. Features selected (or conflated) will often have strong relationships with concepts for which there is extant insight and research. This can be used to inform the feature selection process.

3. Enactment

The deployment of analytics is essentially a technical challenge (computational and mathematical) and therefore largely outwith the scope of *CB&A*.

4. Results

Analytics will often provide results in short time frames but the longer the time frame the greater the potential for effective assessment. Results boil down to the return of outcomes based on the deployment of a predictive algorithm or the various cluster solutions for descriptive analytics. Validation and testing may require revision of the application and this might require several iterations for descriptive and predictive applications.

5. Validation and testing/reconfigured algorithm

For predictive analytics this entails assessment against previous approaches or through testing on historical data in which the outcomes are known (i.e. an assessment of the algorithm's ability to predict churn for customers who have already left vs. its ability to predict churn in real-time) or through an A–B test online. Any algorithm deployed in reality will also 'learn' and optimize after deployment (re-trained). For descriptive analytics (and purposive research) validation is both mathematical (e.g. holdout samples, reconstruction error) and via triangulation with 'ground truths' or purposive research results. At this stage the differences between predictive and descriptive approaches are self-evident in the two figures.

6. Interpretation and visualization

Prediction is often relatively easy to express. For example, previous prediction accuracy for churn was 46% and is now 62%. Descriptive output requires careful interpretation (in light of validation and triangulation insights). Obfuscation of output is not helpful. Clear visualization of data is enormously important (see Chapter 2). Interpretation of cluster analysis or other descriptive output is best undertaken by a team with a mixed skill set.

7. Sense-making

Sense-making entails the process of converting insight into actions and practices that have the ability to be operationalized. Sense-making can be a relatively discrete and confined process (informing 'tactical' marketing – e.g. how people thought to be at risk of switching patronage should be targeted via MC) or be charged with determining how something should be used to fundamentally challenge marketing strategy (e.g. how a new segmentation structure should inform a step-change in product development and MC). Visualization and persona construction (vignettes) of segments need to be clear and accurately reflect the results. They need to be in a form that is close/true to the results of the data but readily assimilated by non-specialists (people with limited analytics training, though ideally these deficiencies should not exist with basic analytics knowledge embedded throughout the team).

8. Marketing outcome

Ultimately the marketing objective/s identified and addressed during the configuring stage require assessment against the actual outcomes achieved through deploying the marketing practice, changed and informed by the analytics process. Once again this is relatively easy to do for predictive applications; e.g. has the new form of individualized MC reduced churn? However, the issue of noise is a factor. Assuming that cause and effect for the improved outcome is entirely due to the improved predictive algorithm is potentially fallacious. If the deployment of the improved prediction protocol coincided with the demise of a leading competitor then the assessment is compromised; notwithstanding the testing and validation stages outlined and described above.

For descriptive applications this issue is even more difficult to assess. How can an organization be sure that the new segmentation structure is better?

This assessment should be both qualitative and quantitative. The issue of noise is relevant again. Sales, retention and increased customer acquisition are relatively easy to measure but linking them with specific marketing practices can be tricky; although sometimes the apparent impact is stark and self-evident (e.g. a targeted sales promotion based on the new segmentation structure coincides with a reduction in churn and uplift in sales above and beyond market conditions). The final two stages will feed back to future analytics configuration as depicted above.

Modular Adaptive Dynamic Schematic (MADS) as a contribution to KDM

The MADS solution is designed to address the issues of complexity and the need for a coherent way of exploring the influences on consumer decision making and behaviour. It is not a model it is a form of mind mapping; an adaptive format for intelligently considering the influences on consumers (in the age of analytics) reviewed in the preceding chapters. It is therefore a representation and form of schematic. It is important to note that MADS cannot be used to provide 'wrong' or 'right' solutions. The approach allows for each element or influence to be weighted according to the context. It is a dynamic apparatus for thinking about consumer choice and behaviour.

A 'structure' or format is required that is cognizant of complexity, as discussed in Chapter 4. This format needs to be able to account for complexity and be applicable to account for various contexts (including temporal dynamics/variations). It must also allow each of the 'traditions' of consumer research to 'speak' or be heard; but it must also acknowledge the fundamental changes and issues outlined above, specifically the existence of EC.

The proposed format/solution was derived via the input of analytics practitioners and scholars with a knowledge of analytics and consumer behaviour over an extended period during a funded research project (the Neo-demographics project – EPSRC EP/L021080/1; please refer to the Acknowledgements for more information). MADS (the Modular, Adaptive, Dynamic, Schematic) is modular because each element or feature represents a discrete theme. It is adaptive because it can be changed in order to account for different consumption and purchase contexts or for different consumers/segments etc. It is dynamic because it accounts for the temporal realm – i.e. it can be used to explore the dynamics of various features or elements, pre, during or post consumption or at different consumer life stages. It is a schematic because it is based on a network premise; not a linear premise. It is a dynamic apparatus for thinking about consumer choice and behaviour. Table 8.1 reviews the various themes and elements developed in previous chapters; these form the modules for MADS.

Table 8.1 MADS elements

Overarching category of antecedents	Review
Behavioural biases	Essentially this distils to loyalty and variety seeking propensities and their relevance to given markets or consumers. Chapter 2 deals with these issues.
Exogenous cognition (EC)	This concept highlights the role of analytics in decision making and influence as presented in Chapter 4.
Utility–hedonic blend	Two elements conceptualized as a blend that can co-exist within the consumer decision process/response. Perceived use value exemplifies this. A variety of elements from brand image and design to practical outcomes determine utility. Refer to Chapter 5.
Economic	This feature (see Chapter 5) encapsulates the basic effects of price and also sales promotion in the era of individually targeted offers.
Deliberation–impulse blend	Again, an element conceptualized as a blend that can co-exist within the consumer decision process/response. Chapter 5.
Image and semiotics	Brands and products are signs and vehicles for communication. Marketing is a form of communication and marketing communications specifically are increasingly individualized, real-time and data-driven (due to EC). Chapter 6.
Responses to marketing communications (MC) and information (distinct from exogenous cognition)	A feature comprising of learning and the anatomy of persuasion. Chapter 6.
Heuristics and perceptual bias	EC has elevated the importance of these features, although they have always been central to marketing and consumer responses to it. Chapter 6.
Socio-cultural	An element that encapsulates the complex of influences and interaction of the individual and the social realm (including conformity, norms and group processes). Chapter 7.
Socio-familial milieu	This essentially explores the micro elements of the socio-cultural realm by focusing on the influences associated with family and/or household and close friends on consumption and purchase. Chapter 7.
Ethics	Ethics can have an insignificant impact on choice or be fundamental depending on the person, market and other contextual factors. EC has increased the power of ethics-driven issues to influence the consumer. Chapter 7.
Emotion	Emotional responses are often key to purchase. They are transient and can endure; they can also underpin attachment and loyalty. Chapter 7.
Psychological biases	Consumers have underlying psychological biases and propensities due to variations in personality and perceptions of self. Chapter 7.

MADS: Worked examples and applications

MADS application and practical utility is best illustrated through a 'worked example'. All of the MADS elements are deemed to be important and (potentially) influential enough to be regarded as a substantive antecedent of choice and behaviour as reflected in previous chapters and in Table 8.1. It is important to re-emphasize that there are not 'wrong' or 'right' applications of MADS. It is a toolkit to facilitate 'armchair' thinking, planning and sense-making in analytics-driven marketing applications in consumer markets.

Core characteristics of MADS deployment:

- The primary driver is placed at the centre of the diagram. The distance of any theme/feature from the central driver is not relevant. Selection of a primary driver.
- The features/themes are organized in a way that best reflects the primary connections and associations of those themes. Connections are depicted with lines in common with schemas and network analysis. It is important to emphasize that only primary or core connections are represented. In reality all the themes are interconnected (indeed this notion of inter-dependence lies at the heart of *CB&A*). The diagram is a summarization of the key associations; it is a representation of reality; an abstraction of what influences the consumer. Proximity is also used to represent the most strident associations where possible.
- Features are weighted according to their perceived impact and importance for the context in hand. The larger the circle the more likely/powerful the influence of that antecedent on choice and behaviour.

Scenario 1

> *The replacement of the family car is the task of a member of a four person household (two adults and two children of school age). She is typical of a segment of consumers with the following characteristics: UK resident, marginally above average income (per adult); suburban and peri-urban dwelling, semi-professional/professional and skilled employment (often in the public sector); both adults work; two/three children between 5 and 18; active leisure pursuit; tend to rely on one vehicle and supplement with public transport and two-wheel transport; replacement takes place every 5+ years.*

Purposive research can then be employed to *determine the veracity* of the initial MADS proposition and *to inform* the initial MADS proposition (it will certainly inform some of the segment insight that will feed into it).

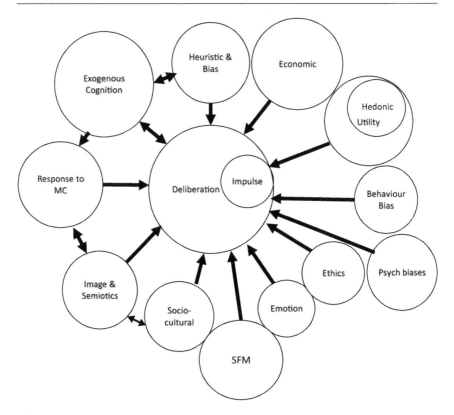

Figure 8.3 High involvement product – pre-purchase

MADS is not designed to be fixed; it is designed to be adapted and changed according to segment, context and incoming insight from analytics or purposive research. MADS is a design that aims to facilitate a blending of insight from extant knowledge, analytics/transaction data and purposive (context specific) insight.

How is this segment likely to approach the purchase decision? Figure 8.3 suggests how a marketing analyst might initially configure, connect and weight the various MADS features.

The following commentary is not exhaustive and deals with the likely and known primary effects and impact of each feature and the initial implications for marketing analytics (once again, these are illustrative and not exhaustive). It goes without saying that any accessible purposive research relating to each of the features (relevant to the sector, market and segment in question) requires attention.

Behavioural biases

- Any loyalty or desire for change might exist in equal measure and will vary from consumer to consumer. Initially, a low weighting is attributed to behavioural bias given the slow cycle of purchase and the ambiguity about any strident variety/entropy or inertia effects.
- Analytic issues, questions and applications stemming from these observations: The analyst should seek any insight into loyalty (inertia) or entropy (switching) for this segment/individuals within it. If inertia is the norm then this will have implications for MC spend (inertia will typically require higher spend) and investment in sales promotion. Car retail franchises will have good data on loyal customers but will also have data on customers who never came back to buy again. The brand owner should access and mine this data. Purposive research can seek to find some explanation for the inertia (e.g. risk aversion). If high entropy is the norm the questions are simply a reflection of the above; equally the balance between entropy and inertia might be more complex.

Exogenous cognition (EC)

- Exogenous cognition is a powerful factor in this scenario. The decision maker is unlikely to eschew an online search. This will be informed by the consumer's own EC and associated bias. The search is likely to override or subordinate weaker behavioural biases and at the very least will reinforce them. Their smart device and computer will be deployed; EC will occur. EC will inevitably have a two-way relationship with deliberation in almost any scenario (this being the essence of EC as outlined in Chapter 4). The impact of EC will tend to increase with involvement.
- Analytic issues, questions and applications stemming from these observations: Any browsing behaviour linked with this segment and the individuals within it will prove valuable. Likewise in terms of sentiment and review data. The insights gained will inform MC and promotional activity. Social network analysis can seek to establish influential nodes (e.g. web pages or people) for the segment.

Utility–hedonic blend

- This purchase for this segment will tend to be a utility-driven event; hedonic factors will still be in play but will often be subordinate to more functional utility factors oriented around issues of practicality, safety and usability.

- Analytic issues, questions and applications stemming from these observations: Purposive research is suited to addressing or measuring perceived use value (PUV) and its dimensions. Browsing, sentiment and review data is potentially powerful if it is associated with the segment in question (or related groupings or sub-sets). An A-B test could be employed to indicate if this segment responds differentially (either to direct to consumer MC or MC that identifies the consumer if they click) to MC that emphasizes either hedonic or utilitarian factors or blends the two.

Economic

- For this segment economy and therefore sales promotion are likely to be significant and influential. Sales promotion will potentially impact/inflate impulse later on in the buying process.
- Analytic issues, questions and applications stemming from these observations: Online sales promotion could be deployed and rated in terms of effectiveness/the responsiveness of this group to offers delivered via online MC. Again, A-B tests are an option. The key issue is to try and establish associations between groups and individuals to variant frames and types of sales promotion driven MC. Again any sentiment or review insights relating to this factor should be sought if possible.

Deliberation–impulse blend

- Deliberation dominates the pre-purchase process with impulse embedded within it; it has the highest weighting and is at the centre of the schematic for this reason. For this segment impulse is a luxury; they are unlikely to indulge it in haste (unless induced by a seductive sales promotion). If the MADS for the segment is accurate then the key inputs are economy, utility and EC.
- Analytic issues, questions and applications stemming from these observations: The anatomy of the deliberative process is constituted by looking at all of the other features in the round (i.e. what are the key inputs and influences, do they tally with the MADS?). The variety of methods mentioned for each other feature (if the principal ones are accurate then they require prioritization).

Image and semiotics

- No one is immune from the effect of image; especially in automobile purchase. They are publically consumed and conspicuous goods. In this case the purchaser/s are likely to privilege utility over image (this being related to hedonic elements in this scenario). Image and semiotics are linked to the factor below (MC) and EC – they form a community or subset of factors in this scenario.

- Analytic issues, questions and applications stemming from these observations: Once again, A-B tests of MC with differential semiotic content are an appropriate option (e.g. which brand associations appear most effective?).

Responses to marketing communications (MC) and information (distinct from exogenous cognition)

- As soon as EC occurs then targeted marketing communications and offers will be generated. The purchaser will also have been subjected to prior communications and ideas about the evoked set based on this (in part). The responses to MC will have a potentially powerful impact on the course of the decision and this factor is inextricably linked/overlaps with EC.
- Analytic issues, questions and applications stemming from these observations: A-B tests and effectiveness of assessment as described above. Purposive research could be deployed to investigate source credibility (this is alluded to above in terms of trusted nodes in any network analysis). Any history of the individual's response to prior MC is invaluable; if it can be linked with purchase (or non-purchase or unresponsiveness) even more so.

Heuristics and perceptual bias

- The buyer is bound to have some perceptual biases in terms of the various competing offers at this search stage.
- Analytic issues, questions and applications stemming from these observations: Biases might be evident in sentiment data linked to the group or individual.

Socio-cultural

- How others view the brands and product configurations will be important. The buyer will not be immune to this. For example, they may have a preference based on the pervasive view that hybrid cars are more socially acceptable (this will also connect with ethics and possibly with economic factors if such cars are perceived to be more economic or come with tax incentives).
- Analytic issues, questions and applications stemming from these observations: Can network or sentiment analysis determine the reference groups for this segment or individual? Can transaction data indicate any

patterns in terms of socio-demographics if cross-referenced with secondary data sets (these are often readily available). Again, any links with subjective data or with transaction data is invaluable.

Socio-familial milieu

- The SFM will have an impact on the decision but at this stage, as well as sharing images, searches and thoughts, the primary decision maker will have an idea about the family members' needs, preferences, opinions and biases. Their ideas on these factors and interactions with family members will have a powerful influence.
- Analytic issues, questions and applications stemming from these observations: Many geo-demographic 'off-the-peg' segmentation software and apps will give an insight (based on probability) of an individual's likely family composition. Sentiment and social media data may also betray insight.

Ethics

- Ethical impact will vary. Extant research tells us that for this income group it is likely to be subordinate to (and synergetic with) economic concerns (somewhere between a 'Billy Liar' and an 'Amélie' as per Chapter 7).
- Analytic issues, questions and applications stemming from these observations: Reliable insight into consumer ethics requires links between transaction data and robust purposive research. Sentiment data and social media data can be misleading here due to social desirability bias and 'virtue signalling'.

Emotion

- Emotional responses to MC and the SFM interactions will underpin various other features notably ethics, image and semiotics. But emotional reactions will provide an undercurrent, an undertow to what is essentially a deliberative cognitive (but not necessarily rational) decision process.
- Analytic issues, questions and applications stemming from these observations: Whilst it is important to acknowledge the importance of emotion as an antecedent it requires elaborate and expensive purposive research. Emotion is also transient and elusive. Sentiment data and review data might reveal traces of it but they are likely to be unsubtle and biased.

Psychological biases

- Whether the consumer is risk averse (underpinning behavioural inertia) or more adventurous (possibly underpinning an openness and desire for a change of brand and style), their sense of self and personality will affect other factors (e.g. ethics). There might be common psychological characteristics for a segment, but the segment will not be psychologically homogeneous. Psychological biases underpin the process in common with emotion.
- <u>Analytic issues, questions and applications stemming from these observations:</u> These issues mirror those for emotion and inconclusive or negative results are a risk (i.e. low association between personality and product choice).

Clearly, there is an element of 'wish list' in terms of the analytics possibilities (notwithstanding ethical and regulatory issues relating to any acquired or web-scraped data). Purposive research is expensive, sentiment and social media data might be difficult to access, it might pose serious ethical issues, it is also potentially misleading and biased. On the other hand, online A-B tests are relatively cheap, any transaction or customer record data should be thoroughly mined and cross-referenced. Transaction data, even for one purchase, will release a host of possibilities. It will record the name and address, the full details of the model purchased, financial data, it could record how decisive they were (among other data in the salesperson's notes), they might have been subject to a survey after purchase (or non-purchase), it is likely that they would be required to rank and rate the salesperson even if they didn't buy, all of this can be cross-referenced with any proprietary purposive research or public data or off-the-peg geo-demographic data. The parent company may have an owners' club and its own review site or facility or discussion group (this will be consulted by but exclude non-purchasers – but they can then be tracked via cookies) or even a consumer panel to report product usage after purchase. In fact there are myriad opportunities to generate and 'own' data. So, on the face of it, a slow-moving market doesn't seem to provide much in the way of analytics relating to transactional data when, in reality, a switched-on dealership franchise in unison with guidance and support from the parent manufacturer can build up an enormously rich data set around the transaction (or interaction/inquiry from non-buyers). If this is cross-referenced with other data sources then the transactional element lies at the heart of a constellation of associated data.

It will not be practical or cost-effective to interrogate all of the analytic relevant implications and questions cited above. Priorities will have to be set. If the weighting attributed to each element has a sound basis in either extant research, purposive research and transactional and browsing/sentiment analytics

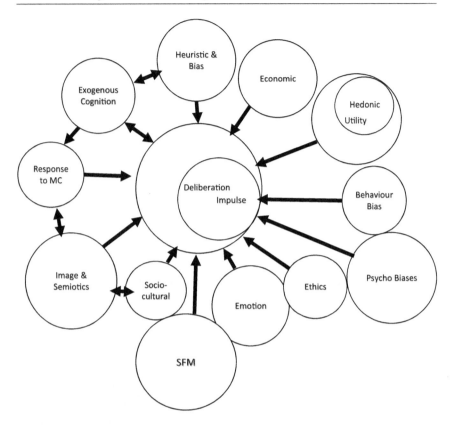

Figure 8.4 High involvement product – during purchase in-store

then those areas are likely to require prioritization. The more significantly weighted elements will require greater attention and review to extant and generic research (as outlined throughout *CB&A*).

MADS can account for how the relative significance of elements change according to time (it is dynamic). Indeed, the MADS pictorial can be 'animated' for various stages (pre, post, during purchase etc.). Clearly, this is not possible in a book; however, a 'partial equilibrium' approach is accessible. Figure 8.4 depicts the potential change in the MADS configuration consistent with the automobile purchase scenario outlined and applied above. Once again, the premise here is that purposive research and anecdotal managerial insight is an input into the re-configuration; again the case is illustrative.

Various elements now have an inflated role. SFM effects have grown because this segment often makes showroom visits as a household unit. Each will express their view and likely exert more influence than during the search stage/pre-purchase stage. When a product is experienced 'in the flesh', image and semiotics are even more powerful. The design elements become real and tangible. Psychological biases might also come to the fore. At the decision stage the consequences of the purchase (financial, social and image risks) are all the more real and immediate; the purchase is no longer a 'thought experiment'. The tendency to impulse is also inflated given the likelihood that the sales interaction will lead to various offers and inducements and other powerful persuasive effects (MC is reduced but this does not include the actual sales interaction – this being a function of the context/temporal change). Economic considerations shrink slightly as image effects inflate. The viewing and testing of products will provoke an emotional reaction as the consumer and their associates project and share ideas/images about how the car will fit into their life, what it will feel like to go on holiday in it etc. Any showroom located survey, sales interaction appraisal or any email questionnaire post-purchase (or non-purchase) can therefore be designed to address the elements that have inflated. For example a couple of questions exploring the SFM dynamics on the day (subtly framed of course).

For the sake of balance and breadth another scenario requires consideration in order to demonstrate the variability and adaptability of MADS. Figure 8.5 illustrates how the features/elements morph when the context is quite distinct from the one comprehensively considered above. Here the product is organic cow's milk; a product with a high rate of repeat purchase. For the sake of consistency and brevity the illustrative example is based on the premise that the segment is the same as the scenario above. The key changes from Figure 8.3 are as follows. Behavioural bias is now at the centre; inertia drives the essentially low involvement purchase (although not void of cognitive effort); heuristics and other perceptual biases will tend to underpin this choice (e.g. 'organic = sustainable'). The decision to buy this variety of milk will be reviewed by the consumer as new information comes to light so MC and EC will inform their background knowledge and nourish their opinions on related issues (e.g. environmental degradation). There is an increased weight for basic utility. The product in question is more expensive and this is reflected in the reduced role of economic factors. Ethics is also a key driver of the purchase in this context (the primary drivers being utility, ethics and behavioural bias). All of the other MADS elements still have an impact, but they are underlying factors (secondary and tertiary drivers).

Application of MADS

Table 8.2 outlines and cross-references the stages of an analytics project as specified in Figures 8.3 and 8.4 with the application and contribution of the MADS framework for summarizing extant research. The table primarily deals

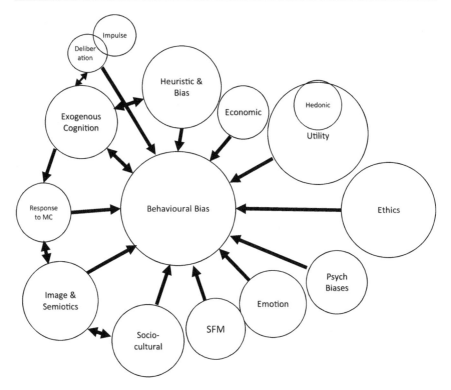

Figure 8.5 Low involvement product

with descriptive analytics but is also pertinent to predictive utilization (predictive application in the subsequent paragraph specially considers relevance to predictive applications).

The table for predictive applications would differ at certain key stages and MADS is most useful at the first two stages (Capture and Configuring) and the final three (Interpretation, Sense-making and Outcome) since the validation stages for predictive analytics are driven by a mathematically informed process; however, MADS still has a 'background' role in validation. For example the key features that seem to underpin prediction might be a reflection of extant research. This insight can be used to feed back into any augmented algorithm. If a predictive study establishes that the key features/variables that determine holiday/vacation destination choice are family composition and income, a consideration of MADS sub-elements (the sub-themes/subsections of Chapters 4, 5, 6 and 7) could be employed to feed into the interpretation stage. Otherwise the application of MADS is similar to Table 8.2.

Table 8.2 Descriptive analytics and MADS application

Analytics process stage in descriptive analytics (as per Figure 8.1)	Application of MADS
Data harvest and capture	A structure to systematically review the opportunities for the collection of any additional data at any interaction or transaction event. How can any indications at all of any of the MADS elements be gathered?
Configuring analytics	Does extant research or accessible purposive research provide any insight that can help to avoid seeking answers to questions that have already been resolved? Each MADS element should be considered in turn when addressing this question.
Enactment	This is a technical stage regarding the deployment of the configured analytics.
Results	Does extant research or accessible purposive research provide any insight that can help to make an initial assessment of the results? Again, the review is structured according to the 13 MADS elements.
Validation and testing	MADS application is similar to the stage above and there is some overlap here. According to extant research and/or abductive logic do any of the MADS elements lead to a potential explanation of the behaviour observed or provide a format for triangulation? Additionally, MADS can be used to review the potential and suitability of any purposive research used for triangulation. The review should highlight the MADS elements which are not investigated as yet. If they are heavily weighted elements then additional research should be considered.
Interpretation and visualization	MADS provides a 'lens' through which to view the data; it provides themes that will endure for many variant projects.
Sense-making	As above. MADS provides a lexicon for consistent communication. Many terms (e.g. loyalty) are used polysemically in marketing management. MADS provides a consistent structure of meaning.
Marketing outcome	An audit of the lessons from the project can include a review of data capture and knowledge gaps that endure (the audit structured on the MADS themes as well as other elements relating to data science and marketing applications and deployment).

A cautionary note on ethics

Ethical data management and usage should not be an afterthought (indeed, *CB&A* highlights ethical pressure points throughout). Ethical decision making begins with the acknowledgement that there is an ethical problem or potential pitfall. Many industries have fallen foul of a cursory attitude to business ethics (think the tobacco sector in the 1960s); too many simply feel that adherence to regulatory structures is a proxy for ethics or 'good behaviour'. The tobacco industry knew what it was up to and resisted increased restriction and regulation at every turn. It serves as a warning to any industry that appears unassailable; an industry or brand is in its greatest danger when in its pomp. Regulation is merely the step-daughter of ethics, regulation follows ethics; regulation is the last resort and often lags technological progress and innovation. Foucault (1985) observed that surveillance will tend to exploit or be at the frontier of technology. Analytics is surveillance and it is driving technological change not just exploiting it. So, practice will always be ahead of regulation; therefore the only effective restraining force is ethics.

Various research has highlighted the drivers of this cursory or even cavalier attitude to customer data. There is a tendency for dehumanization, to see people as data or artefacts. Frankly, this is almost impossible to avoid in analytics, since it is all about data and reduction (this section might therefore appear anachronistic and that fact exemplifies an issue at the heart of analytics – how to serve the brand's and the consumer's interests simultaneously). At the very least, the custodians of the data should continually remind themselves that the data represents a person; that harm can be done (dangers include data breaches and hacks, inappropriate targeting among others), that access to people's data is a privilege not a right. A 'Wild West' attitude is fuelled by and a function of distance from the consumer. Some companies find ways of engendering data use and communications that is sensitive, cautious and driven by delivering increased value to the consumer. Notwithstanding the impenetrable terms and conditions that people don't read, the unwritten contract or covenant is 'OK, you can have that data if I get something that's worth it', at least for the more savvy; that consumers get value for the service, the pay/price is the data. Not all consumers are savvy in terms of their beliefs about the use of the data they volunteer. How many really know how Google makes money given that most of its services are free? Consumers are either in denial, don't know, don't care, or are informed and accept the trade-off.

Google, Amazon, Microsoft and Apple are truly global in terms of their manifestation and reach. You can purchase on Amazon in the Amazon if you can get a signal. This makes them difficult to regulate. Regulatory structures tend to be nationally grounded (an exception being the European Union). They are powerful entities and somewhat faceless and remote in comparison to analogue services.

Final thoughts

In data or any evidence-driven marketing there is a danger in pursuing a fatuous search for the Holy Grail and the magic bullet in terms of explaining consumer behaviour. Human behaviour is complex and as Chapter 4 asserts the variety of contexts, markets and instances are myriad; the degrees of freedom in consumer research are vast and the environment is dynamic. Ever since VALS there has been a recurrent quest for the 'answer' or more specifically the overriding determinants of choice and behaviour. Inflated claims are often made for new approaches or potential determinants (e.g. passive personality scores). Analytics isn't *the* 'answer', it can provide some answers to appropriate questions. However, like it or not, transactional analytics has led to a shift of focus on what people actually do (with the exception of sentiment and social media data); indeed it has led to an entirely new form of consumer marketing. However, this does not utterly supplant all that went before. This is the whole point of *CB&A*; analytics insight informed by extant insight.

It is often risky to think that you have the definitive and complete 'answer' to any question; that is *the* answer as opposed to *an* answer. There's always more data, evidence and answers out there.

Note

1   Learning comes in two forms: supervized and unsupervized. Supervized learning is a form of machine learning in which the 'teacher' or the analyst determines what is to be learnt or what the objective of the algorithm is. It is a process where the search for the answer drives the process and is common for predictive analytics and descriptive analytics with a specified objective or question. For example, 'can we find groups of customers with certain characteristics in order to account for their spend/customer value' – this requires a *descriptive* outcome. 'Can we predict which customers are most likely to leave us (churn)' – this requires a *predictive* outcome. In unsupervised learning we are not trying to find the answer for a specified problem/explain a 'dependent' variable. An example of a question to inform an unsupervised learning problem or algorithm might include the following: 'can we group our customers according to two dimensions that provide actionable segmentation?'

References

Deka, G.C. 2014. Big data predictive and prescriptive analytics. In P. Raj and G.C. Deka (Eds.), *Handbook of research on cloud infrastructures for big data analytics* (pp. 370–391). Hershey, PA: IGI Global.

Foucault, M. 1985. *Discipline and punish: The birth of the prison*. Harmondsworth: Penguin.

Zwitter, A. 2014. Big data ethics. *Big Data & Society*, 1(2), pp. 1–6.

Index

CPSIA information can be obtained
at www.ICGtesting.com
Printed in the USA
LVHW082301070720
660035LV00011B/1496